DRUG

Graham Johnson is former investigations editor at the *Sunday Mirror* newspaper. His first book was the bestseller *Powder Wars: The Supergrass Who Brought Down Britain's Biggest Drug Dealers*. He is also the author of Football and Gangsters: How Organised Crime Controls the Beautiful Game.

NOTE: Several individuals in this book, who took part in very serious crimes, have not been named. Their identities cannot be revealed for legal and security reasons. In such cases, they have been given false names. However, their real identities are known to the author and the authorities.

Druglord contains an account of John Haase's criminal experiences given by Haase himself. The information was gathered in a taped interview with Haase at Whitemoor prison, during which he swore an affidavit. Both the author, Graham Johnson, and Liverpool Walton MP Peter Kilfoyle were present. Haase made the confession freely and without duress in the hope that he would receive credit from the authorities, possibly in the form of a reduced sentence, even though no guarantees were ever made.

Some of the quotes attributed to Haase about his background and childhood are extracted from interviews he gave to the *Liverpool Echo* and *Daily Post* newspapers.

First-hand accounts from other sources quoted in this book were gained in a variety of ways, including formal interviews, covert surveillance and witness statements.

GUNS,
POWDER AND
PAY-OFFS

DRUGLORD

GRAHAM JOHNSON

MAINSTREAM
PUBLISHING

EDINBURGH AND LONDON

This edition, 2007

First published in Great Britain in 2006 by
MAINSTREAM PUBLISHING COMPANY (EDINBURGH) LTD
7 Albany Street
Edinburgh EH1 3UG

ISBN 9781845962401

A catalogue record for this book is available from the British Library

Typeset in New Baskerville and Trixie

Printed in Great Britain by
Cox and Wyman Ltd, Reading

CONTENTS

PART ONE

HEROIN DEALING

1

INTRODUCTION –
THE GREATEST ESCAPE

On 3 July 1996, Britain's biggest drug dealer, John Haase, was secretly released from prison by Royal Pardon after serving just 10 months and 13 days of an 18-year sentence for heroin trafficking. His nephew and partner-in-crime, Paul Bennett, was also freed as part of the same deal. More than 17 years had been wiped off their prison terms overnight – an unprecedented act in over 1,000 years of British judicial history.

The decision had been brokered by the highest powers in the land, a Holy Trinity of senior lawmakers and enforcers: Customs and Excise, a top judge and home secretary Michael Howard, who went on to lead the Conservative Party into a general election. Nothing like it had ever happened before, and, not surprisingly, the extraordinary event was shrouded in secrecy. The big question was, and still is, why did it happen?

The official explanation was simple, but again kept under wraps: Haase and Bennett had turned supergrass while in prison and their freedom was a reward for disclosing sensitive information about the underworld to Customs and Excise and the police that enabled crimes to be solved. Unfortunately for the authorities, the story leaked out – despite the government's attempt to prevent newspapers, TV and MPs from talking about it – immediately scandalising Michael Howard and raising a series of important issues. The questions thrown up were the key to unravelling the mystery, because the answers, piece by piece, led politicians and journalists closer to the full, astonishing truth.

The first question – posed by an MP – was the most obvious: why was the government putting the public at risk by freeing from jail two of the most dangerous criminals in Britain? Haase and Bennett were no ordinary villains – they were top-five UK gangsters who trafficked drugs on an industrial scale and ran guns as proficiently as the IRA. The serious threat to public safety was blindingly self-evident. Blood-curdling violence, kidnappings and torture were their stock-in-trade. They were rootin'-tootin', shoot-'em-up outlaws as ruthless as anything that had come out of London, Chicago, Moscow or Sicily in the last 50 years. Before his capture, Haase was the UK kingpin of the Turkish Connection, a gang that pioneered the mass importation of cheap Afghani heroin across southern Europe and into Britain. During his reign between 1991 and 1993, the gang had flooded the streets with Class A drugs, triggering the first measurable drug epidemic in the UK, quickly followed by an exponential rise in the number of drug addicts. Haase's outfit was Sigma Six efficient; it did for opium what Motorola and Vodafone had done for mobile phones. It was the first to replace piecemeal heroin smuggling with systematic mass importation. Under his instruction, regular 100-kilo loads poured into the UK, causing the market to reach saturation point quickly, which led to the biggest single fall in the kilo price of heroin on Britain's streets ever. Allowing Haase back onto the streets was to unleash a vicious, one-man crimewave back onto an unsuspecting public. Granting his freedom was tantamount to government-sponsored organised crime.

The second question – raised on the front pages of several national newspapers – was more political: why was hang-'em and flog-'em home secretary Michael Howard putting his career at risk by freeing exactly the type of criminal he had sworn to stamp out? Why was he blatantly going back on his right-wing 'prison works' policy, putting the credibility of Prime Minister John

Major's government on the line with a scandalous decision, ahead of a general election?

Howard was a Tory golden boy who had made his name as a hard-line crime fighter. He had come to the Home Office job on a ticket of longer prison sentences for drug dealers and violent criminals. He had rallied the grass-roots membership in a series of vote-catching law-and-order speeches at conferences. Destroying Haase and Bennett's gang was the biggest single success that Customs and Excise had ever achieved against international heroin traffickers. To authorise Royal Pardons for them was an unusual U-turn for Howard that would not go down well with the blue-rinse brigade. So what exactly had motivated him to do it?

The plot thickened when the Sunday Mirror newspaper unearthed a remarkable link between Haase's underworld gang and Howard. Astonishingly, Howard had a relative in Liverpool who knew Haase's mob bosses and had allegedly been in touch with Haase himself in the days following his release from prison. The man's name was Simon Bakerman. He was Howard's cousin. He even carried a picture of the home secretary in his wallet. He was also a cocaine-snorting drug dealer and petty criminal with strong connections to Haase's Liverpool 8 gangland manor. It is unclear whether Bakerman had known Haase *personally* before he went to prison for the heroin offences in 1993, but there was definitely strong evidence linking him to Haase's partner Bennett.

Bakerman had met Bennett through contacts in the world of drug dealing and had visited his flat in the Woolton area of Liverpool before his imprisonment with Haase. In the same story exposing the link between Howard, Bakerman and the drug dealers, the *Sunday Mirror* sensationally revealed that Haase and Bennett had been in contact with Bakerman just days after their release. This underworld link between the serving home secretary and the criminals he had just pardoned begged the next question: what role, if any, had Bakerman played in the scandal?

Howard did not comment on the Bakerman allegations but finally defended the extraordinary decision to release Haase and Bennett, amid growing conspiracy theories, by confirming publicly for the first time that the pair had indeed turned informants in jail and helped in the fight against organised crime. However, the statement did little to dampen the outcry nor draw a line under the scandal as Howard had intended. Instead, it raised a series of other questions, the most important being: just how big a supergrass was Haase and what crucial information had he supplied to Customs and the police to warrant an exceptional, 17-year discount on his sentence? Royal Pardons are rare. Most have been granted to convicts for helping to save the lives of prison officers in jeopardy. Again, the details of Haase and Bennett's informant value were kept secret, but a leaked Customs memo revealed that the pair had led police to a string of massive arms caches all over the UK, crucially including a gun hidden inside Strangeways prison, where Haase was on remand. Preventing an armed hostage situation inside a prison was the key to clinching a Royal Pardon, as set down in legal precedent.

However, this raised another question, this time posed by some of the UK's most feared crime bosses and IRA terrorists: if Haase and Bennett were supergrasses, which underworld figures had they betrayed to the police? To be freed from prison so remarkably early, in such mysterious circumstances, many senior criminals assumed that Haase and Bennett had fully cooperated with the law, and had inevitably 'grassed up' some seriously heavyweight villains into the bargain. How else could such a good deal have been achieved? For instance, it was assumed that Haase and Bennett had led police to the underworld owners of the gun caches that they had so accurately located, some of which were linked to Republican terrorists in Ireland. Only supergrasses of the highest calibre are rewarded with a Royal Pardon. Just who exactly had Haase and Bennett named in their statements to the police? These were the chilling questions that UK gang-bosses began to ask themselves.

This led to another question, this time asked by a sharp-eyed underworld watcher in Liverpool and switched-on reporters at the *Liverpool Echo* and *Sunday Mirror* newspapers. If Haase and Bennett were supergrasses, then they were dead men walking, as laid down by the underworld code. If they stayed in Liverpool, they were living on borrowed time. Why, then, were they walking around their home town 'without a care in the world', as reported in the

Sunday Mirror? In many ways, this was the most important question, and the answer is an important clue to unlocking the mystery.

As supergrasses, Haase and Bennett would have to face the wrath of their underworld peers on the street, and that usually meant execution – the traditional punishment meted out to informants big and small. The alternative, in similar cases, had been for the authorities to spirit away supergrasses into the witness-protection programme, where they were given a new identity and a new life in a faraway place. They were protected by armed guards.

However, for Haase there was no such arrangement. Following his release from prison, Haase had returned to his home in Liverpool almost immediately. Instead of hiding from his underworld pals, Haase threw parties for them to celebrate his freedom. In other cases, he visited the homes of rival gangsters he believed had taken liberties while he was in jail, to settle old scores. Haase had a hit-list of top villains he wished to confront. One after another, he knocked on their doors and asked, 'Have you got a problem with me?' The answer was invariably no – many of the gangsters were too shocked that he was out of prison and too scared to stand up to him. For Haase, this lack of resistance was a green light to go back into business – as a Liverpool Mafia godfather specialising in heroin smuggling and gun-running. This was not the behaviour of a man who had informed on his peers and was in fear for his life.

Bennett was more cautious. After prison, he flew to Mexico for a three-week holiday to ride out the media storm that had blown up following his sensational release, before returning to Manchester airport. On touchdown, he was debriefed by his Customs handlers before returning to join Haase in Liverpool. Neither Bennett's nor Haase's behaviour was in keeping with that of a supergrass in danger. Quite logically, Britain's top gangsters concluded that they weren't 'real' supergrasses after all. This led to the final question, the last piece of the jigsaw: if Haase and Bennett were not supergrasses, then how exactly had they won their Royal Pardons? Finally the killer question had been reached. Possible answers to this, and many other questions, are revealed in this book.

The evidence suggests that Haase and Bennett were never

supergrasses – they simply conned their way out of prison, pulling off one of the most audacious and devious escapes in the history of British prisons and at the same time orchestrating one of the most evil miscarriages of justice.

The plan seemingly had three phases. First, they pretended to be informants by organising the pardon-clinching gun plants themselves, setting up phoney arms caches and then directing police to them in an elaborate self-serving scam. The second part of the plan was aimed at covering up the deception by making sure their web of carefully choreographed lies was not exposed. Testimony is given in this book that certain officials were bribed with a string of payments from a 'war chest' containing a staggering £3.5 million. Certainly, the bribes would have enabled awkward questions to be avoided, and sceptical investigators were prevented from digging too deeply into the quality of Haase and Bennett's 'supergrass' information. The third phase was apparently to ensure that the Royal Pardon process went through quickly. Once again, testimony is given in this book that illegal payments were used from the war chest to grease the wheels of justice.

For Haase and Bennett, any such pay-off would have been a double whammy. They got their freedom and their criminal credibility remained largely intact, hence they escaped retribution from the underworld. Although they were officially registered Customs and Excise informants, the evidence they had supplied to police had been fabricated and no arrests had resulted from any of their phoney crimes. Far from being maligned, their status in gangland shot up. Haase and Bennett had pulled off the perfect crime.

In legal terms, such a con is likely to amount to a massive perversion of the course of justice. As a result of evidence first unearthed in this book, the Metropolitan Police's Specialist Crime Directorate immediately set up a probing investigation called Operation Ainstable, spearheaded by one of its most senior officers, Tarique Ghaffur. At the time of going to press, one member of Haase's gang has been charged with serious criminal offences and between six and eleven others, including Haase himself, are facing a similar fate.

2

HAASE BACKGROUNDER

John Haase was born in Liverpool on 1 March 1949. He was raised in the slum-ridden district of Everton, in the north of the city. He was the youngest of four brothers and two sisters in a family of respectable working-class Scousers of German origin with no criminal history. Haase was the black sheep.

Along with many of his childhood pals, Haase followed a well-trodden career path to narco superstardom: juvenile petty criminal to armed robber to drug dealer. However, the descent was not necessarily inevitable and his family tried hard, and not without initial success, to stop it. Until his teens, Haase was largely kept on the straight and narrow by a disciplinarian father and even landed a job as an apprentice plumber. He attended Calder Street infant school in Everton and went on to Major Lester Primary. Though bright and articulate, he finished his education at Breckfield Secondary Modern with little more than the basics before leaving to get a job. None of his family had criminal tendencies. One of his brothers, who was close to him during childhood, later moved away from Liverpool and did very well in life, having little more to do with his wayward sibling. Haase lost touch with the others but stayed close to one sister.

Haase went off the rails in his early teens, carrying out small-time thefts and burglaries. He was prevented from escalating to more serious offences for a period by his no-nonsense father. At 14, he picked up his first conviction for minor offences in December 1963. He was given a conditional discharge at Liverpool City Juvenile Court. One year later, he was arrested for larceny and breaking into a shop, and in January 1964 he was sentenced to probation for the offences, again at Liverpool City Juvenile Court.

Haase's father was convinced that his son was under the influence of a bad crowd and was determined to put a stop to his deterioration. He made him get a job. At 15, Haase won a trade apprenticeship at a firm in the Dingle neighbourhood, a tough dockside area in the south of the city with strong criminal ties. The Park Road and Granby Street areas would go on to be world centres of excellence in drug trafficking and gun-running, churning out some of the biggest gangsters on the planet. But in those days, all that Haase wanted to do was go out with his mates and blow his wages in the docker pubs, getting to know some of their seedier customers in the process. 'But I had a very strict father who made me be in early. All my mates were out until 11 and 12 at night,' recalls Haase.

In later life, Haase's pals blamed his violent and jealous tendencies on his father's influence. Chris No-Neck, an extremely violent criminal who cannot be named for legal reasons (because he has only two very minor convictions), said, 'Haase had a rough upbringing with his auld fella [father] beating him up. That made him think, towards other people, "If I haven't got it, then why should you have it?"'

Despite his new job, Haase continued to commit crime on the side and his eventual refusal to stay away from trouble upset and embarrassed his parents. He spared them the shame by moving into a flat of his own. He spent much of the time in the nearby house of a pal called Jim Thomas (not his real name), who lived in Toxteth. The boys were like two peas in a pod. Like Haase, Thomas had got into crime early and grew up to be one of the city's top gangsters, eventually helping Haase as an international drugs courier. Haase said, 'I was brought up well but my dad was just too strict. So at 16 I left home and got a flat on my own.' No longer under the watchful eye of his parents, Haase's life spiralled downwards into a cycle of petty crime.

Like many a youthful scallywag before him, Haase invaded the relatively peaceful pastures of North Wales to pillage the rich pickings and run amok. In March 1964, he was sentenced to 14 months in Borstal and given two years' probation at Llangollen Juvenile Court for unlawfully taking a mailbag. It was an unlucky collar. Haase had stolen the bag from a village post office and made his getaway on foot and at speed – right into the arms of the local bobby. Years later, after Haase had been convicted of being Britain's number one drug kingpin, he would relate this story to his gang as an example of how bad luck had plagued his criminal life from the outset.

One of his top heavies, a contract-violence specialist known as The Debt Collector, recalled, 'Haase was from a well-gotten background, a nice family. He wasn't dragged up like most poor kids in those days and he had no need to get into crime. But the badness was just in him from birth. John was a one-off, a tearaway. He used to tell us this one story – that he should have given up being a criminal after his first job went wrong. He robbed a post office in North Wales, put the money in a bag and ran round a corner – straight into a copper riding a pedal bike. He knocked the copper off the bike. But the copper got up and arrested him on the spot. John used to say that he should have stopped being a criminal there and then. That he'd had bad luck ever since.'

On the same incident, Haase remembered, 'When I was 16, I was arrested for larceny and burglary in North Wales. There were five of us in a gang and we all went down. It was my first court appearance and I was sent to Borstal.'

Complaining about the severity of the sentence – a theme that would be recurrent in his criminal life – Haase blamed everything other than his own dishonest behaviour for the sentence. He said he had been unduly punished for being a

Scouser by an anti-Liverpudlian court. Like many of his peers, Haase had a chip on his shoulder about being a Scouser, a perceived persecution which stayed with him through his later life but bonded his gang closely together. He went on, 'I think the court wanted to make an example of a gang of thieves who had gone to North Wales from Liverpool. I got Borstal because I was a Scouser who got caught out of town. Borstal was like a holiday camp, except you could not come home. I was there for 14 months.'

Haase has always maintained that this was the turning point in his life, the criminal record marginalising him in society and forcing him to commit more serious crimes. He said, 'One thing I learned was that once you had been inside, it was hard to get a decent job. People did not want to know you once they discovered you had been inside. Would things have turned out different if the judge had given me a chance and released me? I'll never know. I was on my own again when I came out and I got a labouring job building 22-storey council flats in Cantril Farm [a '60s development in Liverpool].'

But no sooner had the two-year probation period for the post-office theft expired than Haase was back in court, this time for stealing a box of grapes. In 1966, he was fined £5 at Liverpool Magistrates Court. Later that year, in April, he was back in court for another offence, this time larceny of lead. At Denbigh Quarter Session, Haase was handed down a six-month suspended prison sentence.

By the late 1960s, the juvenile court system was losing patience with Haase's repeat offending. The leniency he had been shown because of his youth was rapidly drying up. In March 1969, the courts got tough and he was sent to adult prison for the first time after breaching the conditions of his six-month suspended sentence. Haase had been caught taking a car without consent – a rather insignificant offence, but in criminal terms it was another turning point. By going to prison proper, he had stepped up a rung on the ladder. Haase enjoyed jail; he learned to network with other villains and was introduced to more serious crime. Shortly after he was released, he was back inside again. In March 1970, Haase was jailed for 18 months at Liverpool Crown Court for burglary and theft. Then, for a string of similar offences, he was given two years' probation at Preston Crown Court in June 1972.

In 1973, encouraged by the seasoned criminals he had met in prison, Haase made a quantum leap into the semi-big-time and became a professional armed robber. Haase said, 'I upgraded to armed robbery and had a shotgun. I turned to crime because I wanted money. I cannot blame anybody for leading me down that path. It was all down to me.' It was the beginning of a lifelong love of guns and an addiction to the adrenalin buzz of violent crime. Years later, even after fulfilling his ambition to become a multimillionaire druglord, Haase refused to hang up his beloved balaclava. He still went on raids 'just for a buzz' right up until his late 40s, boasting that drug dealing was easy money compared to armed robbery. He considered 'blagging' to be the premiership of gangsterism and the only 'real crime' left, the best test of a criminal's bottle.

On 1 March 1973, on his 24th birthday, Haase's first wave of terror as a full-time blagger came to an end. He was sentenced to seven years and three months in jail for his part in five raids on post offices, two assaults on police officers and breach of probation. Passing sentence, Judge Rudolph Lyons was to express himself in terms that would become familiar to Haase in subsequent trials: 'The time has come for your reign of terror in Liverpool to come to an end. You are an evil, dangerous man.'

During his early post office raids, Haase had demonstrated a singularly callous side to his nature, particularly in the aggressive use of what would become his signature weapon: the single-barrelled shotgun. One female victim who came face to face with Haase during a raid on her employer's office suffered a nervous breakdown. In the words of an investigating police detective, she was so 'totally traumatised by what happened to her' she feared she would never recover from the ordeal of gazing down the barrel of Haase's shooter. By the time he got out of prison, Haase's reputation as a gangland hard-man was set in stone. Ambitious and smart, he was now a rising star in the Liverpool underworld, despite the fact that his personality was becoming unstable as a result of being locked up. A darker side was beginning to emerge, touches of evil that were noticeable to his friends and family.

Incarceration had increased his aggression and shortened his temper. On the street, he was getting a reputation for being a bully, prone to bouts of psychotic fury. His rivals began to fear his love of violence. Paul Grimes, the supergrass who eventually brought down Haase's drugs-and-guns empire in the late '90s, had first met him 20 years earlier, shortly after he had got out of prison. Grimes revealed the story in the book *Powder Wars*. Haase was trying to bully his way into a nightclub where Grimes worked as a doorman.

———————

PAUL GRIMES: One night a man called John Haase was trying to get into my club. He was giving all sorts of abuse to the girl on the door till but none of the other doormen would intervene in case he shot the place up – he was one of these new generation of gangsters who were mad on guns. I just said to him, 'Listen, I don't give fuck who you are but you are going to have to leave now.' Haase was a vicious bully, but if you stood up to him, he respected you. Eventually, we became mates.

As I got to know him, I found out he was an armed robber into post offices and security vans. He wasn't a chancer; he was a pro. People were afraid of him. Physically he was nothing, but people were afraid of what he could do with the hardware.

I taught Haase how to wash money. I taught him the value of using straight businesses as a cover for criminal activities. He later went on to use these tricks to great effect when he became a drug dealer.

I was a villain but I also had a legitimate waste-disposal company on the side. John Haase invested £170, just a token gesture, so he could say to the police that the money he was robbing was straight.

In between robbing post offices, he'd turn up for work, as

though to prove he was a regular blue-collar guy. Even though it was shite-removing, he'd wear an expensive suit and an ironed white shirt. He insisted on rubbing barrier cream on his hands to keep them smooth. He was vain but he wasn't scared of hard work. When he did commit crime, he'd disappear for weeks on end robbing post offices. Or sometimes it was because he'd been nicked. The business was sound for him in this respect because it provided him with alibis and that. I'd vouch for him when the busies came, asking where he was on such-and-such a date, but one time a private detective I knew turned up and said, 'I believe you've said Haase was working for you on the day such-and-such a warehouse was robbed. Just to let you know, we've got him on camera doing a robbery. You'll end up going inside yourself for perjury if you are not careful.' So I had to pass on that.

Then I remember he went to prison on some charge. I was starting to realise that Haase was too hot to handle. He was too ambitious, too dangerous, and I started to put a bit of distance between myself and him. After he got out of prison, I gave him £300 and told him that that was his stake in the business. There was no point him being involved in my legitimate businesses. He was too ontop. I didn't want him fucking me up.

Among the many gang-bosses and crime families in Liverpool, Haase was a loose cannon, hell-bent on challenging the old order. Even minor slights would launch Haase into hellish rages, leading to all-out gang war, triggering shootings, stabbings and beatings. He was given the nickname 'Loony Tunes' for his unpredictable bouts of violence and his almost suicidal bravery in confronting other gangsters face to face regardless of their reputations. In 1980, Haase went to war with members of a tough south Liverpool gang made up of two notorious families, the Ungis and the Fitzgibbons.

The Ungi and Fitzgibbon families hailed from the dockside area that Haase had made his home. The Ungis were descended from Filipino sailors and the Fitzgibbons from Irish immigrants. But in the melting pot of Liverpool's slums, they had formed a strategic alliance based on close familial and marital ties and driven by a desire to be the number one mob in south Liverpool. Over the next 30 years, they would outperform their own local ambitions and grow into a national syndicate with international links, pursued by Britain's top serious-crime policemen and intelligence agencies. But on the face of it, to the outside world, they remained no more than petty, unpredictable criminals with a penchant for street-gutter violence.

In 1969, 18-year-old Tony Martin Ungi was sentenced to Borstal for killing 16-year-old drinker John Bradley at the All Fours Club in Liverpool. Ungi slashed the main artery in his neck with two broken pint glasses. Twenty years later, twenty-three-year-old Colin Ungi was jailed for five years after blowing the head off his best friend, Nathan Jones, with a sawn-off shotgun as they played around while smoking cannabis.

The family's history was littered with hundreds of such incidents, most of which went unreported. But such bouts of inexplicable violence formed their power base. On the streets, they were feared. This fear was systematically exploited to racketeer. By the mid-'90s, their hunger for power had landed the Ungis at the centre of one of the bloodiest gangland feuds ever to take place on the mainland, against drug smuggler Curtis Warren, the wealthiest and most successful criminal in British history, worth an estimated £200 million. The war cost the family their nominal leader, David Ungi. The 36-year-old father of three was gunned down in a hail of automatic bullets as he drove his low-key VW Passat through the streets of Toxteth. Scores of gangsters were killed and maimed in revenge.

In 1980, Haase took on the full force of the Ungi/Fitzgibbon crew. The feud had been bubbling along for some years, perpetuated by a series of failed deals and rip-offs for which both sides blamed the other, but it needed a reason to explode into fully-fledged warfare. One soon presented itself: Haase's wife, Vera Aldridge, claimed she had been slighted in a local pub by a member of the opposing gang. It was a pretext which Haase used to seek revenge for a dodgy deal that had recently gone wrong. Haase kicked off the feud by slashing one of their gang. Another associate, John Fitzgibbon, was attacked with a baseball bat and a senior adviser called Tony Murray was shot at point-blank range.

PAUL GRIMES: One night I was on the door in Caesar's Palace and I got a call from Haase. He was looking for one particular member of the Fitzgibbon family. He asked me if this lad had been into the club that night.

'He's just left now,' I told him, literally watching this lad get into a cab and get off.

Haase picked up his trail and followed the cab. When the man in the cab got out, Haase jumped him near his flat and cut him up ruthlessly with a Stanley knife. He always used a weapon. He never used his fists.

Local hard-man James Turner (not his real name), who knew both sides, attempted to mediate to prevent the conflict escalating.

JAMES TURNER: Haase beat up John Fitzgibbon and then went for Tony Murray over an argument with his wife, Vera Aldridge. An argument did take place; she was screaming at John Fitzgibbon. But John Fitzgibbon never said anything bad to her. Haaser was a good fella; it was just a case of he'd been told lies by his wife. That night, they [Haase's gang] took a bulb out of the landing where Fitz went up to his flat [so he couldn't see] and done him there with a baseball bat. It didn't hurt him bad; it was just a baseball bat.

Anyway, the next day we're all in this flat with John Fitzgibbon and the discussion is 'What are we going to do about it?' A few of the lads was there, absolute toerags, all of them. I said, 'John Haase is my mate, so the answer is nothing.' I explained to John Fitzgibbon, 'No one's scarred, so it's just one of those things.' But John Fitzgibbon was there with that dirty fiend Tony Murray. Murray was giving it the big I am. I warned Murray, 'You want to be very fucking careful. You don't know this man, Haaser. Be very fucking careful.' I told him to shut his fucking mouth [about a revenge attack] because if it got back to Haaser that he was talking like this, he would be in trouble.

Sure enough, someone blew Murray up to Haaser and Haase and his men went down the next day and Murray ended up getting shot. What can you say?

PAUL GRIMES: Haase roped me in on that hit. Six weeks after he was out of jail in February 1980, I got a visit from him. He turned up with one of his best pals, Bernie Aldridge, who was his wife Vera's brother, and said that he needed me as back-up to help him sort out a dispute between himself and the Ungi/Fitzgibbon gang. Haase was fuming. He's going off've his head saying how he's going to kill them.

As far as the fight was concerned, I thought it was just gonna be a straightener with fists, iron bars and maybe the odd machete – but no shooters. So I grabbed a couple of pickaxe hangles off've one of my wagons for good measure. But Haase was getting more and more angry. He then decided to shoot them, so he asked a mate of mine called Johnny One Eye to go and pick up a shooter from his house and to meet us in Kitchen Street, near the Dock Road in Liverpool.

Haase found out that one of the senior members of their crew was at a mechanic's garage owned by Tony Murray. When we got there, he and Johnny One Eye steamed inside and started smashing the place up. Haase was dressed like he'd just walked out of a Burton's window as usual. Tweed jacket, black kecks and a nice white shirt. He was also wearing a balaclava.

First, they smashed up Murray's car. Then Haase pointed the shotgun at his head and threatened to blow him away. At this point, Johnny One Eye, who is a very trigger-happy bloke, got impatient with the talk, grabbed the single shooter off 've Haase and blew a hole in Murray. He was aiming to kneecap him from behind the knee, IRA-style, but he just ended up shooting him in the back of the leg. There was blood everywhere. Murray's sidekick, a fella called Desmond Fox who was in the garage as well, also got bashed up. They smashed his kneecaps in with an iron bar because they were busy reloading the shotgun. All the while, I was stood outside in my ovies with the pickaxe hangles to make sure no one gets in. Suddenly, Haase and Johnny One Eye ran out and we get off.

In the car, I asked Haase why he had done it. He just said that they had insulted his bird. Haase's bird was called Vera Aldridge. They had a kid together. I thought Haase had gone way over the top, to shoot someone over basically pub talk.

Anyways, we thought no more of the shooting. It was one of them. Allday. I went back to running my business. Haase went back to planning his bank robberies. Little did we know. The thing blew up out of all proportion. I mean, out of all fucking proportion. You'd have thought we'd shot the president by the way the papers were going on.

The victim Tony Murray was rushed to hospital and a surgeon battled to save his leg. The local papers said he was hanging on to his life by a thread. They described him as a garage boss. The busies said it was a gangland attack and they were determined to bring the culprits to justice.

Three days later, Haase and Bernie got nicked and charged with attempted murder on Murray and GBH on Foxy. They were sent to Risley Remand Centre. Then my uncle Billy Grimwood got it sorted. He was the biggest gangster in Liverpool at the time, old-school, and he had a secret meeting with Murray and persuaded him to drop the charges. That was normal.

On the day of the court hearing in July, Murray was persuaded to go missing, of course, and not turn up. The papers ran a story begging him to come forward and give evidence. They even had the prosecution barrister pleading with him in court to come back, saying that his leg would fall off within seven days of peritonitis, which would kill him if he didn't get to a doctor fast.

As we predicted, the court said that if Murray didn't turn up within seven days then they'd discharge John and Bernie. The police knew that we had nobbled the case so they launched a manhunt to find Murray and save the case. For a brief period, Murray came out of hiding and gave himself up to calm them down. He told his solicitor that there was nothing to worry about and he would go into the witness box before the seven-day court extension expired.

But on the day of the court, at dawn, Murray goes and has a freak car accident. Instead of going to court, he was rushed to hospital with his shot-up legs even more mangled and pumped full of drugs by the docs, meaning that he's in no fit state physically or mentally to give evidence in a court of law.

The police were so desperate to get him into court that they went to the hospital and tried to drag him from his bed to court. But the docs refused to allow it. In a last-ditch attempt to keep Haase behind bars, the most senior busies in the city plead with the court not to drop the case, but the judge discharges the case and Haase and Bernie walk.

That was the first time Haase started to get a reputation as someone who could beat cases and manipulate the system.

3

THE TRANSIT MOB

During this period in the late 1970s/early '80s, Haase put together a notorious gang of armed raiders called the Transit Mob, a name derived from their trademark use of Ford Transit vans. The gang terrorised Britain, targeting post offices, security companies and high street shops, stealing tens of thousands of pounds.

The Transit Mob was the dark secret Haase was trying to hide from the outside world by pretending to be a part-owner of Paul Grimes's waste-disposal company. Grimes noted that Haase would often disappear from the job for weeks on end without telling anyone what he was doing. Haase used these secret breaks to carry out armed raids. Most of the time was spent meticulously gathering intelligence on the target using surveillance, covertly logging the movement of security vans before attacking them with overwhelming firepower.

The seeds of the Transit Mob had been sown in the early '70s while Haase was serving his seven-year sentence for armed robbery. In prison, Haase met other, more experienced raiders and decided to recruit them for a superstar team once he got out. Career villain Danny Vaughan was the first to enlist. Haase was impressed with Vaughan's credentials. Vaughan picked up his first conviction at the age of 14 after stealing a million cigarettes from a kiosk in the Formby area of Merseyside. Later he was jailed for possession of a .45 Smith and Wesson and 50 rounds of ammunition. He was handy with a gun and noted in the underworld for his unflinching bottle, qualities which Haase admired and was determined to instil in the Transit Mob. A villain called Roy Grantham also caught Haase's attention. Jailbird Grantham was a powerfully built man, 5 ft 10 in., with a nerveless temperament in the path of a storm. Haase got him on the firm.

The Transit Mob's MO was simple but deadly. First, the gang's Ford Transit van rammed the target vehicle off the road and then its passengers pounced mob-handed from the back. Clad in overalls and balaclavas and armed to the teeth, the raiders relied on terrifying their unsuspecting victims into submission.

The Mob struck many times in the late '70s and evaded capture because of their careful preparation. Convicted heroin dealer Ken Darcy, a gangster who later went to work for Haase as a drug mule, estimated that Haase carried out 42 armed robberies. But by 1979, just as the gang were growing in confidence enough to increase the frequency of raids, the police were catching up. The key offences for which they were later convicted took place between 8 September 1979 – when the Transit Mob robbed a security van after ramming it off a dual carriageway in Netherton Way, Liverpool – and the day of their arrest on 9 April 1981. During this 18-month period, they were the most feared highwaymen in the north-west of England. The gang also raided high street shops including Marks and Spencer's, W.H. Smith's and Woolworths.

The police put the Transit Mob under surveillance, suspecting that Haase and Vaughan were the authors of a string of as yet unsolved robberies. However, officers failed to catch them red-handed and much of the evidence against them was intelligence-based. Vaughan recalled, 'There was no personal admissions, there was no forensic evidence, no IDs, no eyewitnesses, nothing from the day of the robberies.'

When Haase and Vaughan were arrested, the police believed

they had enough evidence to link the pair to two robberies in Ormskirk, Lancashire, and another in Maghull, a suburb of Liverpool. They were transferred from Liverpool to Manchester County Court for committal.

During the investigation, Roy Grantham turned supergrass, to the delight of the police. Using his evidence, officers had the confidence to widen their investigation to cover more than just the two sample offences they had charged Haase and Vaughan with. Police were able to link Haase and Vaughan to a backlog of unsolved offences, known as 'out of date' crimes, some stretching as far back as 15 years. Haase never forgave Grantham for informing on the Transit Mob. Several years later, Grantham allegedly committed suicide after mysteriously disappearing at sea on a boating trip. Underworld sources maintain he was killed in revenge for betraying the Transit Mob. Other sources claim that he took his own life out of fear, after a series of threats. However, the inquest into his death found no foul play, and Haase and his associates deny any involvement.

To seal the case, the police turned to a second supergrass called Dennis 'the Menace' Wilkinson. Wilkinson was a career con who specialised in luring his cellmates into making confessions during off-the-record conversations inside prison while they waited on remand. He was a vicious kidnapper and sex offender who had served time in jails all over Britain. His credibility within the close-knit prison system made him an ideal double agent. Wilkinson had few problems gaining the confidence of his victims, convincing them he was a hardened gangster, staunch and trustworthy.

At the time, Wilkinson was facing a possible 20-year sentence for kidnapping, torturing and sexually assaulting a man, so he agreed to help police in exchange for a reduced tariff. Wilkinson befriended Vaughan in jail and claimed to his police handlers that he had wheedled sensitive information out of the talkative Scouser. He started to report this back to them. Later, in his legal statement to police and under oath, Wilkinson swore that Vaughan had admitted the robbery of a post-office van 'during conversations in the last few weeks'. Wilkinson claimed the explosive confession took place in an exercise yard, despite the fact that he was being held in a different part of the jail from Haase and Vaughan. His evidence helped police win a conviction for the Transit Mob robberies. In July 1982, Haase got fourteen years for armed robbery on two post-office vans. Haase was then 33. His co-conspirator, 31-year-old Danny Vaughan, was jailed for 13 years. They had both pleaded not guilty. Haase remained at Liverpool's Walton jail but Vaughan was transferred to Gartree prison in Leicester.

Furious Haase waged a war of violence against the prison system, beating up guards and sparking a string of mini-riots in an attempt to get back at the authorities he blamed for stitching him up. He spent four years in solitary confinement as punishment, becoming increasingly embittered and cut off. He caused fights with other prisoners and took on the daddies and godfathers of the system without care. For comfort, he befriended other Scousers and took it upon himself to defend them against bullies, increasing his reputation in his home town on the outside. Haase was convinced that he would die in prison and at every turn looked for any excuse to appeal.

An opportunity arose. Supergrass Wilkinson's evidence was later discredited after he was exposed as a fraud. Haase and Vaughan tried desperately to appeal on the back of the revelations, getting solicitor Paul Baker on the case. Baker learned that Wilkinson had appeared as a key prosecution witness in at least eight major criminal trials, where he alleged that fellow prisoners confided in him about serious crimes. He had been used by police to give evidence against more than 20 men, who had been jailed for a total of 90 years. He was first exposed in 1984, two years into Haase's fourteen-year sentence, for irregularities in his evidence after he made his own confession in taped conversations with David Capstick, a private detective and former police officer. Mr Capstick said, 'He was nothing less than a professional witness.' When Wilkinson himself appeared in court later that year accused of kidnapping, torturing and sexually assaulting a man, police attended to praise his evidence in the robbery trial. The judge took the credit on board and sentenced Wilkinson to just six years.

Haase and Vaughan were confident that Wilkinson's sensational new evidence would help overturn their convictions. They instructed their solicitor, Paul Baker, to interview him in Wakefield prison. Wilkinson told Mr Baker that he would help his clients because his relationship with his police handlers had by then turned sour. He was bitter at his treatment by the police, who he claimed had promised him a new identity in Canada but later reneged on the deal. Mr Baker took a statement from him and contacted solicitors from other trials in which he had been involved. However, none of the convictions were overturned.

In a further bid to get back at the police, Wilkinson later retracted his original statement against Haase and Vaughan, claiming in a *Sunday People* story that he fitted up the pair on the instructions of a bent copper who had passed him Vaughan's confidential file and told him to memorise the evidence. Wilkinson claimed that he had perjured himself.

In 1984, friends and relatives of Haase and Vaughan climbed the 120-foot Wellington Monument in Liverpool to protest at the miscarriage of justice that had brought about their imprisonment. Vaughan's wife, 32-year-old Kathy, and Haase's brother-in-law Eddie Thompson barricaded themselves inside the stone plinth, which is similar in design to Nelson's Column in London's Trafalgar Square, and climbed to the very top. A police inspector using a fire ladder eventually persuaded them to come down. The protest, which later inspired the 'Free George Jackson' campaign in the soap opera *Brookside*, was in vain. Haase's and Vaughan's convictions were not overturned. They stayed in jail and served out their remaining sentences.

Haase was devastated, but the incident had taught him a lot. He noticed the increasing influence that supergrasses – the police's latest secret weapon – were having in the legal system as the law battled desperately to stay on top of organised crime. To him, it seemed as though the authorities would do business with anyone, no matter how crooked, as long as it got results. Haase also noticed how supergrasses were able to manipulate the system to their own advantage, bargaining tariffs for intelligence whether it was credible or not. It was a lesson he never forgot.

Personally, the long stretch in prison – without the prospect of early release – had a dramatic effect on Haase, as he later revealed to the *Liverpool Echo*.

JOHN HAASE: I got a long stretch and served 11 years out of a 14-year sentence. I spent the first four years in solitary confinement. I just could not handle such a long sentence and I rebelled. It seemed like the end of the world. I was violent and gave the screws a lot of trouble. I lost remission and the years were just piled on. I was a Category A prisoner with a history of trouble and violence and I was shunted between prisons . . . Parkhurst, Albany, Armley.

There did come a turning point and I realised that if I was to get out, it would be down to me. I had done four years in solitary, completely on my own in prison. No contact with my family. After 11 years, I was out. I had won back two years' remission, otherwise it would have been thirteen.

There were other spells in prison and since I left school I have spent most of my time either in Borstal or behind bars. You have to harden to it all and you eventually become conditioned to life in prison. It was tough but I took it on myself to look after the underdog and, of course, fellow Scousers behind bars.

But friends say Haase was underplaying the effects, that the sentence left hideous mental scars that never healed. He became vengeful against society, savagely, psychotically violent and hell-bent on taking huge risks to claw back the lost years by living hard and trying to earn money at an impossible rate. According to his friends, he had always been a 'hard-knock', a man who took no shit from anyone and was always up for a fight, but now he lost his temper more rapidly and did not know when to stop, even when his victims were unconscious on the ground. He had apparently lost control of his bloodlust.

Vaughan recalled that by now prison had changed Haase

irrevocably. He said it affected Haase mentally, making him cold, hard and bitter. Another pal said, 'The 11-year sentence changed Haase into what he is today. He went in a criminal. But he came out evil. That was the difference.'

However, he also emerged a more accomplished villain. He had gone into prison an amateur and come out a mastermind. Now back on the outside, he began to win the respect of his underworld underlings with his professional attitude and by not being afraid to go out on jobs himself.

KEN DARCY: Haase is very polite. His expression never changes. Cold and callous but he is very civilised. I've done graft with him. I've had 100 kilo of weed [cannabis] thrown in the back of the car and he's followed me home. I've bought all kinds of guns and he's followed me home. He's not afraid to be there when it's going off and get his hands dirty – and stay with it until the job gets done. A lot of the major criminals distance themselves from the graft, getting joeys to do their running around because they fear getting caught. But he wanted to do things himself. Everything I'd done with him was spot on and I'd had good wages out of him. You could see he'd done 11 years, see he's been en route – he was staunch.

But a new associate called Chris No-Neck, who was dealing drugs with Paul Bennett while Haase was in prison for the Transit Mob robberies, noticed a sinister, venal side to Haase.

CHRIS NO-NECK: My bird got on to him, the real him, before I did. He said something which summed him up one night, which gave us an insight into his true character, when we were all out on Valentine's night. Haase said, 'I would do absolutely anything for money.' Women get on things. Their instincts are better. She understood what that meant. That defined him.

4

JAIL AND THE BIG-TIME

In 1982, Haase may have been depressed by the 14-year sentence that lay ahead of him, but he was determined to make the most of it. Just as he had done during his previous stretches, Haase used jail to his own advantage. 'Make the time work for you' was an old lags' saying, and Haase did exactly that. He networked with Britain's top villains, plotting and scheming on the criminal activities that would make him rich when he got out.

Haase was constantly on the lookout for the crimes of the future, new opportunities that would pay better and pose less risk than the more traditional armed robberies that had landed him in jail. It didn't take long for his market research to throw up the Next Big Thing: drugs.

In Long Lartin prison in the late 1980s, Haase was introduced to an inmate who would change his life: a Turkish-Cypriot heroin dealer called Mustafa Sezazi. The former policeman turned vineyard owner was serving 18 years for mass importation of heroin into Britain. Sezazi was an early pioneer of the Turkish Connection, a ruthless gang of Turkish babas or godfathers who controlled the Southern Route, a heroin-smuggling network from the poppy fields of

Afghanistan to Britain via Turkey, the Balkans and much of Europe.

The Turkish Connection had refined their smuggling into a military operation. Successfully, they had used immigrant Turks in Britain and other European hubs to get their gear in from the east. The organisation grew in efficiency because of the deep-rooted, Sicilian-style values that held it together. Toughness, honour and a strong code of omerta (silence) were paramount. Soon they began to push the traditional competition – including the Chinese Triads, Pakistanis, Indians and Iranians – out of the heroin market to become Britain's number one suppliers. Ninety per cent of heroin in Britain originates from Afghanistan, the bulk of it coming through Turkish hands. Customs and Excise assistant chief investigator Phil Connelly, whose 100-man team was dedicated to stopping heroin at the time, said, 'It was big business. They were handling a hell of a lot of heroin even then. When this all started, it was all Pakistanis. In the '80s, it was virtually all Pakistanis. In the late '80s, the Turks then became very big in it.'

But, as Sezazi had discovered to his own misfortune, there was a weak link in the chain. The Turkish Connection could get heroin into the country but they didn't have control of the end-user distribution networks in British cities outside London, such as Liverpool, Manchester, Birmingham, Bristol, Glasgow and Edinburgh. To put it bluntly, the Turkish Connection did not have good contacts with established, mainly white British villains who had the muscle, the firepower and the know-how to distribute large amounts of heroin into local markets once it was in-country. The Turks – or Diesel Mercs, as they were known in cockney rhyming slang – couldn't get a handle on the local crime families and gang-bosses in these regions who controlled the council estates and the tower blocks where heroin addicts lived, who had the confidence to dish out kilos of heroin on tick to middle-ranking dealers, assured that the debts would be repaid out of respect. At street level, these local hard-men had fearsome reputations, ensuring that the heroin would not be stolen by rival dealers and that drug money could be transported safely without being hijacked by specialist tie-up gangs.

The Turkish babas were experts at getting 10- or 20-kilo parcels of heroin into the UK. But what was the point if they couldn't shift it en masse once it was within these shores? Selling dribs and drabs, ounces and half-kilos, to opportunists over a period of months and months would not sustain the production-line throughput the ambitious Turkish Connection was aiming for, nor generate the profits to sustain such a well-organised network. The bottleneck thrown up by imbalanced distribution, of having large amounts of supply but little demand, also posed security risks. The longer stocks remained unsold in the UK, hidden in safehouses or in transit, the more chance police and Customs and Excise had of finding it.

Enter John Haase – a potential solution to the problem. In Haase, Sezazi recognised an ideal business partner for the Turkish Connection, even if he was in jail. Haase was intelligent, fearless and hungry for riches. He had a bona fide reputation as a gangster and was as respected in Liverpool as in other parts of the country. The penal system had allowed him to befriend senior cons, such as London's most notorious enforcer Mad Frankie Fraser and leading figures from all over the UK. At that time, Haase had a reputation for being staunch, refusing to grass on his fellow criminals even when faced with long stretches in prison.

In addition, Haase was one of the new breed of gangsters who understood the potential of narcotics. Mostly former armed robbers, these upstart villains were completely amoral and had none of the old-school, Godfather-style hang-ups about dirtying their hands with drugs. To Haase and his contemporaries, it just came down to cash. Dealing in death was no different from harming the public during an armed robbery. It just made more money. They understood that theirs was a dying trade. The police now had armed robbery under control. Better security, improved intelligence, specialised squads and lengthy sentences were bringing to a close the glory days of blagging. Drugs, however, were virgin territory, in which the underworld had stolen the idea wholesale from the hippies and stolen a march on law enforcement at the same time. The villains were streets ahead of them all.

Hitherto, the drugs trade in the UK had been controlled by small-time opportunists and cannabis-smuggling long-hairs in the mould of Mr Nice, Howard Marks, a hangover from the 1960s. At first, the Turkish Connection tried to befriend the hippies, but they found them unwilling to diversify into Class A drugs. And when they did, some of these dealers were flaky and risk averse. In contrast, the new breed of armed robbers turned drug barons had no such inhibitions; they thought big and acted big and were vicious enough to stamp their control over the existing networks and flood them with heroin.

In their Long Lartin cells, Sezazi struck a deal with the Turkish Connection's new-found protégé, and appointed him de facto head of UK heroin sales for the organisation on his release. Sezazi promised that when Haase got out of prison, even though Sezazi himself would still be inside finishing his longer sentence, he would arrange for an introduction to leading members of the London-based Turkish Connection so that business could get started. It was fortuitous for everyone. Haase's plans to turn the Turkish heroin racket from a cottage industry in the UK into a multimillion-pound business coincided with the rise to power of the young Turks. Some of these next-generation smugglers were British-born, making it easy for Haase to do business with them. It was a match made in heaven, timed to perfection.

While Haase was in jail, a young north London hoodlum called Suleyman Ergun and his brother-in-law Yilmaz Kaya were both making their mark on the Turkish underworld. Ergun was a highly energetic, fast-talking wheeler-dealer in the rag trade. Kaya had interests in sweatshops manufacturing clothes.

Ergun lived in a 1930s council tenement block a stone's throw from Euston station with his Turkish immigrant mum, dad and younger sister. He was a street kid at heart, as much a

Londoner as he was Turkish. He spoke with a cockney accent and ruled the notorious Somerstown council estate in Camden with a heady mix of violence and charm. Though slight of frame, he was a tough fighter and a natural born risk-taker. He was known to be stubborn, fearless and trigger-happy, if need be. The fast-moving 21 year old, known as Slay on the street, was loved and feared in equal measures by everyone he did business with because of his infectious nervous energy and quick-fire intelligence. He was a doer, not a talker. Ergun had an egalitarian approach to the underworld, an ability to do business at all levels of the gangland hierarchy. On the one hand, he could sit down with the top bosses of the Adams family, London's gangland ruling elite, or international drug smugglers from Turkey, Sicily or Colombia. On the other hand, he had no problem doing business with Jamaican yardies or scallies from Liverpool and Manchester. It was a quality that served him well on his meteoric rise to wealth and power beyond his wildest dreams.

Ergun rose to become the effective number three in one of the world's biggest heroin-smuggling gangs. He was the right-hand man to his brother-in-law and deputy boss Yilmaz Kaya. Kaya reported directly to the main man, the Turkish boss of bosses and Istanbul-based baba The Vulcan. The Vulcan's real name was Zulkiv Topuz (also spelt 'Topaz', by Customs, amongst others) but he frequently used the alias Nuri Yazici. He was one of the world's biggest heroin dealers, near the top of Customs and Excise's hit list. But in the late '80s, while Haase was in jail, Ergun was still a petty criminal.

SULEYMAN ERGUN: When I first got into dealing, it was only with small amounts, nothing great. The reason was we couldn't really find someone to take the amounts we were bringing in. Ever since I was young, I've known heroin comes from Turkey. I knew that Turks – the underworld – were the main heroin dealers in other countries. It was all done by word of mouth. Eventually, Turkey became the main supplier to the world.

They get the opium base from Afghanistan and Pakistan, transport it to Turkey through the mountains or sometimes by boat, oil tanker or cargo ships into the Black Sea ports. The base is brought in in tonnes. Then five chemicals are used to break it down, refine it into heroin. I believe most of the chemicals – the acids – come from Belgium and Germany.

In the late '70s to early '80s, it really took off. Although the transport and technology wasn't as sophisticated as it is now, the business routes suddenly opened up, with trucks and wagons able to ship it west in bulk. The routes out of Turkey were the same as they've always been, just over the old routes by land and sea. By land from Istanbul through Bulgaria, sometimes to Greece and into Yugoslavia. Then into Czechoslovakia (now Czech Republic), Hungary, Austria, then you're in Germany and Italy.

These countries have got the key roads. One good route, which I used many times, is from Bulgaria through Yugoslavia, Austria, Germany, Belgium and into France. Then straight over here. You can miss one country and go to another. It's dead flexible. Getting from Istanbul to France or Belgium is easy. No one stops you.

In the 1970s, when the Turks were just getting it sussed, it was just brought to England in small amounts. They were doing it [hidden] in clothes or by post. For instance, someone works in the post office and knows it's coming in, how and everything else about it, when and where from. Then they intercept it before it goes to the main sorting office. Or you can post it to someone's address and they sign for it. Customs don't go into the post office, only if they get a tip-off. And the Customs in the other countries en route don't mess with it either. Royal Mail regulate everything – even overseas. Because a parcel is on a transit route, just passing through a foreign place to its destination in England, they don't open them up in other countries. The back doors of the mail trucks are sealed, preventing Customs from getting into them. At least, that's how it used to be.

Overland, if you take it yourself, you could seal it in a Land

Rover or the roof of a transit van or in door panels, in the gearbox, tyres, dashboard, inside the sashing. A transit van could store 150 kilos in the roof – but those big amounts only came later in the late '80s/'90s when we got involved and Haase was involved. By that time, we had become very good, very efficient, but at first it was all piecemeal.

Later, once we made it big, we even planned to bring it here in an oil tanker along with the Italian Mafia and some cocaine people in Colombia. That was the biggest vessel. It was going to be a superload – heroin, coke and hash in an oil tanker.

But before we made it into a big business, it was only being brought in kilos; ten-kilo parcels at the most. Individual Turks would bring in a little lump, sell it for a few grand, buy a shop and never do it again. But they were still quite clever. The most sophisticated I ever knew about in them days was inside a suit – a suit with heroin soaked into it. You put heroin in water, dissolve it and then put the suit in it. It's sort of washing it in heroin and then letting it dry out. The suit gets heavier but you just wear it. When you get it to the destination, put it in water again and the heroin washes out. The wet heroin powder is then laid out on an absorbent cotton cloth to dry in a warm room or, if possible, outside in the sunshine. A kilo and a half could be done that way. The Pakistanis started that off, but I've seen that done by Turks.

The Turks also brought it in dissolved in whisky, rum and brandy, inside women's heels and inside people's bodies. A human can swallow about a kilo. That was the kind of thing the old Turks were doing before we took over.

My introduction into heroin came because I knew Yilmaz [Kaya] through the rag trade – the factory business. Yilmaz wasn't involved with gear at first. He got involved in Turkey. We knew each other. I was only young but Yilmaz trusted me, knew my family, liked me. Yilmaz had always liked me when I was a little kid. He was 15 years older than me, about the same age as Haase. He was like a brother to me. Trust, honour and respect is what I had that Yilmaz liked. I wanted to go into it, the heroin business, but at first he didn't want me to get into it.

He was trying to dissuade me. But I was stubborn; I said I would do it anyway and I'd rather it be him than anyone else.

Haase and Mustafa Sezazi were together in Long Lartin doing time, Haase for armed robbery and Sezazi for heroin. They became jail friends. Sezazi was an ex-policeman from northern Cyprus. Yilmaz got to know him through the underworld, and when he was in jail we would send in money to him so he could fund his appeals. He would be visited by his son and we would give the money to his son beforehand. To return the favour, Sezazi introduced Haase to us when Haase got out of jail. We gave Sezazi a 'drink' for introducing Haase to us. At that point, Yilmaz was giving heroin to too many people, in small amounts, so he wanted someone who could take more at once, in one go.

The less people that were involved, the less chance of getting nicked, so he was looking for someone who could handle a lot in one go. Sezazi was still in nick at the time but Yilmaz went to Liverpool for the first meet with Haase when he got out. They talked about how much Haase could move, then shook on a deal. Kaya offered to supply Haase with as much gear as he could take.

Haase had no experience of the drugs business but when he got out of Long Lartin, he found out that his nephew Paul Bennett was doing brown at the time in Liverpool. That was pure coincidence. Bennett was not getting it off us and they were only doing small kilo loads. But the point was Bennett knew about drugs, the technical side of it. So Haase was able to tap into his knowledge. It was a good partnership. Haase was the muscle and the brains. Bennett was the doer, the dealer.

Immediately after he got out of jail, Haase told Bennett that the business was going to change from now on, that he was taking over. He told him that they were going to get bigger. Bennett's partner at the time, a villain called Chris No-Neck, was muscled out by Haase. So Haase became the boss and Bennett his sidekick.

The first amount Haase moved was 90 kilos. Yilmaz gave it to him. I wasn't with Yilmaz at the time. I came on board a bit later to collect money. It was only after a good few months of Yilmaz working with Haase that I was introduced, after trust had been established. Collecting money was my first job.

It started with a phone call out of the blue, then going up to Liverpool – that was my first meet with Haase and Bennett. Bennett was a loudmouth – immature, he was. But Haase was cunning. I would be collecting money from now on. I was told not to give it to anyone. Until then, Yilmaz had been using a gopher called Joey the Turk (not his real name). Haase and Bennett didn't like him because he was a boaster. He got off on being in the underworld, liked to tell everyone. But Haase and Bennett did like me. I could speak better English. At the end of the day, Joey, like his partner in crime Manuk Ocecki, who also worked for us, was just that: a joey. When I took over, I saw the job of being Kaya's number two as important. I got more involved in managing things. I took on more responsibility.

The first meet was in the Rocky Lane sauna in Liverpool. I collected £68,000 that day. You are told when and where to get it from. Even in those early days, a million pounds' worth of business had already been established. Haase and Bennett had been given, say, 50 kilos at £20,000 a kilo. We became Haase's single supplier. For 18 months, it was big business.

5

THE LIVERPOOL MAFIA AND THE DRUGS REVOLUTION

It was no coincidence that Haase had been able to take a leading role in Britain's biggest heroin gang without much effort. A lot of villains who had gone before him had paved the way, laying the groundwork, grooming him for a top slot in the corporation without him really knowing it but for which he would gratefully take the credit. These villains came to be known as the Liverpool Mafia, and in the 1970s and 1980s the small group of Scouse gangsters pioneered large-scale drug smuggling and distribution in the UK. By the 1990s, the foundations had been laid for a second generation of Liverpool barons, such as John Haase, to take stewardship of this phenomenon – taking drug dealing to a stratospheric level, generating billions of pounds and spreading death and misery on a previously unknown scale. The '90s drug-dealing boom was good timing for Loony Tunes. In 1992, he was just getting out of prison armed with a series of fortuitous introductions into the Turkish Connection, and all the pieces of the jigsaw were in place to make it easy for him.

Other narco superstars to graduate from this school of

excellence at roughly the same time as Haase included drug legends like Colin 'Badger' Borrows and Curtis 'Cocky' Warren, today revered household names in the underworld and in popular culture. Like Haase, these two had started out as armed robbers. Borrows went on to become Britain's first crack-cocaine dealer, responsible for introducing man's most addictive banned substance into the UK and getting Middle England hooked. Warren rose from a rootin'-tootin' scallywag to become Interpol's Target One, moving up the Class A ladder from street dealer to wholesaler to importer. By the time he was successfully prosecuted, he was worth an estimated £200 million. *The Observer* had the following to say about the event:

> The mythology of British villainy needs to be rewritten. Next to Warren, the Krays were pathetic minnows. The Great Train Robbers and Brinks Mat robbers, who were swaggering highwaymen from the pre-drugs era, were way down the division. The plain fact is Warren is the richest and most successful British criminal who has ever been caught.

Haase and Warren were at different times business partners, rivals and then bitter enemies – a normal relationship in the drugs world.

The second generation of drug dealers such as Haase, Warren and Borrows had 20 years of local narco heritage to draw on, knowledge that would be passed down from villain to villain, ensuring that the successors were even better at it than those who went before them. For instance, the second generation began to use professional enquiry agents, including private detectives and former special-services soldiers, to boost their counter-surveillance capability. Gangster Andy Shacklady regularly used former SAS soldiers to debug meeting venues and to spy on rival villains and police patrols. He used a former regiment soldier from Manchester – now serving in Afghanistan – to track down a drug dealer who had stolen a large consignment of amphetamine base. He was successfully traced to a caravan in North Wales and punished.

Ominously, the second generation were quick to rip up the traditional gangland codes that had loosely defined the behaviour of the old-school. For the first time, police and Customs officers became legitimate targets for drug-dealing gangs who wanted them off their backs. The second generation thought nothing of putting out contracts on law officers, raiding their homes, firebombing their cars and even shooting them.

Gangsters in other parts of the UK were also dealing drugs, but the villains in Liverpool were quickly able to dominate the trade, turning the city into an international distribution hub, dubbed by one senior policeman the Amsterdam of Britain. The main reason was simple – Liverpool was a port and its underworld was well versed in trading in contraband; it had been doing it for hundreds of years. But a number of other factors also helped propel the Liverpool mobsters into the premier league, where they played alongside billionaire legends from shady places like Medellin, Sicily, Istanbul and Amsterdam to great effect. The emergence of a group of wealthy, white, middle-aged villains dubbed the Liverpool Mafia was one such factor. Most of them were former armed robbers looking to invest their winnings in a safer, cleaner industry. It was these perma-tanned, golf-clad underworld speculators who put up the money to underwrite the big drug deals, forming an alliance with a younger generation of Afro-Caribbean criminals from the city's Toxteth ghetto – dubbed the Black Caucus by police – to help them run it.

Culturally, the Toxteth Riots and Liverpool's seemingly endless economic recession during the '80s and '90s also helped promote organised crime, providing an army of desperate anti-establishment foot-soldiers infected with the city's trademark scallywag subculture, the swaggering, pro-crime 'Spirit of Whacker'. Scallies were to drugs what yuppies were to stocks and shares. Technologically, mobile phones, computers, electronic counter-surveillance, cheap air travel and financial deregulation also played their part. People in the West were now richer than ever, with the spending power to consume drugs in mainstream amounts. On the supply side, modern industrial farming methods had now reached places like Colombia and Afghanistan and were quickly adapted by drug-crop growers, enabling them to churn out harvests on a massive scale. The cocaine produced from just 500 coca leaves in South America could fetch half a million pounds in a city in Europe or the USA. All this meant one thing: the '80s and '90s were the golden age of drug dealing, and Liverpool was knee deep in it.

Police and Customs officers were quick to realise that there was a sea change under way and that Liverpool was the epicentre of a drugs tsunami. Phil Connelly, former assistant chief investigator of HM Customs and Excise, said, 'In the early '80s, Customs formed two special units to tackle the increase in drugs. One targeted heroin and one targeted cocaine. I was in charge of the one that was after the heroin dealers. There was 100 to 150 men in the team.

'At first, we concentrated our efforts in London, for obvious reasons. That was where a lot of the big players were. Then we started following the drugs and money. And we ended up in Liverpool. We were surprised how big the operations were in Liverpool.

'As drug dealers, they were the best. The drug dealers in Liverpool were streets ahead of everyone else. That was mainly because they were smart. They were very good at covering their tracks. Some of them were very intelligent. For instance, Paul Bennett was very clever.'

A detective-sergeant from the Metropolitan Police's Specialist Crime Unit revealed how drug dealers in Liverpool were quick to use the legal system to protect themselves in a way that had never been tried. He said, 'The drug dealers in Liverpool at around this time were quick to take advantage of the legal system. A colleague in the Merseyside Police told me that just about every drug dealer in the city was rushing to the police or Customs to become a registered informant. That was for two reasons. Number one: they could learn how the system works from the inside. Number two: if they got caught, they could use it as an insurance policy. They could say, "I was only dealing to cover my tracks as an informant," or, "I was gathering info for the police." They used it as a get out of jail free. That was very different from how villains behaved before drugs came along. Because it was the early days of big drug dealing, a lot of mistakes were made by us, the police and Customs, in falling for criminals who abused the supergrass system by using it for their own ends.'

Another leading Customs investigator described Liverpool as 'the number one UK centre of excellence for drug smuggling'. The situation was becoming a law-enforcement embarrassment and it was not long before politicians were demanding action. Gradually, the authorities began to respond. First up were Customs and Excise, who agreed to train their biggest undercover informant on the city like a guided missile. Former Greek-Cypriot freedom fighter and gangster Andreas Antoniades, who has worked for HM Customs and the American CIA for over 30 years infiltrating the world's biggest narco networks in the Middle East, Africa and Latin America, was instructed to bring down the Scousers with immediate effect. The colourful Antoniades, who shot one of the Krays' gang before turning supergrass, had dozens of successful big convictions under his belt, leading to three attempts on his life, and went on to take part in a US intelligence-service plot to buy back Stinger anti-aircraft missiles from the Taliban in Afghanistan. Posing as a buyer, he befriended members of the Liverpool Mafia but quickly realised he was dealing with some of the most violent and calculating men he had ever encountered. To boot, they had learned about the supergrass system well, which made it difficult for him to turn them over. He said, 'I did a job in Liverpool involving over 1,000 kilos of cocaine where [my fellow undercover man] was almost killed.'

In March 1982, Merseyside Police Chief Ken Oxford recognised the trouble in his own backyard. He declared war on the drug dealers. He said, 'We are talking about millions of pounds. It is essential that money does not go back into the international syndicates because as one gang is busted there is always someone to take its place. There is no diminution of supply and the key to the supply is the exchange of large sums of money. It is important that these people do not gain from their criminal activities.' But even by then it was too late. The seeds had been sown a decade or more earlier and now there was nothing stopping it.

Almost all of the members of the Liverpool Mafia had served their criminal apprenticeships as professional warehouse raiders stealing from the city's docks in the 1950s and '60s. For organised crime back then, the Port of Liverpool was the answer to their prayers – a ready-made wealth-creation scheme on their doorstep which they could tap into any time they wanted. Eight miles long and poorly protected, the warehouses were jam-packed full of millions of pounds of every conceivable consumer good ripe for the picking. In a post-war era which had created a ration-starved public used to meddling in the black market, it was a match made in heaven.

For the Liverpool Mafia, the bonus was that warehouse robberies were largely risk-free. The docks were totally under their control and had been for generations. Dockers, lorry drivers and security guards were mostly friends and family, whose cooperation was bought with bribes if not loyalty.

During the Second World War, the US Army had tried in vain to stamp out the gangs that were a threat to war materials. Special platoons were created to prevent Army cigarettes from being stolen en masse. But unlike New York, where the US Navy had got the dockers onside by doing a deal with their union-boss mobster Lucky Luciano, the attempts in Liverpool to stop warehouses from being looted failed miserably. In fact, the plunder rocketed to new heights. By the 1950s, the problem was putting the economic viability of Liverpool's port at risk. Marine insurers began to baulk at losses no longer covered by special wartime indemnities. In desperation, cargo handlers began introducing bizarre security measures. The shoe exporter Timpson's began splitting up its cargoes – left feet on one ship, right on another – so that the hijackers were left with lorry loads of stolen but unsellable single shoes. The electrical goods company Remington removed the magnetic motors from its top-of-the range razors and stored them in separate warehouses, miles apart from their plastic cases. But the raiders simply slipped the cargo handlers bigger bribes to pinpoint the exact locations of the various components so they could be robbed and reassembled later. Finally, in the mid-'60s, faced with huge losses from theft, the Port Authority of Liverpool invested millions of pounds into containerisation – the transport of cargo in relatively secure steel containers.

Containerisation spelled the end for this type of crime. But by this time, the Liverpool Mafia had moved into contraband smuggling, armed robbery and protection racketeering. This set them on the route to drug dealing, which would turn out to be their field of excellence. The advantages afforded by living in a port soon paid serious dividends, including good money-laundering contacts and strong historical and family links with the Dublin-based IRA, the most ruthless and efficient contraband smugglers in the world.

Another key to success was the UK-wide underworld distribution network which the Liverpool Mafia had been running since the war – a ring of fences, middlemen, money-men, drivers and couriers across the country that was the envy of their land-locked rivals in other cities, who traditionally feared to tread outside their 'manors'. Using the network, they were able to sell stolen goods far and wide quickly. And in the '70s, the same contacts experimented with sales of cannabis. In the '80s, they moved into heroin and by the time the cocaine boom of the '90s came around, the network was flooded with cheap Colombian powder, trafficking drugs to all corners of the UK. The Liverpool Mafia, as controllers of this system, grew rich as drug addiction in the inner cities soared.

A power shift away from the traditional gangsters towards the new drug dealers began in the early '80s, corresponding with the ascent of Mrs Thatcher and the Toxteth riots of 1981. By

1985, the drug dealers reigned supreme, their power base built on vast wealth. The new drug dealers were quick to ditch the traditional underworld codes. Forging profitable and strategic partnerships was now the source of their power, sometimes by passing information to the police and Customs and Excise, becoming double agents who protected their own empires by ratting on others, and at other times by linking up with new criminal gangs. For instance, the predominantly white, middle-aged gangster elite began forming unprecedented links with the young, black drug dealers of Toxteth's Granby ghetto – a partnership that led to mutual success.

The founding fathers of the Liverpool Mafia included leading luminaries such as Tommy 'Tacker' Comerford, Tony Murray, brothers Michael and Delroy Showers, a super-rich godfather known as The Banker and crack baron Colin Borrows. These were the pioneers who got a foot in the door, allowing Haase to boot it in and open the floodgates. These were the gangsters to whom John Haase would owe his good fortune.

Tommy Comerford was an armed robber turned safe-cracker who blazed an early trail in heroin trafficking. Comerford had been behind an infamous robbery dubbed the Water Street Job in 1969, a commando-style raid on a Liverpool bank carried out by international jewel thieves. After spending two days tunnelling into the strong room of the bank, the gang made off with £140,000. They were the first in the UK to use state-of-the-art thermal lances during a robbery, and Comerford was later jailed for seven years. Following his release, Comerford invested in cannabis but soon clocked up another seven years for recruiting dockers in a smuggling conspiracy. In 1983, Comerford was arrested with a half a kilo of heroin at Heathrow airport and later jailed for 14 years for masterminding what Customs officers described as 'Britain's first Class A drugs cartel'. In the prison system, Comerford was noted for his Jimmy Tarbuck-style '70s Scouse humour, a trait which made him many friends and enabled him to put his often ruthlessly violent and unstable peers at ease.

In the late '70s and early '80s, Comerford set up his HQ in the city's Holiday Inn hotel, which later became a Moat House, to market heroin: the new drug of choice amongst unemployed youth. His objective was simple: the ruthless exploitation of the relatively new phenomenon of cheap, mass-market drugs. Comerford used the Holiday Inn to cut up his freshly smuggled heroin with Minotol baby-food powder in a kitchen blender. Minotol, he discovered, was a perfect blending agent for heroin. It was the same colour and consistency and it melted at the same temperature as heroin crystals. That meant that on the foil of the addicts who smoked it, Minotol 'ran' across the surface indistinguishably from the active ingredient heroin. Such was the demand for Minotol that when supplies ran out in the Liverpool chemists, gophers were dispatched on planes to Amsterdam to clean out the shelves there, where it was openly sold as a drug-traffickers' product. Comerford was also an early kilo-cocaine speculator who experimented with buying powder in bulk at a time when most of his criminal contemporaries were still dabbling flakily in cannabis.

In between trips to Germany, Amsterdam and on the QE2, Comerford and his team of Lacoste-sporting scallywag urchins ostentatiously held court at the Holiday Inn. Touring pop groups and visiting football teams playing at Anfield and Goodison were lured up to his comped (complimentary) suites – the hotel management had been bribed – for all-night snorting sessions.

For Customs and Excise, he was the missing link in the evolutionary chain of drug-dealing gangsters. As they watched him, investigators observed that they were seeing something new – Comerford was essentially an opportunist drug dealer, a lay criminal who got into drugs because it was easier and more profitable than stealing. Like many of his narco-pioneer contemporaries, he came from a family of Liverpool dockers, steeped in the tradition of pilfering merchandise and smuggling contraband. Comerford saw drugs as an extension of this custom and was able to use his old knowledge and contacts in his new illegal enterprise. Comerford's unique selling point was his professionalism, and this enabled him to make a quantum leap from being a small-time dealer to a big-time smuggler. In this sense, Comerford was the stepping stone from an era of '60s hippy dealers and '70s opportunists to today's ruthlessly dedicated international drug dealers.

A major criminal player called Tony Murray was also quick to realise the potential of drug dealing, along with the importance of covering his tracks in this extremely fickle business. He became an expert at leading a double life, to shield his activities not only from the police but from his underworld peers as well. Playing your cards close to your chest was an essential tool of survival in the new culture of drug dealing. There were too many informants, too many anti-drugs vigilantes and too many villains looking to rob or 'tax' drug dealers of their super-profits.

In a bizarre bid to distance himself from the new phenomenon, Murray publicly declared war on the city's drug dealers in 1985. The stunt, solely designed for public consumption, was triggered after Murray's 14-year-old nephew Jason Fitzsimmons died of a heroin overdose. The tragedy was one of the first teenage deaths from drugs in the UK, sparking a media frenzy. Murray attacked the drug dealers responsible on local TV and vowed to 'wipe them off the face of the earth'. Jason's death then triggered a national outcry. Even PM Margaret Thatcher commented, 'Jason's death reminds us of the threat drug misuse poses to the well-being of all our young people, their families and society.'

Murray went further in a statement to the *Liverpool Echo*:

> When I find out who did it, then they are dead. I will do it with my bare hands if I have to. These people are nothing but rats. They are scum of the earth. They should be wiped off the face of the earth.

Ten years later, the stunt spectacularly backfired. Murray was jailed for 12 years for plotting to supply £1 million worth of heroin. He was caught red-handed offering to sell one kilogram of heroin to undercover police officers and conspiring to traffic a bulk load. In September 2002, a car carrying 10 kilos of heroin with a street value of more than £500,000 was discovered in Beech Street, Kensington. Realising the game was up, Murray fled to Spain after a car chase in Cannock, Staffordshire, in which he crashed into seven vehicles. British police launched an international hunt for the man who had shot to the top of their wanted list. He was arrested at his villa in Malaga and extradited to the UK. In March 2005, Murray was jailed again, this time for 13 years in a second plot to traffic heroin, in partnership with a Turkish gang. Judge Jonathan Foster QC told him, 'The supply of drugs is a sophisticated business. It involves knowledge and dealing with a producer or wholesaler. I find you were the principal participant of the Liverpool end of this conspiracy.' Murray had reaped rich rewards from his career as a drug dealer, including a luxury house in Cheshire. Of all the Liverpool villains who made the leap from traditional villainy into drug dealing, Murray was the most symbolic.

Toxteth brothers Michael and Delroy Showers led the charge amongst the black community and soon broke into the heavyweight league. Michael Showers rose from barman to doorman to racketeer. He was evil, violent and feared, and began drug dealing on a small scale by travelling abroad and sending parcels of marijuana back to his girlfriends in Liverpool.

Between 1977 and 1979, Michael's brother Delroy increased their imports, flying to Kenya on a false passport and sending suitcases of cannabis back to Liverpool by sea. Delroy had close links with south London mobster Charlie Richardson. In 1980, Delroy was jailed for nine years for being 'the ringleader' of the smuggling operation.

Meanwhile, his brother Michael was covering his tracks by carving out a political career as a self-styled spokesman for the riot-torn Toxteth ghetto. Astonishingly, he was given a £16,000-a-year job by Liverpool City Council and appeared on BBC's *Question Time* and *Panorama*. It came as a great shock when Michael was jailed for 20 years for smuggling 12 kilos of heroin into Britain from Afghanistan.

The Banker is the undisputed godfather-king of the Liverpool Mafia, a drug baron worth hundreds of millions of pounds. He cannot be named for legal reasons because he has never been caught with drugs. The former docker was so secretive about his Class B and Class A drug-smuggling operations in the beginning that his closest friends did not know he had got involved. He became an expert money-washer through property deals and various businesses. But his strength lay in his ability to overcome the race prejudices held by other villains of his generation and do business with the black gangs who knew the drug scene back to front. His claim to fame was that he started off super-dealer Curtis Warren.

Colin Borrows slipped secretly into the history books on Wednesday, 8 June 1988 as the first person in the UK to be arrested for the manufacture and supply of crack cocaine. Officially, he had become Britain's first crack dealer. The lorry driver's son turned gangster had begun dealing crack cocaine three years earlier, in 1985. During that period, he had revolutionised the cocaine trade and changed the social and criminal landscape in Britain forever. Borrows' rags-to-riches story was textbook business. He had started out with a little-known niche-market product and turned it into a household name almost overnight. He compares himself to Richard Branson, Bernie Ecclestone and Alan Sugar, apportioning his success to the application of a peculiarly British brand of 'stack 'em high, sell 'em cheap' entrepreneurism to an amateurish cottage industry. And it was a formula that struck gold.

Today that market is worth £1,817 million in the UK, boasts more than 200,000 loyal customers and employs thousands of people, many from deprived inner-city backgrounds. If it were any other business, it wouldn't be difficult to imagine Borrows being lauded at 10 Downing Street as a particularly exciting example of British free-market capitalism. But his business was crack cocaine, the most addictive street narcotic known to man. Borrows is unrepentant and proud of his achievements.

BORROWS: In April 1985, I got out of prison after serving nine months for burgling a detective-inspector's house. Liverpool was a grim place to come out to. There was no graft whatsoever. It was bang in the middle of all that Militant crisis with Derek Hatton. No cunt had a job – there was fuck all going. I had two kids to support. But all's I knew was robbing. In the end, I went back to being a doorman on a nightclub in Liverpool.

I never set out to be a drug dealer. It happened purely by accident. It all happened because there was a patch of waste ground near Lodge Lane where drug dealers would often stash their stuff while selling on the frontline in Granby Street, which was nearby. There was a campaign in the neighbourhood to keep heroin out of the ghetto. There was graffiti saying 'This is Toxteth not Croxteth' on the wall, referring to a district that heroin had turned into Smack City. Vigilantes were going around having dealers off. And grassing them up. So no one wanted to get collared with Class As on them. They all had their little stashes on the sly.

I knew this and I would always walk carefully over this patch of ground to see if I could find anything. I was skint. I never found nothing, of course. Except for one day. I was just looking out of the window. This fella walks straight over and I watch him try and drop something on the ground. I waited for him to go and then I went down to where he'd been standing – and I found a bag of white powder. It was just there, under an old Coke tin. Nothing dramatic. Just like that – in a resealable plazzy bag.

That was it. That was my point of entry into the drugs business. I didn't even know what it was, but I knew it was good so I was buzzing. I took it to a friend's house, who immediately said it was cocaine. Up to that point, I'd only ever come across cocaine twice before. Both times it was back in the '70s, when I'd seen a few of the lads, armed robbers and what have you, snorting in a couple of pubs. It was rare and expensive then and it was a bit of a thing to have it, showing off. It turned out to be a quarter-ounce of powdered cocaine that was worth about £350. But my friend said if I bagged it up, it was worth twice as much.

We split it up into eight bags, each with a gram inside, and sold them for £80 each. They took over a week to sell. I soon found a reliable source of cocaine and doubled up. I bought a half-ounce and bagged that. Business picked up.

After a few weeks, my friend said that he'd heard about a new form of cocaine in America. He said the dealers there could sell it quicker because they made it into crack. People smoked it in seconds rather than snorting it over hours. Instant bonus if you're a dealer. The rocks were also small and easy to conceal. I began to find out more.

My friend said he would introduce me to a yardie who could wash up a few days later. I was buzzing. My friend took me to the yardie's house. It was a nice flat and it turned out that we knew each other from around the place. The yardie was not a dealer, just a user. I took out an ounce of Charlie and put it on the side in the back kitchen. The yardie put on a pan of water to boil. I started to build a joint while the yardie got out the scales and weighed the cocaine into four quarters. He said, 'I will wash the first quarter and then you do the next,' and so on.

The yardie showed me how to wash the impurities out by heating it with baking soda, to make crack cocaine. After about 30 seconds, I could see the white froth begin to crystallise on the surface of the boiling water. I was buzzing. Even then I was thinking about how much money I could make. We dried it on the cooker; I paid him for his services and left.

Again it took me a week to sell, mainly because no cunt had tried the rocks before. But I made £1,000 profit. Then I doubled up and bought two ounces, washed it up and sold it from my car on the frontline in Toxteth. I then set about learning by myself how to manufacture crack on a big scale, how to do it properly. The first time I did it by myself, the mixture blew up all over the walls because of the baking soda. I lost £1,000 worth of cocaine. But it didn't matter. The punters who I had sold it to a day earlier were now craving for it, begging me for more. By trial and error, I got it right. I used bicarb, ether or ammonia, depending on what quantity I was washing up. It was done in a test tube or a Lucozade bottle, in a jam jar or a microwave.

Within weeks of selling my first rock, I got my first crack house, a flat in Faulkner Square in Toxteth. It was an ordinary flat, but high up and in the middle of the red-light area. I installed a huge gas fire and had it burning 24 hours a day so that the gear could be vaporised in the event of a police raid. The customers would be sweating like pigs but it kept me out of prison for three years.

The secret to my success was I learned how to wash up cocaine in large amounts and get a production line going. That was the turning point. Up to then, people used to do it themselves like a cottage industry. My first premises generated between £2,000 and £5,000 a day.

Within three months, I opened three more crack houses in the Lodge Lane area of Liverpool and I got ten street dealers also selling for me. They were open 24 hours a day. As more people got into crack, each house made between £5,000 and £10,000 a week. Then I began to make an astronomical amount of money. Forty thousand a week became a pittance. A pittance. I expected to make that per day sometimes, never mind a week.

I literally became famous for being able to wash up cocaine better than anyone else. Other dealers paid me £3,000 per kilo to wash up their cocaine to make crack. When I first started, I didn't spend any on drugs for myself and it was strictly business. I was a millionaire in a matter of weeks. Not months. Not years. Not like Branson, who's taken so many fucking years to make so many millions. You could do that in a matter of months back then.

I lived an extravagant lifestyle. I bought a BMW, a Jag, American imports, Mercs, a Bentley – all new and for cash. I still wore tracksuits, whether I had millions or not, for doing business on the street. But for going out I wore Armani, Moschino. I'd spend £2,000 a night on Chinese meals and champagne.

I bought a nightclub and two massage parlours, one with a swimming pool. I found out quite early on that sex makes money as well as drugs. It goes without saying that I got the girls on the rocks, so it cost me nothing. I bought two shops that sold TVs and videos, like electrical shops. I'd sell them from the front. But I'd still have someone selling crack out the back. I bought a clothes shop. Then I started investing in antiques, mainly because I had two houses to fill with them.

Soon I had Liverpool saturated with crack. I then moved into other big cities such as Manchester, Birmingham and London, in which crack had started to appear. But as far as I was concerned, they were untouched. No one had gone in there and really caned it yet. Crack was around those places but no one was doing it big, no one was doing it like me. Also, there were little towns in the suburbs and in the country with no drugs. Places like Ellesmere Port on the Wirral and Chester and rural places. I moved into places like that, too.

Wherever I went, I had a sales pitch, like a system to get new customers into crack. I'd go to private parties where people with plenty of money would be snorting cocaine. I'd take one or two people with me into the cellar and I'd start taking crack cocaine. Curiosity would draw them in. I'd say to them, 'The shit in the powder does you more damage than anything. This is pure.'

They got the first rock for nothing. The high only lasts 15 seconds. When the rock's gone, they craved another one. Then they'd have to pay. No one sat there and smoked for nothing. Then they'd tell their friends and it just escalated. All of a sudden, I had a lot of people taking crack cocaine, which was all the better for me because I'd make a lot more money.

I've lost count of the number of girls I've put on the game through crack. One was a lovely-looking girl who used to do a bit of modelling. I met her when she was 15, still at school. I gave her the first rock for nothing, of course. Within two days, she was a prostitute on the street. Then I moved her into my parlour. She made a lot of money for me. Now she is back on the streets and will do anything for the crack cocaine. I don't feel anything. I had to make a living.

I've had people offering me their girlfriends and wives for sexual favours just because they were £10 short for a rock. Normal, respectable people – teachers, civil servants, taxi drivers. All's I was interested in was money. I didn't care how they got their money – if they were prostitutes, shoplifters or muggers. I treated everybody with the same respect.

I've had armed robbers turn up at my crack house with £10,000, £20,000 in cash in a Kwik Save bag, still sweating from running away from a post office. I sat there smoking it with them until the pile of cash slowly moved across to my side of the table. Then they would give me their watches, their clothes, their trainees. Eventually they would leave, three days after they'd arrived, wearing just a pair of stinking jeans and a pair of old slippers I'd lend them to walk home. I used to keep a pair handy exactly for this.

I have a young daughter these days. Lo and behold if I find anybody who sells my kids crack cocaine. I would be their worst nightmare. I'm their father. Other parents may allow their kids to get into crack. But if my children decide to sell drugs, then that's fine. All's I would do to them is give them advice on how to do it properly. I wouldn't stop them. If they listen to me, they'll make a hell of a lot of money. If they don't, then they will go to jail.

People thought crack was a fad that would die out. But I made it big so that it will run and run and be there long after I die. No one can take that away from me. I created an industry. I made something from nothing. I feel a sense of fucking pride in that. It's an achievement.

It's impossible to put a number on the amount of people I've got into crack – thousands, tens of thousands. Every one of them will have been fucked up in one way or another. Many will have died. But if it's killed 100,000 people, I couldn't give a fuck. I'm not interested whatsoever. I feel no remorse or sorrow. I don't regret anything. Fuck all. A lot of people will call me a cunt. For ruining their sons' lives or whatever. But again,

I could not give one fuck. It's of no consequence to me. I don't think anything about being a crack dealer.

Because I was the first crack dealer in Britain, people expect me to have something to say about what has happened. They expect me to feel sorry. But I don't feel fuck all. In fact, I'm fucking pleased about it, to be truthful. At the end of the day, it was a product that people wanted and I manufactured and sold it to them. I had a family to support at the time with no qualifications whatsoever. It was in the middle of a recession. All's I did was what Mrs Thatcher was telling us to do – get on your bike and make money on your own. Fuck everyone else. Being a criminal was all I knew.

As far as I was concerned, selling crack cocaine, to me, I didn't see it as illegal. Obviously, the government thought it was illegal. But I just thought that was their problem. I just thought they were fucking stupid for not trying to sell it themselves. To me it was a business opportunity. I never stole anything. All's I done was made a product, realised there was good money to be had and bladdered it – to death. I realised it was a commodity that people wanted and made sure they got it. I manufactured crack cocaine from powder. And sold it, masses of it. I don't think that's illegal.

It's just like someone selling cigarettes from a shop or alcohol from a pub. It's given a lot of people jobs. There are whole communities who now rely on drugs to make a living. It generates billions. I'm proud of that. I've contributed to society. Without me, they'd have fuck all – no cars, no tellies, no trainees, fuck all.

The difference between me and other drug dealers who went before me was two things – the scale of my operation and the fact that I got onto a new thing first, fast. I steamed right in there, no messing around. When I got involved, crack wasn't around in Britain. It was just something we read about in the papers from the States. But I realised it could be big. Just like any other businessman with an idea, I did my homework. I went out and found how crack cocaine was made. I found out that a few yardies were the only ones making it in this country.

But they were small, flaky operations making it for personal use only. Once I found out, I just started making it, fucking loads of it, 24 hours a day, seven days a week.

In the early '80s, supergrass Paul Grimes was a prominent enforcer in the Liverpool underworld. He was anti-drugs, but in the book *Powder Wars* he recalled how dozens of his criminal associates were dropping everything to become drug dealers.

PAUL GRIMES: All of a sudden they'd all started to get into it. Even my partners. Even my relative Johnny One Eye started flying it in direct from the Dam without a care in the world. He kept this a secret from me because he knew how I felt about drugs. Eventually he was jailed for ten years for organising a parcel worth £135,000, which came into Liverpool and Harwich. It was like a kick in the teeth, knowing that someone so close to you had become a drug dealer without you knowing.

Then there was another mate called Glyn. He asked me to take over his scrapyard in Wavertree so he could concentrate on running a car-ringing scam in a hidden shed at the back. But later Glyn got nicked for dealing in the heavy stuff. Again, I was gobsmacked.

Another mate called Charlie swore blind to me that he wasn't having anything to do with drugs, but later I found out that burglars had screwed his flat and took a telly with two kilos of cocaine hidden in the back. That's where he used to hide his stash, in the back of his Trinitron. But he never banked on a couple of smackheads screwing his flat and having the telly off. They probably sold it for £50, not knowing there was 60 grand's worth of tackle in the back of it. Charlie came to me because he wanted someone to find those responsible and get it back. No way.

The list goes on: a gangster mate called Leslie, another called Brian – all what folk would normally call, at a push, ordinary decent criminals who got mixed up with the gear.

The city's underworld was soon split in two: the drug dealers and those that were against drugs and didn't believe in it. They had kids, like me, who were growing up and all that and they didn't want the likes of that shit on the streets. They were terrified in case their kids got involved with drugs. It was all over the papers – 'Generation in Peril' and all that.

It was purely down to morals. The drug dealers said that it was down to jealousy, but we were making plenty of money so that didn't come into it. My main motivation was that these scumbags were killing people. They were making lots of dough, but they were killing innocent people as well. End of. For the first time in my life, I was actually facing up to the fact that there were victims of crime. It wrecked my head at first.

A lot of the big villains who I knew were anti-drugs also looked down on drug dealers as something that the blacks done. They were in pure denial, but they were very shocked when it turned out that it was whites what was doing it as well, and what's more, it was their own – their families, mates, partners, brothers, sons. They all had blood on their hands.

I wasn't totally against all drugs. For me, there was a big difference between cannabis and Class As. I wasn't arsed about the little dealers knocking out a bit of speed to their mates. The difference between them and this new crowd was the sheer scale. This new lot just wanted to get everyone bang into it on a fucking industrial scale. I watched them. One minute you had a nice auld neighbourhood somewhere where everyone knew each other and that. The next minute it was *Escape from New York* cos these cunts had flooded the place with brown. These new gangsters would have been made up if everywhere was reduced to smoking ruins, so they could run amok selling their drugs.

A lot of the big gangsters who were anti-drugs just started keeping quiet about it, not wanting to ruffle any feathers. They never had the bottle to tell the dealers that they didn't like what they were doing. Some of us even had a meeting. They were that fucking worried about the dealers finding out it was in total secret and they whispered their concerns like old women. I said that I was prepared to make a stand. To shoot some of these cunts if necessary. But they just ummed and arrhhed and said, 'We admire your stance and that but . . .' And they didn't know where to look.

These were big names. Hard-hitters who had killed and maimed in pursuit of wealth with their own hands, but they were behaving like pathetic kids who purely did not know what to do. They gave up the fight before it even started. After that, drugs just became acceptable. It was because of drugs that I got out of being a criminal. Ironically, my son Jason got addicted to heroin. That was the reason I turned supergrass, to get back at the dealers. He eventually died of a drug overdose.

I still had gangsters coming in to try to tempt me into getting back into crime but it was just drugs, drugs, drugs with them. One day in the early '80s, before he went to prison for the Transit Mob, John Haase came in with Bernie Aldridge. They had 20 kilos of cannabis. They were desperately trying to break into the drugs market for the first time. Haase didn't even know how to sell it so he thought with my connections I'd be able to get a buyer. They'd already squeezed all the oil out of it. They offered me a £1,000-a-kilo commission. I told them I wasn't interested, but they even left behind a kilo sample to try to tempt me. I looked at it. Even though it was crap stuff, I knew I could have sold it with one phone call, but there was simply no question, 20k or not.

Grimes struck back by informing on the biggest criminal to emerge from the second generation of drug dealers: Curtis Warren. Warren was a mixed-race mugger from Toxteth who rose from the ashes of the 1981 riots to traffic cocaine in 1,000-kilo loads. He was one of the new bucks like John Haase who capitalised on the Liverpool Mafia's drug-dealing gains. He was Haase's one-time partner and then bitter enemy, and their criminal careers were both brought to an end coincidentally by the same supergrass: Paul Grimes.

In the winters of 1991 and 1992, Customs and Excise, aided

by Grimes, sank Warren's cocaine-smuggling operation. Two consignments supplied by the Cali cartel were recovered, weighing 500 and 1,000 kilos. Curtis Warren was later put on trial for the crime, but, learning from the mistakes made by his Liverpool Mafia mentors, he got the best lawyers money could buy and fought every technicality in a complicated case that was littered with them. The strategy worked and he was dramatically cleared of all charges. However, the ordeal led to a second surveillance operation which later resulted in his conviction for similarly huge consignments in Holland, where he is now serving a 12-year sentence.

Warren's conviction had bigger knock-on effects, leading to the capture of several key members of the Liverpool Mafia. But the biggest coup for the Dutch authorities was the subsequent arrest of one of the world's most successful drug dealers. On 8 October 1998, Cali cartel godfather Arnaldo Luis Quiceno Botero, the figure who had allegedly supplied Warren with cocaine, was jailed for six years.

6

MICHAEL HOWARD
BACKGROUNDER

Michael Howard's and John Haase's lives could not have been more different. Michael Howard was born into a Jewish middle-class family on 7 July 1941 in Gorseinon General Hospital, near Llanelli (a small mining town in South Wales). He followed a model academic and career path that made him one of the most powerful and successful men of his generation: from grammar school to Cambridge to barrister to politician to cabinet minister to Tory leader.

Haase's angry view of the world, meanwhile, was formed during a childhood of crime and violence. He has spent much of his adult years in jail, mainly as a high-risk prisoner or in solitary confinement, which compounded his disturbed outlook and made him callous and hard, at times psychotic. When not in jail, Haase lived on the streets of Liverpool in the company of some of the most disgraceful and dangerous members of society. Worlds apart, but Haase's and Howard's fates were set on a collision course that would explode into scandal, the fallout from which had long-lasting ramifications for both of them.

Even before Michael Howard was born, events were

occurring in his family that would come back to haunt the political leader in later life. The first controversy, which would embarrass the leader of the opposition nearly 70 years later, involved the immigration status of his Jewish immigrant father, Bernard. As Tory leader, Howard fought the 2005 election campaign on a ticket of get-tough measures against asylum seekers and illegal immigrants, attacking Labour MPs for being a soft touch. However, to Howard's chagrin, it was revealed that his own father had been turned away from Britain as an illegal immigrant before the Second World War, four years before Michael was born – and that only the intervention of a humanitarian Labour MP had saved his father from being sent back to Romania to certain persecution at the hands of the Nazis. Not for the first time, Howard was accused of double standards and hypocrisy.

The theme is recurrent throughout Howard's life. The two great scandals that have dogged his career – the Haase and Bennett scandal and the Al-Fayed–Lonrho DTI affair – have both involved associations with dodgy cousins dragging his name through the mud.

Michael Howard's real name was Michael Hecht, but his father changed the family name to Howard in March 1948, seven years after Michael's birth, as they settled down and became more anglicised. His father, Bernard, then 23, and mother, Hilda, then 28, were from orthodox Jewish families and had recently opened up a drapery shop. They had married a year earlier in June 1940 at the synagogue in Llanelli. Hilda had been introduced to Bernard by her wealthy cousin Harold Landy. Michael Howard's associations with his second cousin Landy, a powerful man in the Jewish community, would later come back to haunt him.

Bernat Hecht (his original name) first tried to land in the UK on 21 March 1937, aged 20. He arrived at Dover from Ostend in Belgium aboard the mail ship SS *Prince Leopold* with a Romanian passport and described himself as a synagogue 'cantor' or singer. When quizzed by immigration officers, Mr Hecht produced a letter from the president of a synagogue in

Whitechapel, east London, which stated that it wanted to consider employing him for just one month as a cantor. However, Mr Hecht – born in Romania on 13 November 1916 in the town of Ruscov – was 'refused leave to land' because an immigration official found that he had not been granted a vital Ministry of Labour work permit. Howard's father was sent back to Ostend that day on the same ship. However, just two days later, Labour MP James Hall hand-delivered a letter to the then home secretary Sir John Simon pleading for help. The MP for Whitechapel wrote, 'I beg to submit the application for your favourable consideration and would regard it as a personal favour if an early reply could be given me because of the urgent character of the situation.' Four months later, Mr Hecht was granted a visa allowing him to stay in the UK for a month by the Home Office at the British embassy in Brussels. He finally set foot on British soil on 20 July, after sailing from Ostend on the SS *Baudoin*. He then took up a month-long 'trial' at the Kehelath Moishe Anshei Belz synagogue in Fairclough Street, Whitechapel. For the next year, Mr Hecht obtained a string of visa extensions on the back of offers of work from the Whitechapel synagogue, allowing him to stay.

On 11 April 1940, the Home Office granted Michael Howard's father 'leave until further notice' provided he did not change his employment. But within a fortnight, he had moved to Llanelli in South Wales to live with the family of Hilda Kershion, whom he married two months later.

It was another six years before Bernat Hecht applied for British citizenship. By then, he was known as the Revd Bernard Howard, a title commonly used in Britain by Jewish ministers lower than the office of chief rabbi. At that stage, he falsified details on his paperwork, claiming that both his parents had died in Romania. In fact, his father Maurice – Michael Howard's grandfather – was still alive and had been living in London since the 1930s. He was a synagogue warden. Maurice's wife Leah perished in 1943 at the Nazi death camp of Auschwitz in Poland.

Many members of Howard's family were tortured by the

Nazis, including his Aunt Rose, who survived Auschwitz. Howard has suggested a possible motive for his father's false statement: 'I have speculated on the reason and I suppose one possibility is that my grandfather might have entered Britain unlawfully.' Mr Howard acknowledged that, while Nazism was on the rise in Europe, at the time he settled in Britain his father was primarily an 'economic migrant'. He died aged just 49 in 1966 in Llanelli. His widow, Hilda, is now aged 94 and lives in Stanmore, Middlesex.

Further intrigue surrounds the circumstances of how Michael Howard's mother entered the UK. The former Tory leader once hinted that Hilda's Jewish parents, Max and Chaika Kershion, fled Tsarist Russia to escape persecution. They arrived and settled in Llanelli, South Wales, in about 1912, when Hilda was six months old and her brother Jack was two. As is known, Hilda later wed Howard's father, Bernat Hecht, after being introduced by her wealthy cousin Harold Landy. However, so far no trace of a family with the name Kershion or similar has been unearthed in the Ukrainian town of Ostrog, where Howard's office has said his maternal grandparents came from. Immigration records also fail to shed any light on how the Kershion family came to enter the UK. Howard's grandfather Max died of an epileptic fit aged just 30 on 26 January 1913. The name Kirson – rather than Kershion – is recorded on his death certificate. Hilda is thought to have been born in Ostrog on 30 December 1911.

Michael Howard was raised in Llanelli, in orthodox fashion amid the small Jewish population of 120 people. Howard attended Llanelli Grammar School from about 1951 to 1959. Rebelliously, he used to leave school at lunchtime for the 'nefarious purpose' of honing his skills in Jack's Snooker Hall in the town. To the annoyance of the school authorities, he was notoriously anti-rugby and pro-football and played the guitar in a skiffle band. 'Lonnie Donegan, that sort of thing,' he said later. He joined the Young Conservatives at the age of 15. From there, he obtained a place at Peterhouse College, Cambridge, where he was president of the Union in 1962 – some two years behind former vice-president of the EC and home secretary Leon Brittan QC. Howard was known at university as a bit of a dandy. While the others went for zip-up jackets, his soft lambswool pullovers and high-sided elastic boots earned him many female admirers. He was a bright star of the Union in the 1960s, a formidable debater with a killer political instinct coupled with fierce ambition. With contemporaries such as Kenneth Clarke, Norman Lamont, John Gummer, Leon Brittan and Norman Fowler, Howard and this group of friends became known as the 'Cambridge mafia'. Two decades later, they provided much of the upper reaches of the Thatcher and Major cabinets. The gang was close-knit. When Howard made a rare attack on his old friend Lamont, saying that he would 'cut a ridiculous figure' if he stood against John Major, Sandra Howard told Lamont's wife, Rosemary, that 'it's just politics; it's not worth destroying a friendship for'.

After leaving university, Howard pursued a career as a lawyer with an American firm, becoming a barrister in 1964 at the age of 22. He shared a bachelor flat in Harley Street during the '60s with Norman Lamont. Following a period working on criminal cases, he went on to specialise in industrial-tribunal work then planning and administrative law. He took on tricky planning appeals such as the Sizewell B power station and Okehampton bypass.

At about this time, Michael began to travel to Liverpool more frequently. In 1966 and again in 1970, he stood unsuccessfully as Conservative candidate in the Edge Hill constituency, a Labour stronghold in the city. During 1970, he was chairman of the Bow Group, again following in the footsteps of Leon Brittan. Between 1970 and 1973, he was a member of several leading Conservative groups promoting links with Europe, and was chairman of the Coningsby Club during 1972 and 1973. He resigned from the Conservative Association committee over its decision to invite Oswald Mosley to speak and later joined the Campaign for Social Democracy, a minor political party in the 1970s formed by an ex-Labour MP.

On 1 August 1975, at the age of 34, he married former model Sandra Paul, also 34, at Winchester Registry Office. She called him 'an extraordinarily romantic man' after he gave her a copy of F. Scott Fitzgerald's *Tender is the Night* after they first met. This was her fourth marriage and she already had one child. Her previous husbands included Robin Douglas-Hume, a nephew of the former Tory prime minister. They went on to have two children together. Howard's best man at his wedding was Norman Lamont, the former defence minister, and he in turn was best man for Lamont.

By the time he was 40, Howard was rich enough to become an underwriting member at Lloyds, and he was appointed a QC in 1982. In June 1983, he was elected Conservative MP for the safe Tory seat of Folkestone and Hythe. With a foot in the door, he rose through the ranks quickly. In 1984, he was appointed parliamentary private secretary to the solicitor general, and in September 1985 became parliamentary under-secretary at the Department of Trade and Industry, with responsibilities for corporate affairs. He stopped being a member of Lloyds and ceased practising as a barrister. In March 1986, he was appointed a recorder, although he couldn't carry out this function while a minister.

Howard was a member of the Carlton Club and, in 1985, he and his wife were members of the St John's Wood Liberal Synagogue. During his time as a junior Trade and Industry minister under Margaret Thatcher, Howard became embroiled in his first scandal. He was involved in an official takeover report on a business – but did not declare that one of his relatives was involved. Ten years later, while home secretary, he became embroiled in a related scandal – the refusal to grant millionaire Harrods boss Mohamed Al-Fayed a British passport. Again, the same relative was lurking in the background of the case.

Both of the scandals were related because Howard's shadowy second cousin, millionaire tycoon Harold Landy, was at the centre of the storm. On both accounts, Howard was accused by his rivals of allowing his ministerial position to be unduly influenced by his cousin. Landy was born and bred in Llanelli and was a powerful figure in the local Jewish community before Howard's dad arrived from Romania. Landy had signed Howard's father's naturalisation papers as sponsor. In return, Howard's religious father blessed Landy's wedding. Landy's brother Maurice married Howard's parents at the local synagogue.

Landy subsequently moved to London, where he set about building a family business empire. He became a pillar of Jewish society on a national level and sat as a JP in Hertfordshire and Middlesex. In 1974, the Israel-Britain Bank (London), which he controlled, crashed with initial debts of £2.8 million and threatened the survival of his other company, London City and Westcliff Properties (LCW). Later it emerged that the bank, with a parent company in Tel Aviv, had combined deficits of £60 million relating to loans – mainly irrecoverable – made to companies under the control of Landy in Liechtenstein and Switzerland.

The senior official receiver's report blamed his conduct for the collapse of the bank. Landy and four other bank executives were charged with conspiracy to defraud the bank's customers. In July 1979, Mr Landy was jailed for five years and fined £350,000 for his part in the bank's collapse. The conviction was quashed three months later on a legal technicality and Landy escaped prison, but his fellow director in Israel was jailed for 24 years.

The key to the scandal which later engulfed Michael Howard was Landy's friendship with controversial tycoon Tiny Rowland. Before the court case, Rowland's company Lonrho bought a 29.9 per cent stake in Landy's property company LCW for £5.73 million. Rowland helped with the appeal and after his conviction was overturned Rowland installed Landy as his deputy in Lonrho.

The collapse of the bank prompted Landy's niece Francesca Pollard, then 46, to start a campaign against her uncle, claiming he had deprived her of her rightful inheritance from her grandfather, who had founded the bank. She wanted £90 million, which she claimed Landy had siphoned off for himself and his business mates, including Roland. Pollard, who was Michael Howard's cousin, went on the rampage against Howard too, blackening his name at every turn and publishing libellous pamphlets such as '20 things you didn't know about Michael Howard'.

Ten years later, the scandal would resurface during Howard's reign at the DTI when Tiny Rowland complained that Harrods had been unfairly taken over by Mohamed Al-Fayed. As a minister, Howard was instrumental in the department's decision to set up an inquiry into the Fayeds' takeover in 1987. Howard had been the Trade and Industry minister in 1985 when Lonrho was desperately campaigning for an inquiry to be set up. But to his peril, Howard failed to declare his interest through a link with Landy, a director of a Rowland company, to Lonrho. Fayed did not believe there should be an inquiry and claimed that Howard was being pressed by his cousin Landy to help Lonrho.

Howard, who had helped set up the inquiry, did not disclose to the House of Commons his or his parents' close family links with the Landys and their close links with Tiny Rowland and Lonrho. He was challenged in the House by Dale Campbell-Savours and five other opposition MPs to explain why he had failed to reveal this link, which 'provides legitimate cause for public concern'. Howard did not respond. He also refused to comment on whether it was right to answer a series of questions, as Minister for Trade and Industry, about Lonrho and House of Fraser in the House of Commons between September 1985 and 1987.

When Fayed first made allegations about the link, Landy denied the claims, saying of Howard, 'We may be second cousins but we are not exactly close. We don't even send each other Christmas cards. I haven't seen him for two years.' He stated, 'I never spoke to him [Mr Howard] once, either by telephone or face to face during the Harrods takeover inquiry. Why should I? Mr Al-Fayed is a very bitter man. If ministers had to declare every distant relative, government would grind to a halt. Michael Howard's mother is my cousin and I keep in touch with her but that is it.'

In 1994, Howard's irate cousin Francesca Pollard alleged that Fayed had paid her £2,000 a month to finance her smear campaign. In return, she had sent out hundreds of malicious letters about Rowland. She later 'defected' to the Lonrho camp. At the time, Al-Fayed's camp denied Pollard's claims. A House of Fraser spokesman stated that everything she said should be 'taken with a fairly large sack of Saxa [salt]'. The allegations have been raised in court cases and Pollard repeated them in a sworn statement. But the alleged payments have never been fully investigated.

A further ten years later, while Howard was home secretary, the spectre of Harold Landy appeared again. The scandal was still rumbling on. The Home Office had refused to give Al-Fayed a British passport. Al-Fayed claimed that the home secretary was pursuing a vendetta against him because of a 'blood debt' he owed to Landy. Fayed claimed he was being victimised because Landy was the pal of his bitter rival Tiny Rowland, whom he beat to buy Harrods. By that time, Landy had suffered a stroke. But his wife Gertrude, then 82, denied family links could have had any influence on the home secretary's decision to deny citizenship to Mr Al-Fayed. She said, 'My husband and Mr Howard have nothing in common. If they met, they would have nothing to say to each other. They have had no contact for years.'

Mohamed Al-Fayed fought on and claimed that Howard had taken a bribe from the Lonrho team during the DTI inquiry. But another inquiry cleared Howard. In a report, Sir Gordon Downey, parliamentary commissioner for standards, dismissed Al-Fayed's bribe story. He said, 'Mr Al-Fayed has discovered fragments of evidence which, when pieced together, seem to support the explanation of a bribe,' and stated, 'I have no reason to think that Mr Al-Fayed is not telling the truth as he sees it.' Al-Fayed kept pursuing the story, repeatedly demanding an appeal for a judicial review, which was refused. Eventually, the scandal blew over, but to some degree the damage had already been done.

In all, Howard went on to get ten years' ministerial experience under his belt, seven in the Cabinet, mostly as home secretary. He served, briefly, as Employment secretary under Margaret Thatcher before being promoted, via Environment, to the Home Office by John Major in 1993. Were it not for the prime minister's strong Euroscepticism, John Major might even have appointed him chancellor or foreign secretary. He reached the Cabinet in 1990, in which he served until the meltdown of May 1997 – one year after he released John Haase from prison.

Howard then spent years in the political wilderness after a miserable bottom-of-the-poll showing in the leadership contest of 1997. That is when Ann Widdecombe made her famous 'something of the night' comment about him. The phrase will always be associated with Michael Howard even though the row that created it has almost been forgotten. It arose from Howard's decision to sack Derek Lewis, the then head of the prison service, in the light of an official report into escapes from Parkhurst prison in January 1995. Widdecombe, then Howard's junior minister for prisons, disagreed violently with that decision and almost resigned over it. It was a very difficult time for Howard, and only his parliamentary skills and a disastrous performance by his shadow, Jack Straw, in the key debate saved Howard's career. Matters rested until the Tories went into opposition, and it was then that Widdecombe coined her special nocturnal sound bite. It was seen by many as a faintly anti-Semitic smear of the nasty, whispered type that Howard has had to cope with throughout his career ('oleaginous' is another). Widdecombe denies this and says that it was in fact taken from the title of a thriller by the American author Mary McMullen. She adds that, 'The further you get away from God and heaven, the deeper the dark. My picture of hell is complete with devils and tridents and burning lakes and darkness . . . my image of badness is dark. You hear a lot of people saying "there is a dark side to a character". So if I'm saying somebody's been bad, yes, there is a dark image there.' All that, damaging enough, was followed up by a Commons speech by Widdecombe that demolished Howard's reputation. His attempt to regain ground with an appearance on *Newsnight* turned to disaster when Jeremy Paxman asked him the same question 12 times, an exercise that succeeded in making him seem shifty and evasive. Even now, Howard is reluctant to discuss the Widdecombe–Paxman experience. However, it sank his leadership ambitions at the time. He received only 23 votes from his fellow MPs. Howard switched allegiance to William Hague, who rewarded him with the job of shadow foreign secretary, although he did have to serve for a time in Hague's team with his tormentor Widdecombe. In March 1999, he announced his voluntary retirement from the front bench. And that was that for Michael Howard, until his surprising recall later by Iain Duncan Smith. He went on to become Tory Party leader in 2003.

Friends say Howard is an urbane man, who enjoys watching baseball on Channel Five and is still capable of jiving to The Crickets. John Major said in his memoirs that:

> Michael is clever and able, but in private is a shy and charming man, with an unstuffy, self-deprecating manner. He was always at his best without an audience; in public he could not help stirring things up. Too many people saw the polished barrister on the surface, and took against what they saw. They missed the substance underneath.

7

THE TURKISH
CONNECTION

John Haase was released from prison in 1992 after serving the greater part of a 14-year sentence for the Transit Mob robberies. Immediately he launched back into a life of crime, recruiting Liverpool's most feared enforcer and arming himself to the teeth. Springing back onto the scene sparked resentment from some members of the Liverpool Mafia, including the supervillainous Tommy Gilday.

THE ENFORCER: I was a best friend of John Haase from early 1992, having met him shortly after he came out of prison having served a lengthy sentence. He became close – we went on holiday and socialised regularly. We saw little of one another during the day but saw each other at night. I introduced him to my friends and work colleagues.

The first time I had concerns about Haase was when I was at his house and he asked me to guess which hand a gun was hidden in. I guessed – he showed me a .22 handgun and revealed he had three of them. He had only been out a few months. I remember him being stopped by the police outside his home and having the gun taken off him.

I knew people – a lot of people. He was trying to involve me in his business and asking me to enforce for him. Two people who I recall he had problems with at that time were someone called Hannah and someone called [Tommy] Gilday.

On another two occasions, when I accompanied him to meet people, he was carrying a gun. I had asked him not to. I said I would talk to the people as I knew them well. After the first occasion, I had said that it was better to talk to people. He said he wouldn't take a chance and showed me the gun that he had been carrying, even though I had asked him not to.

On the second occasion, I told him we were seeing two people over a problem I had and we were meeting them in the Adelphi Hotel. John phoned 'Ben' up. He said he had a few quid that he needed. Again, when we left the Adelphi, he showed me another gun. He said he wasn't rolling around the floor with anyone.

After this incident, I didn't see as much of him, although we still spoke on the phone. The two people we went to see at the Adelphi, he became friendly with. After settling in, Haase then turned his attention to his new job – drugs.

Haase recalls: 'When I came out of prison in the early 1990s, the world of crime had changed. Suddenly all of the big firms had switched from robberies to drugs. So I got involved in heroin. Again, it was all down to money; no other reason.' On this score, Haase had an ace up his sleeve, potentially worth millions of pounds – an introduction to the Turkish Connection promised by his old Long Lartin lag pal, Mustafa Sezazi. But the cunning Scouser was in no rush to get involved in a trade he wasn't quite master of. Haase didn't make contact with the Turks immediately. He wanted to find out more about dealing drugs himself, to get a feel for the market. He hung up his shotgun and picked up the tools of his new trade – a purity-testing kit, a pair of surgical gloves, a handful of resealable plastic bags, a roll of brown package tape, a holdall for the gear and black bin bags to carry the stacks of cash he was going to make. Haase teamed up with his errant nephew Paul Bennett, who was busy dealing kilos of cocaine – or whatever he could get hold of – to and for the rising stars of the next generation of Liverpool mafiosi. Haase and Bennett began buying drugs off Chris No-Neck. No-Neck was Bennett's pal, supplier and partner. When Haase got out, he made Bennett more ambitious – but some say at the expense of caution.

CHRIS NO-NECK: Before John came out, Ben was doing stuff. Me and Ben had been doing it for five years. We made sure no one fucked with us. We did it our way. We fucked people off. For years turned them away [refused to sell them heroin because they didn't know them]. But Ben turned when John got out. He wanted what John had. However, he never really had the bottle. He'd never pull the trigger himself. That's why he's got little Joey [a well-known hit-man linked to at least six hits] to do it for him.

The relationship between No-Neck and Haase reversed when Haase later became big and No-Neck went to work for him.

Haase was spending a lot of time in Bennett's flat in the upmarket Woolton area of Liverpool. Many of the city's criminal fraternity were to be found coming and going from the flat, talking shop, gossiping, partying. Interestingly, a young wheeler-dealer called Simon Bakerman was often to be found there, buying and taking drugs. He was a figure of curiosity in this Fagin's den, being related to the esteemed Michael Howard.

Another of Bennett's visitors was cocaine baron Curtis Warren. Again, Haase's timing was fortuitous. In the same year that Haase was released, Warren was taking his leap into the big-time narc scene as well. He had stopped trafficking 50-kilo loads from Europe and started to import 500- and 1,000-kilo loads direct from Colombia.

In 1991, police first became aware of Warren's independent smuggling operation after an informant in Operation Bruise, a Midlands-based taskforce targeting organised crime, named him as a maverick middle-ranking operator who specialised in 50-kilo-a-time shipments. But in the winter of 1991, Warren brought in a 500-kilo load in lead ingots – the first consignment to be grassed up by Paul Grimes. Customs and Excise let this load go in order to catch a bigger fish, a 905-kilo load expected a few months later.

It was cocaine from the first 500-kilo load that almost certainly started John Haase off as a drug dealer. As they got to know each other, Warren began to like and respect Haase. He felt sorry for the legendary armed robber who had just got out of prison and was skint. Warren, like all career criminals, knew the feeling and was sympathetic. Poverty was an affront to a big man's pride. Magnanimously, he offered Haase the 'arse end' of the huge consignment to help him get back on his feet. Most of it had already been sold, but Warren gave Haase a parcel of about 20 to 30 kilos 'on tick'. The young buck trusted Haase because he was old-school with a fearsome reputation. At about £30,000 a kilo wholesale, Haase's stash was worth between £600,000 and £900,000. He would have to pay back Warren for the initial amount after it was sold, but the profits were staggering. By 'dancing on' or 'cutting up' the powder with a bulking agent such as glucose, Haase could turn the 20 kilos into about 25 immediately. Then, by 'bagging it up' or splitting it into ounces or quarter- or eighth-kilos, he could increase the profits by mind-boggling multiples until it ran into millions. And that's exactly what he did. He told Bennett to take care of these production details and also relied on Bennett to use his contacts to sell it.

Bennett enjoyed the lifestyle of the new drug-dealer elite: champagne, Cream nightclub, Chinese meals, snorting, hotels, glamorous women, clobber from Wadies (an expensive Liverpool clothes shop). But little is known about the secretive trafficker, referred to as the 'Pimpernel' because of his frequent moving around.

His family's twee home in Norris Green, Liverpool, was the image of respectability masking the shameful truth. On the front window sill stood a neat row of porcelain figures alongside pictures of the children. However, there were a few clues as to the occupation of the owner. The house was surrounded with security gadgets. A spotlight and closed-circuit television camera were trained on callers.

Bennett was laid back about selling the cocaine that Warren had given to Haase. However, Haase was impatient. To him, he was in direct competition with the city's numerous other drug dealers. When Bennett wasn't selling the cocaine fast enough, Haase discovered a new technique: bullying dealers lower down the chain to sell his cocaine exclusively and stop selling drugs from a rival. Haase began bouncing around the city bashing people up if they didn't sell for him rather than others. Other mobs had tried this method but it seemed to cause more hassle than it was worth; the threats led to bitterness and arrangements soon fizzled out if not policed. But Haase had the power and the violence to pull it off – to make the new rules stick.

The £20 notes began to roll in, enabling Haase to get back on his feet – new clothes, car, apartment, etc. Then, once Haase had learned the basics of drug dealing, he wanted more. Enter the Turks. Haase remembered the promise made to him by Mustafa Sezazi in Long Lartin. Contact was made with Kaya and arrangements were made for him to travel up to Liverpool for a get-to-know-you session.

Both men liked and trusted each other. Kaya, who was now one of the Turkish Connection's senior bosses, welcomed John Haase in. Within the hierarchy, at first, Haase was offered the role of being the Turks' north-west distributor of heroin – but he soon outgrew the position and was so good at his job that he had quickly eclipsed all of the other salesmen the Turks had on their books in the UK. He became their number one UK distributor. But he was still not satisfied. Within months, Haase got involved in trafficking the heroin, insisting that his men help the Turks transport their cargoes on the last leg of their journeys through France to the UK. Then he pushed for a role in manufacture back in Istanbul.

In the early days, Haase was given 10- to 20-kilo loads. Kaya and Bulent Onay would travel to Liverpool to make arrangements and collect the cash. (Onay was Kaya's right-hand man who ferried money and drugs to all parts of the UK before Suleyman Ergun replaced him.) During 1992, as trust increased, Haase's 'tick' increased to 30 then 50 kilos and beyond. Haase was selling it as fast as the Turks could bring it in. They were flabbergasted.

The Turks quickly realised that Liverpool was now the hub of Britain's drug distribution network, a fortuitous fact they were delighted to discover because they now had one of the city's top men working with them. They began giving the vast majority of their imports directly to the Liverpool gang, bypassing London and other cities.

From this point on, a loose structure began to emerge. With a flexibility that was key to its strength, the shape of the Turkish Connection's outfit began gently to morph. It changed from a triangular hierarchy with The Vulcan at the top, overseeing his deputy Yilmaz Kaya and third-in-command Suleyman Ergun, to more of an axis of power. The Vulcan was still in overall charge at the centre of the see-saw, but at one end were the Scousers and at the other the British Turks led by Yilmaz – two gangs joined at the hip with roughly equal standing. The business became so huge so quickly that it had a momentum of its own. Even after Onay was arrested in Christmas 1992, following a roller-coaster but bumper year, the operation steamrollered on without a care in the world. Suleyman Ergun blossomed into an even bigger player.

Based on official Customs and Excise reports, the role of each member of the gang was as follows:

1. THE VULCAN
The Vulcan was one of the world's biggest heroin dealers, supplying most of Europe, including the key markets in Britain, Germany and Italy. He was vastly wealthy and owned a

Turkish travel firm with a fleet of coaches – in which he smuggled drugs – a huge property empire and a hotel chain.

The Vulcan survived because of his anonymity. He was middle-aged, short and non-descript. Despite his millions, he dressed like a dad who bought his clothes from Asda: patterned polyester crew-neck jumpers, shapeless suit jackets and dark, cheap slacks. He had bought off powerful connections in the Turkish police and government. He had bought himself out of prison in Turkey several times. He was always armed, sometimes carrying two heavy-calibre pistols, and travelled in a fleet of bullet- and bomb-proof limos specially made in Italy. Whenever he landed at Istanbul airport, he was whisked through security at a police checkpoint. If he was flying out again, before he took off he was able to deposit his guns in a special safe with airport security for collection on his return. On one occasion, when a rookie cop threatened to arrest him for carrying the guns, The Vulcan threatened to have him sacked if he didn't do as he was told. On finding out who the passenger was, the copper begged for mercy.

The Vulcan had his HQ in a faceless office block in the capital. One visitor recalled that it was stacked with military boxes of Kalashnikovs, rocket-propelled grenades and bombs – ammunition in his ruthless quest to get and keep control of the heroin business. He was powerful enough to have one-on-one meetings with the godfathers of the Italian Mafia. He arrived at hotels in southern Italy flanked by men with machine guns.

The Vulcan trusted few men. One of the exceptions was Yilmaz Kaya. They had met when Kaya was staying at his relatives' near a secret safehouse used by The Vulcan. The godfather was impressed by his old-style sense of honour and the calm way he dealt with people.

One of the strangest sights observed by Customs officers investigating the Turkish Connection was The Vulcan's appearance in a suburban street in Liverpool. What was one of the world's biggest drug dealers doing in Liverpool on a summer's day walking down the road without a care in the world, his jacket tossed casually over his shoulder? It was a bizarre image, and one which symbolised just how important the city had become in the international drugs market. The scene got even more surreal when he was greeted by Haase and Bennett dressed like a pair of scallies going to the match. Haase was sporting a pair of tennis shorts, a stripy T-shirt and a pair of blue Reebok trainers. They were discussing a drug deal worth £10 million.

2. YILMAZ KAYA

Kaya was the Turkish-based suppliers' main representative in the UK. He was in charge of the heroin-distribution organisation, the collection of the money and its transmission back to Turkey.

Before drugs, Kaya worked as a storeman and delivery driver for a Turkish-owned clothing business in the Green Lane area of north London. One day, he told his colleagues that he was leaving to make his fortune. He accompanied them to the local café on Green Lane which they had frequented every work day for years. The café was popular with workers and Kaya and his pals enjoyed one last bite to eat together. He was well liked, always polite and helpful to everyone he knew within the Turkish community. As he got up to go, he told the assembled crowd, 'The next time I walk past here, I'll be carrying a suitcase full of money.' Two years later, he returned to keep his promise, showing off his new-found drug-wealth to his astonished pals.

Kaya travelled extensively throughout Europe on a number of different passports in various names. He first appeared on Customs' radar after being linked by observations to other members of the Turkish Connection in the second half of 1992. Customs connected him to large amounts of cash that were being exported from the UK to Turkey, and also the heroin seized from Bulent Onay in December 1992. Kaya was observed personally transporting large amounts of cash through Heathrow and was seen many times at meetings with the principal conspirators in Liverpool, when money was handed over.

3. SULEYMAN ERGUN

Ergun was Kaya's UK-based lieutenant, responsible for the organisation's interests during Kaya's visits abroad, and a constant companion of Kaya on meetings in Liverpool with Haase and Bennett. He was usually seen carrying the bags of money that he and Kaya collected from Haase and Bennett.

Ergun was a key suspect in the conspiracy to import into the UK as Kaya's right-hand man and in the conspiracy to supply because of his strong and frequent links by mobile phone to Haase and Bennett. He was observed making 23 drug-related visits to Liverpool in the first six months of 1993 alone. He travelled to Turkey with Kaya on 15 May 1993, when their baggage for the trip was searched. Currency and false passports and driving licences were found hidden inside. He had also changed large amounts of currency at a travel agent's in the West End.

Ergun was sharp. He had made the travel-agent contact after noticing a neighbour in his London tenement block wearing one of the company's uniforms. He befriended him in a local pub and asked whether he would be able to change up large amounts of pounds into different currencies for transport without attracting too much attention. Ergun charmed the man and he agreed. Dollars were good because the large denominations made it easier to reduce the size of a bag of sterling and they were accepted anywhere in the world.

A legal document based on Customs intelligence states:

> One thing is absolutely certain. Ergun was no 'bagman' or a 'chauffeur' simply driving, fetching and carrying for Kaya. He was twice seen changing large sums of sterling to US dollars . . .
>
> Ergun also travelled abroad, though not as extensively as Kaya. He made two trips to Ostend from Dover (on one trip he was accompanied by two others), one trip to Calais from Dover and he accompanied Kaya to Turkey on 15/05/93. Their baggage for this trip was searched and found to contain currency, false passports

and driving licences. It was not therefore a trip with an innocent purpose. Ergun also met Topaz [The Vulcan] on his visits to the UK and was in constant attendance along with Kaya. Ergun was not only aware of the conspiracy but played his own vital role within it.

4. JOHN HAASE

Haase, together with Bennett, was initially a distributor of the drug in the north-west. However, he quickly took on bigger deals. After December 1992, observations showed that both men were involved in arranging importations from the European mainland as well. On 17 May 1993 – two days after Kaya and Ergun had landed – Haase flew to Turkey under a false name with his girlfriend Debbie Dillon [though there is no suggestion that she knew of Haase's involvement with drugs] to meet with members of the organisation there. Both men were regularly seen meeting Kaya and Ergun in Liverpool.

Haase and Bennett got so big that they were present at important meetings with Topaz [The Vulcan], proving that they were central players in the operation.

5. PAUL BENNETT

Haase's flash deputy in Liverpool. Career drug dealer and hands-on expert from the Croxteth and Norris Green area of Liverpool. Known on the street as Ben or alternatively the Ben Fella, the B-fella and B-Man. Even before joining the Turkish Connection, Bennett was dealing big amounts of heroin with No-Neck – a fact that didn't go unnoticed by neighbours. A constant stream of limos and heavyweight villains advertised the murky world inside Bennett's semi, where he had lived for five years with his partner, Cathy, and their children, Carl, then nine, and Cerys, then two. One neighbour said, 'Big men dripping with gold in even bigger cars were always coming and going.'

His-and-hers matching BMWs – hers was a soft-top – were always parked outside. A luxurious camper van added to the line-up.

'We knew they weren't a normal couple by the hours he kept,' said another neighbour. 'They would spend so much money on the place but you never saw him going out to work. There were always lots of comings and goings after dark, not loud parties but often loud music and lots of people in big expensive cars.'

A bull mastiff dog kept guard from behind a high iron gate with spikes at the back of the house.

Haase delegated day-to-day control of cutting up, bagging up, security and transport of heroin to Bennett, who in turn employed a team of gophers to carry out the tasks on a massive scale. Before Haase introduced him to the Turks and their bulk supplies, Bennett was a medium-scale drug dealer who dealt in kilos and below. Bennett was often described as a big kid who liked to eat sweets and say very little. But behind the mask, he was very clever and careful.

6. CHRIS NO-NECK

Extremely tough, clever, cool-headed enforcer who rose through the ranks of Haase's gang. No-Neck was an all-rounder. Haase relied on him because of his no-nonsense and fearless approach to violence. But he was also technically skilled as a drug dealer, familiar with purity tests and methods of chemical bulking out and distribution. No-Neck was also disciplined and well organised, able to carry out complex tasks smoothly and efficiently. He was also loyal and prided himself that he wasn't an informant and could withstand torture from other criminals or 'tax men' intent on stealing drugs money.

7. EDWARD CROKER

First lieutenant to Haase and Bennett, responsible for storage, cutting and distribution of drugs, as well as collection of cash proceeds, which he passed on to them. Croker was also observed meeting Kaya and Ergun in the absence of Haase and Bennett and handing bags to them. He was a regular at a terrace house in Dane Street in the Anfield district of the city. The property was one of the gang's safehouses where drugs were stored and cut up. On 21 July 1993, Croker was observed there in the process of cutting a large quantity of the drug and was in possession of a further 50 kilos five days later, together with £27,980 in cash.

8. BULENT ONAY

Bulent Onay was a founding member of the Turkish Connection and Kaya's deputy before Suleyman Ergun took the job, but he was arrested shortly after Haase began dealing with the Turks. However, he did take part in some early drug deals with Haase during the honeymoon period immediately following Haase's release from prison.

Before his arrest on 24 December 1992 in possession of 36.54 kilos of heroin, Onay had been involved in the transport of money and/or drugs within the UK. Three days before the raid, he had been to visit the north-west with Kaya and two other Turks to collect the drugs seized at his house. In the last half of 1992, Onay had frequently been seen in the company of other members of the organisation. On two occasions, he was seen leaving the UK carrying baggage containing large quantities of cash, together with a false passport and driving licence, for use by Yilmaz Kaya. His role was similar to that subsequently adopted by Ergun.

Onay travelled abroad fairly frequently and joined other members of the operation on a trip to Liverpool on 21 December 1992. On Christmas Eve 1992, Onay was stopped and given a speeding ticket on the M6 travelling south at 0035 and gave his name as Erdal Devrenk. Later that day, Onay was arrested at his home address and 36 kilos of heroin were found on the premises.

9. MEHMET ANSEN

The Vulcan's bagman. Former Turkish army colonel with impeccably clean credentials. Well groomed, well spoken and highly efficient. He was chosen to transport money because no one suspected him. From a well-heeled Turkish middle-class family with a taste for the finer things in life, including a beautiful holiday home. Antiques dealer and bone china expert. Corrupted by offers of cash from The Vulcan.

Ansen's function was the transport of cash in suitcases to Turkey. On 24 March 1993, he left the UK with £120,000 in his baggage. This was less than 24 hours after one of Kaya and Ergun's trips to Liverpool, where they collected a large bag from Haase and Bennett. His luggage was covertly searched during one run and found to contain several assorted boxes which were sealed with Sellotape. One of the boxes had split open and a wad of a hundred five-pound notes was found.

If questioned, Ansen was supposed to say that he thought it was the proceeds of gambling. That was the cover story he and Kaya had agreed on one year before. The Vulcan and Kaya had similar heroin-dealing operations in cities all over Europe. Ansen soon became their EU bagman, going to meetings in various European cities including London, Vienna and Milan with Topaz and Kaya. He transported money for Kaya and Topaz from Italy to Turkey. On arrest, his diary was found to contain extensive details of his travels. His efficiency, together with a former army officer's compulsive desire to keep a record of all his expenses, was his downfall. The diary made numerous references to Topaz, known as The Vulcan.

10. MARK DREW

A minor player who was approached by Eddie Croker and asked to find premises for storing drugs. He duly arranged for a key to a premises which was used by Croker and others for the cutting of a large quantity of the drugs. Observations showed him being present on the day of one big delivery of heroin. It was alleged that Drew provided the premises, knowing full well that they were to be used for cutting drugs.

11. MANUK OCECKI

Armenian descent. At first, he had a role in the Turkish Connection similar to that of Onay and Ansen. He transferred drug money out of the UK to Turkey, where the heroin originated. For example, Ocecki was observed carrying approximately £100,000 to Istanbul on 8 July 1992. He was also responsible for staging meetings and organising safehouses. But, as time went on, the close partners in crime Joey the Turk and Manuk Ocecki became less involved and consequently less valued by some members of the gang. However, in the Turkish tradition, Kaya remained loyal to them, valuing their trust and comradeship above their financial performance as criminals.

12. JOEY THE TURK
Carried out similar role to Manuk Ocecki.

13. NEIL GARRETT
Real name cannot be given, for legal reasons. Childhood friend of Paul Bennett from the Croxteth area of Liverpool. Former heroin addict. Members of family also heroin addicts. Brought in to cut up, bag and distribute drugs.

14. PAUL LALLY
Real name cannot be given, for legal reasons. Drug- and money-runner for Haase and Bennett.

15. THE ESTATE AGENT
Haase's main money-washer through property. Reputedly disappeared with £1 million of Haase's cash to the USA.

The Turkish Connection was now up and running and operating in total secret. Few people knew of the gang's existence. One of the few members ever to talk about the organisation and what type of people were in it is Suleyman Ergun, the number three. Ergun was essentially a normal boy from a decent family who turned into a ruthless gun-toting international heroin baron in his early 20s.

Ergun was born on 30 March 1969 in Tarsus, a city on the south coast of Turkey on a plain in the shadows of a mountain range. It was a world away from the clubs of north London, where he would make his mark by shooting gangsters for showing disrespect. Customs officers would later ask themselves what had changed him so dramatically.

SULEYMAN ERGUN: Tarsus is about the size of Cambridge and cotton is the major industry there.

I was a stubborn kid, very stubborn, and I was the first child and only boy in my family. My dad was a barber who started off as a child apprentice in Tarsus, then worked his way up, opened up a shop and even built a house.

We left Tarsus when I was three years of age. My dad was the first to go. He wanted a fresh start so he ended up coming to London to earn some money so he could get us over. One of his mates, Marmut, was over here, and he got him a job as a chef working in the Aberdeen Angus steakhouse in Piccadilly. He saved up a bit of money, came back and collected me and my mum and brought us over. We first lived in Newington Green.

I didn't want for anything growing up. We were always out of London. My dad used to take us everywhere: Torquay, Hastings, Brighton, every weekend. My dad rented a small place from a fella, which we shared with my aunt. She had her own room, so we could just about live separately.

I started going a bit wild when I was about seven. I burnt the house down playing with matches under a sofa. When it caught light, I just walked out the room and shut the door. Everything was destroyed. We had to start again.

My mum and dad by this time had progressed to the rag trade. The factory was in Hackney. After I was seven, my mum and dad got a council flat in Somerstown, in Camden. I've been in Somerstown to this day.

I excelled in school until the third year in secondary school. That was when I started fucking up. Before that, I was good at sprinting and science. One year, I remember the heatwave when we went to school with flip-flops. I remember getting a Chopper bike, a brand new one, from my dad. My sister was born around 1970. The area I lived in then, you could leave your door open day and night. They were the good times.

But I was cheeky and feisty and got into a lot of fights. I used to take a lot of risks – jumping off sheds, hanging off balconies, throwing big blocks of ice up in the air and head-butting it. Pushing yourself to the edge, adrenalin, I don't know. Even now, I still like the pump of adrenalin going through my body. It was something that made me feel happy; not to impress anyone.

After a couple of years, they put me in the project, for misbehaved kids. I was causing trouble and the truant officers kept turning up at my house. I hated the rules. I smashed a chair over a maths teacher's head when I was about 12. I was suspended and then put in the project class. Outside school, I was drinking and stealing. I used to go round burning the bubble-gum machines with a blowtorch, getting money and bubble-gum out.

My first brush with the police was robbing a pair of trainers out of a shop in Oxford Street. I was 14 years of age. They were Adidas Forest Hills. My dad came up the police station. As soon as my dad seen me, WHACK! Right across the office. Policeman said, 'You can't hit him in here.'

He said, 'He's my son. I can hit him where I want.'

My dad was embarrassed. But I didn't give a fuck. If it's in you, it's in you: crime.

We then robbed cars at about 15, 16. With a slide-pull, a hammer. On one joyride, I nearly got killed in an Astra GTE, but I learnt to drive robbing cars, just going to Epping Forest and doing it trial and error. High Beach, Woodford Way, tumble the cars on country lanes.

The first time I ever took drugs, I was 14. It was pot. I wouldn't rob houses as it didn't appeal to me. I tried to burn our school down with a can of petrol. At 15, my dad's mate got me a job in this factory in the rag trade. One day he was at our house and he said, 'If he is not going to go to school and get an education, bring him to the factory on Monday.'

I loved it. I was an errand boy on seventy pound a week. I was still doing petty crime as well, like robbing fruit machines.

Then I started selling pot on the side – an ounce, two ounces. Chop them up into eighths, sixteenths, and deal them. I used to sell it in the factory. I became a top cutter, marking patterns, cutting the cloth. I used to lay fuize, material to make the cloth harder, stiffer. It was good money. Two hundred pound a week. We used to make clothes for Debenhams, Miss Selfridge, Pineapple, Wallis.

Then I started selling a bit of coke and Ecstasy when I was 17. Getting about a quarter-ounce, breaking it down to half and full grams. I was smoking the pot but not taking the coke. Hash and oil I used to sell also.

I had girls everywhere. Two girls in Hackney, two in Islington, two in Camden. I used to have a room above the Salmon and Ball pub on Bethnal Green road just for partying with girls. Done it up: hi-fi, leather couch. I wouldn't tell them it was mine, so they wouldn't come back looking for me. Just shag 'em and leave 'em.

I was respected on the streets. I was making good money from dealing. I started carrying a gun. I had a BMW when I was 21 – a 323i. B-redged. Six and a half grand. Go in the Camden Palace on a Friday night. Work that a couple of hours; walk out with a grand. Once someone tried to rob me in the toilets. He was a black lad. I just shot him in the leg straight away, stepped over him and walked back into the club. The bouncers smuggled me into the back alleyway and got me a cab. They knew me.

One incident I remember was when a van of coppers pulled up in Somerstown. One copper ran up to me, tried to put a paper knife in my hands he'd found on a wall. Nothing to do with me. So I've held me hands behind my back. Tried to get my prints on it. Takes me down the station and all that. While they were interviewing, tried to put the knife in my pockets. Crown court, fought the case. Copper never showed. Case was thrown out.

I gave up the rag trade at 21. The street appealed to me more. I was still living with my mum and dad but earning over a grand a week. I started taking coke about 22. That was because I was drinking too much. I started to buy an ounce for twelve hundred pound. That was the most I would use. But I wanted more. A more daring adrenalin buzz. From the quantity.

I would sleep during the day; at night I came out like an owl. Buy a bottle of champagne, pour an eighth of coke into it. Drink champagne with an eighth of coke in it. I liked it because it comes on slower. Doesn't fuck your nose up. From lips to your belly, it goes all numb. Nice.

My mum found a gun, a bag of pot, in the drawer once. They pulled me up about it. But they couldn't say nothing, though, could they?

I'm my own worse enemy. I do what I want to do. My best quality was the respect I showed to people, especially my elders. My drug dealing was different. I kept it under wraps. That's why I kept that job for a while. There was no trouble then.

I started getting good coke from Colombia. We would get a mule to go over to Colombia and bring a ki or two back. But the buzz wasn't enough, though. It's nothing like the feeling you get with a hundred kis of heroin in the boot of your car. Just to be near it. That's it, isn't it? Driving along thinking, 'I know what I've got in the car.' Police stopping beside you. A gun under my seat. Taking the risk. At the end of the day, that's why I got into the big-time dealing. Not the money. Or the power. Just the buzz.

Don't get me wrong, all the other perks came along too. Stringfellows, Ra-Ra's, the Hippodrome: they were the places to be seen. Charlie Chan's, Browns in Bethnal Green.

I took over my estate. My mates owned the local pub. Of a summer's night, we'd be in there all night.

I got married in my early 20s. I think 21. She was a Turkish girl. I think her name was Hikmet Malizgit. She was a horrible girl. I kept going back to Turkey all the time. Stay with my cousins, on my mother's side. It was fucking lovely in Tarsus. I'd come back, skin shiny, healthy. I'd spend six weeks out there in the summer. Go back here in the winter. Then spend New Year out there.

I met her through the family. The parents got together, had a chat and then we went out. I was a nutter. Got married. Got divorced a year or two later. I don't even know the day I got married. I didn't even wear a ring after the day of the marriage. It meant nothing to me. Swear to God. I didn't know her age, or what day I got married.

I think I just suddenly woke up. Before I got married, I was going a million mile an hour. Then I ran out of petrol and married her. Filled the tank up again. Realised what I'd done. Sacked her. Back on the road again. That's when John Haase came along and everything just went mad from then on.

8

THE WORLD IS YOURS – BRITAIN'S BIGGEST HEROIN GANG DO THE BUSINESS

In 1992 and 1993, Haase and the Turks were at their peak, smuggling in hundreds of kilos of heroin at regular intervals and making tens of millions of pounds in cash. A tight-lipped underworld source, who has witnessed some of the biggest dealers in the world rise and fall, took his hat off to the gang, giving them an uncharacteristic compliment: 'Let's just say, they were very industrious lads.' The gang were so successful at flooding the market that they caused the biggest single drop in the price of heroin almost overnight – from £24–25,000 a kilo to £20,000 a kilo. For them, these were the good times.

Haase's MO was simple: after receiving the uncut heroin from the Turks in kilo bags, Croker and Garrett would dilute the powder using paracetamol, usually increasing the volume by 25 per cent. Every kilo of high-percentage heroin produced 1.25 kilos of street heroin, immediately boosting profits by 25 per cent with little effort. The street heroin would then be divided into quarter-kilo bags – known as 'corners' on the street

– and sold on to lower- and middle-ranking dealers across Merseyside and elsewhere.

Haase probably sold the quarter-kilo corner bags for a minimum of £6,000 each. Therefore, on a 100-kilo load (at £20,000 a kilo from the Turks, costing a total of £2 million), he could generate 125 kilos of diluted heroin, giving 500 corners selling for a gross of £3 million. A cool million-pound profit on one single load, which could be processed in less than a day and sold in probably two weeks. Half a million a week, if you're lucky. Good work if you can get it.

If Haase was prepared to be more patient, known as 'sitting on it', and sell the kilos in even smaller amounts, then the profits simply went astronomical. Each corner can be divided into nine ounces. That can be diluted further to make 12 or 13 ounces. Each ounce can be sold for £800, making £10,400 on a quarter-kilo valued at £6,000. Or, to boost profits further, each ounce can be split into 28 grams at £50 a time. Each gram can be divided into ten 0.1-g bags at £10 each. All along the chain, further dilutions occur, generating even more multiples of profit.

Ken Darcy, a drug dealer from Liverpool who went on to join Haase's gang, says the secret of Haase's success can be found in four key competitive advantages: cheap heroin, a good credit system from the Turkish Connection, high-quality drugs that could be diluted easily to boost profits, and Haase's ability to impose a sales monopoly through violence and flooding the market.

———————————

KEN DARCY: Haase and Bennett were getting heroin cheap enough and they were getting it laid on – up front and on credit – which gives them a massive edge on everyone else. Then they'd dance on it, bash it. Say you got four kilos, you can make it into five by bashing it, so you've just made an extra twenty grand instantly by bashing it. So, for every four you're making twenty grand on an extra kilo, so if they are getting ninety ki or a hundred ki at a time, they are making a lot of dough without having to do very much. Then, suddenly, they've got that much of it, they've taken over the whole city by selling it. They are able to sell it a little bit cheaper than other dealers because they've made that extra twenty quid [£20,000] already by cutting it up. They are still making a good wage, even after undercutting the other suppliers.

All they want to do then is pay the debt back to these [the Turks] as quick as possible, so they get another parcel of heroin. Because that's how it works. You've got to clear the slate before you get the next load. Sometimes the business goes up and down. One week you can be making brewsters and the next it's dead slow and you're not selling much gear. That's with any drug. But they evened things out by forcing dealers to take their gear. 'Either you buy it off me or you're not selling it at all.' It's as simple as that.

———————

Haase was beset by teething problems which nearly caused his heroin dream to crash before it had even got going properly. In 1992, he was arrested in connection with a gun that had been found by Merseyside Police – but miraculously he managed to escape serious charges and the mini-crisis blew over. The fact that he did not go to jail so soon after being released from the Transit Mob sentence raised suspicions amongst his underworld enemies that he had saved his skin by trading info with the police, that he had turned grass. But there is no evidence of this. Later, officers from the Metropolitan Police were astonished that their colleagues on Merseyside had not jailed Haase for the gun, an event that would have closed down the heroin operation immediately. Haase was obsessed with guns and carried one around because he was having a dispute with one of the city's hard-hitters, Tommy Gilday, who later became an ally.

But in December 1992, just as they were getting into the swing of things, the gang suffered a major setback. They had just smuggled in a massive load of heroin from Turkey via France, but approximately 40 kilos of it and middle-ranking member Bulent Onay had been seized at his home in north London. The police had recovered 148 bags of heroin, each weighing about a quarter of a kilo, hidden in plastic bags in a bedroom wardrobe inside a green holdall. The total haul weighed 36.54 kilos and had a purity of 62 per cent. But there was a discrepancy. Onay remembered that he had placed 40 kilos at the bottom of his wardrobe. That meant approximately three and a half kilos had disappeared during the police raid. Bulent kept quiet but the officers eventually found out and a bent copper was later blamed for the alleged theft. Police estimated that at wholesale prices the load was worth £750,000 and at £100-per-gram street prices, £3.65 million. Onay was subsequently convicted and jailed.

The episode should have set off alarm bells amongst the remaining gang that they might be under surveillance, or that Onay might be talking to Customs to get himself a lighter sentence – especially considering the inside story of how the heroin ended up in Onay's house. The parcel had taken a circuitous route exposing nearly every member of the gang. First it came into the UK from France. Then it went to Liverpool. Some time approaching Christmas 1992, distributor Eddie Croker was told by Paul Bennett to take 40 kilos from the stash and to rendezvous at 8 p.m. in Pirrie Road with the Turks. The heroin was in quarter-kilo sealed bags and Croker loaded 160 into the boot of his car. Haase and Bennett were watching close by as they were transferred into Onay's Carlton, alongside Kaya. The 40 kilos ended up in Onay's wardrobe on Christmas Eve.

But Haase and Kaya did not heed the warnings. They were making so much money and were so confident in their ability, and in keeping Onay from grassing through their fearsome reputation, that they carried on regardless. Suleyman Ergun was parachuted in to take Onay's place, with increased powers to run a tighter ship. For his first day's work collecting money from Liverpool, Kaya gave him £2,500. Foolishly he paid it into his bank account the next day – a mistake he would not repeat.

As business flourished and Haase began selling

unprecedented amounts of heroin in double-quick time, senior Turkish Connection boss Ergun was rushed off his feet. He quickly became lost in a whirl of late-night cash pick-ups and heroin deliveries, driving constantly on the motorway between London and Liverpool and bombarded with mobile-phone calls and pager messages. The gang were selling so much heroin that he was exhausted. He sometimes came home with hundreds of thousands of pounds stuffed into black bin bags. He would tip the money out on his bed in his room at his mum and dad's house and begin to count and box it. But he would simply collapse and fall asleep. There simply wasn't enough time in the day to get through it.

When there was a moment, he would raid his mum's larder for boxes of cornflakes or teabags, tip out the contents and use the containers to package some of the cash so that it could be taken back to Turkey by a courier. Eventually, a system settled down. Shipments of 100 or 110 kilos of heroin would leave Turkey bound for the UK. Ten kilos, worth £200,000, would be shaved off to pay for this transport and the balance of 90 or 100 kilos would be directly given to John Haase in Liverpool or his couriers in Paris.

SULEYMAN ERGUN: The guy that introduced John Haase to Kaya was an ex-policeman from Cyprus called Mustafa Sezazi. He was in Long Lartin prison with John Haase when John was doing the 14 for armed robbery. Mustafa was doing 16–18 years for heroin smuggling. Mustafa spoke very highly of John and said that he was very well respected in Liverpool. He also said that he could sell a great deal of heroin and had contacts all over England. While Mustafa was in prison, we took care of him and his family and made sure they had money. I once went to a factory which made coats and jackets. Mustafa's son was working there. I didn't know him when I arrived, so enquired and the guy was pointed out to me. I walked up to him and gave him £2,000 in cash and said it was from Kaya. I remember seeing him on one more occasion outside a Pizza Hut on

Stamford Hill. He got into my car and I gave him £10,000 to pay his dad's solicitor's fees for his appeal. Mustafa had good contacts in Pakistan and India, where he would buy the heroin and bring it to Turkey and then on to England. He would often buy raw opium and have it made into heroin in Turkey.

Kaya had gone up to see Haase, after he's got out of prison in the early months of 1992, about them doing heroin business together. So that's how it started off, and soon the contact Mustafa had given us began to pay off. Business between us and John Haase started to boom. There were a couple of hiccups early on, like everything else, but they were overcome. One of our people called Bulent Onay was arrested on 24 December 1992 with about 40 kilos of heroin, on his return from Liverpool.

We didn't fear that Onay would talk too much because it was all based on honour and loyalty and respect. And we didn't think that the whole organisation was under threat because we were convinced that he'd been set up in a one-off kind of thing. Business just carried on regardless.

Up until then, Bulent had been one of our main contacts, with Haase under the supervision of Kaya. I was ambitious. I was determined to be better than Bulent and take on more responsibility. I knew I was better at the job than him and I didn't want to let Kaya down. Just days after Bulent was arrested, I was slotted into his boots and business was up and running before New Year. That's how efficient we were. Up until then, I had been working with Kaya in connection with another gang who we supplied, but Kaya wanted me to deal with Liverpool because it was quickly becoming our biggest outlet. I then started getting involved with Haase more. My first visit to Liverpool was with two other male friends: Kaya and Joey the Turk. There we met John Haase. We also met Paul Bennett to collect money, and to introduce me to money pick-ups, people who would courier money and so on. It was also the opportunity to get to know both Haase and Bennett in case I had to run the operations when Kaya was not in England.

This first meet with Haase was at the end of 1992, just after

Christmas. The story behind this meeting was this. Kaya had just brought in a big parcel of heroin – about 90 kilos – which had been given to Haase about two weeks before on about 18 December. Forty kis of this had been nicked with Onay, but that still left fifty to sell. It had come overland from Turkey to France then across the Channel. Haase and Bennett had got the ferry over to Calais to make sure that the last leg was OK, to see that it came into the UK without a problem. As soon as they had come back on the ferry to Dover, they met with Kaya and Joey the Turk in a Kentucky Fried Chicken shop in Islington to discuss them coming up to Liverpool to collect some money for the gear towards the end of December. That's when I came in. I went to Liverpool with Kaya.

When we first met John Haase, the money wasn't ready, so myself, Kaya and Joey went to a hotel in Manchester for the night. We stayed at the Britannia Hotel in Piccadilly. The next day, we drove back to Liverpool and met Haase and were paid. They then took us to a sauna in Rocky Lane and had a chat, the nature of which was more heroin and money talk. It was there that I met Chris No-Neck for the first time. He walked in the room with a black bin bag full of money. We shook hands; we were given £68,000.

John Haase had known Kaya for about 8–10 months by that time. I had been working with Kaya for a while collecting money for heroin from other people who we supplied. When I was brought in to deal with Haase, they owed us for 90 kilos of heroin which Kaya had supplied to them earlier. The sixty-eight grand was part payment on that. If you give someone ninety kilos and you charge them twenty grand a ki, then you're owed 1.8 million, but the payments are spread over the time it takes the dealer to sell the gear, so there is not that much pressure on them. No one has that money knocking around in one go. Also, it's easier to transport little bits of money piecemeal than all in one go. You come up here one week, you'll collect sixty-eight grand. You come up here the following week, you'll pick up a hundred grand. The amounts of money I began to pick up varied. It could have been forty grand one time. It's done in dribs and drabs. But it was all ticked off a mental account that Kaya kept in his head. After that first meeting, everyone in the room was told by Kaya that I was in charge of the Turkish side when he was not in England. Everyone agreed and we then drove back to London.

A few weeks later, I got a call from Turkey that more heroin was being made and that John would be getting some of it. I made a call to John Haase's sister and left a message for John to call me. John's sister was the one who would take most of John's calls and then pass them on to him. She wasn't aware of what was going on. John would get back to me within the hour. When he called me, I told him that I would be driving to Liverpool to collect more money. We arranged a pick-up for the next day. I made my way to Liverpool and got there quite late. I drove straight to the Rocky Lane sauna and parked around the corner. I paged John from a phone box. He called me and said someone would be calling me back. I parked my car about 20 metres from the phone box. After around 20–30 minutes, someone made a call to me from the very same phone box. I could see the male in the box but I didn't know it was the person I was supposed to meet. That was the first time I met Paul Lally. We shook hands, then he handed me a black bin bag. He said it contained £68,000. He got in his car and drove away. I put the bag on the front passenger seat and started to drive.

You had to be alert all the time, switched on, making sure that you weren't being followed, making sure that you weren't under surveillance by the Customs or police, or maybe other villains looking to have you off for the money. Though that was unlikely because of who we were, you could never get sloppy. I never let my guard down.

That day I noticed something strange. As I was turning left, I came to a dead end. Right opposite me there was a light blue Ford Sierra parked on the corner. There was one male at the steering wheel. After I saw him in my rear-view mirror, I pulled in to a petrol station to see whether he followed me. I put petrol in the car, got some fags and a drink. So I then put my bonnet up and made out I was checking the motor's engine. As he was driving up to the traffic lights, I saw him looking at me. We were almost eye to eye. It could have been nothing but I made a mental note of it.

I knew Kaya was returning to England very soon, so I didn't say anything to John Haase about it. When Kaya came back to England, I told him what had happened. Details like that were so important that we set up a meet, bearing in mind what had happened to Onay. The meet was in the Black Horse pub in Old Swan, Liverpool. There was the four of us: Kaya, John, Ben and me. I told them what had happened and asked whether anyone in their firm had a light blue Ford Sierra. John said no and changed the subject.

At that meet, me and Kaya picked up more money. Just before we left, John asked me and Kaya whether we could get them any passports. We said, 'Yes, but they are really expensive.' But they were very good, right out of the Home Office. They were £4,000 each. They wanted one each, so Kaya said, 'Have your photos ready for the next meet.'

We arranged another meet to collect more money. We sat down at the Black Horse again and started talking. They handed over money and some photos for the passports. The man who supplied the passports was Kaya's man named Ozzie, a Turkish-Cypriot from south London. The passports took three to four weeks. When they were passed on to us, John's passport was under the name of John Williams and Ben's was Shaun Ryan. Again, I remember feeling uncomfortable about something I saw out the corner of my eye. Seated a few feet away from us were a man and a woman drinking orange juice. What struck me was the woman's handbag. I cannot explain it but it just didn't seem right. I told John, Kaya and Ben but they didn't seem that bothered.

Business just carried on going from strength to strength. The sooner they'd finish selling one parcel, the sooner they'd get the next hustle. The quicker it sold, the quicker they'd get the next load. That was their motivation. They were quick. They were very, very fast – I'll give them that. Because they were greedy, they couldn't wait to sell one 90-kilo load so they could get their hands on the next. They'd cut it first. The quicker they paid us, the quicker they'd get the next parcel, the quicker they'd get the money. They paid good for about a year and a half. I wouldn't say on time – dribs and drabs, but we got it. One of the reasons John Haase was able to sell a lot quickly was because he was a bit of a bully. He'd force it on dealers and say, 'Look, you're gonna buy off me.' This person, they was getting it for 22 off someone else. Haase and Bennett then were making him buy it for 24 off them.

A good few million had been passed between us. Demand would shift it really quickly. Drop off 40 kilos to Haase one day and a couple of days later go up and collect £200,000, maybe £150,000. Come straight back to London. Count it, stack it, elastic band them and that. Get The Colonel down from Turkey. The Colonel would come – he'd box it up his way. He gets back on a diplomatic passport. Money was returned to Turkey that way.

The economics of heroin dealing are mind-blowing. It cost about two and a half, three grand a kilo in Turkey when we was doing it. We were selling it for twenty. Transport fees would increase the cost to about six or seven a kilo. Most expensive part is getting it across the water from France/Holland/Belgium to here. Most expensive bit – four thousand pound a kilo that. Driver would take the risks. Usually a thousand pound a kilo from Istanbul to France/Holland/Belgium then two thousand pound a kilo from there to here. We were making about fourteen–fifteen grand profit.

Depends on expenses how much of that would go back to Turkey. If we need a couple of cars, we get a couple of cars. We need extra money, we take extra money. I took what I wanted. Out of a £100,000, I could take maybe ten/fifteen from it. We'd tell them back home: 'This much is coming over. We've collected this much and we've kept this much.' Break it down for them. There was never any friction because we were sensible. One collection out the blue was when Haase and Bennett gave us twelve grand. We were expecting about sixty that day. Eddie had it collected because Haase and Bennett were away. That's why it was so shy. But it was sorted.

The money kept on rolling in. A lot of it was burnt money, because the heroin users would roll it up in a tube when they were chasing the dragon. It burns, singes. We had to spend it in shops over here. To go back to Turkey, it had to be a proper note, no holes or rips. In each load, we had three/four grand of them. I'd walk into Armani and buy suits with them.

Kaya was away for a few weeks then. He had gone to Turkey, then to Italy. He phoned me to tell me a shipment was to arrive in England. I was to arrange it so it all went to John and Ben. Kaya told me it was 90 kilos. When it arrived, it all went to Liverpool. Then a few days later, I met Kaya at Heathrow. We drove straight to Liverpool. When we got there, we told John that we wanted 30 kilos of it back. We had promised to give it to two other contacts we had in Manchester. Because we never let anyone down, as a matter of honour, we decided to take some of it from John's parcel. He [Haase] wasn't happy about it but he had no choice. We waited for a few hours, then Paul Lally arrived with the gear. We took it and drove to Manchester and gave it to two friends of ours called Rab and Barney in Manchester. Rab was a very big player in Scotland.

We went to Rab's house. It was very nice. There were guns everywhere. We had a cup of tea with them and gave them the heroin. But when we opened the bags, the heroin was not in its own bags. It had brown tape around each kilo. This is not the way we had supplied it to them. Haase had obviously cut it. But Rab and Barney were happy with the quantity so we gave it to them and we let it go.

Kaya then returned to Turkey. I waited a few days then called John's sister and left a message. John got back to me and I told him I would be coming up to collect more money the next day. It had been OK'd. When I got to Liverpool, I made contact and waited in the Black Horse. This was the first time that I met Eddie Croker. He came in with John and Ben. John said that I would be meeting with Eddie on some occasions. Eddie handed me a carrier bag with around £28,000 in it. We shook hands and parted.

A few weeks later, I got a call from John asking when there would be another shipment. I told him I was waiting for a call and that I would let him know as soon as I heard anything. I told him I had two kilos in London and if he wanted them, I'd give them to him. He said yes. It was just to tide him over.

At the time, I had a 357 Magnum. It was chromium plated and it had a laser sight on it. I'd got it off a heroin dealer called Mehmet Sait, who owned a farm with two lakes on it just outside of London in the countryside. Mem always had good guns. Like all of us, he was very good at counter-surveillance. He even had a handheld bug detector which cost £28,000. Before he got in a car, he would sweep it. Before meetings, he would sweep the room. Sometimes I used to go to the canal near where I lived in north London with the 357 he gave me and have target practice. In between fishing.

While Kaya was in Turkey, I got a call from him telling me to give John the gun I had, the 357 Magnum. So I called John and told him about the gun. He was over the moon. I got to Liverpool the next day and met Eddie and gave him the two kilos. John and Ben came around half an hour later to meet me and collect the gun. I gave John the gun with nine bullets. He then asked me to go with them in their car, a silver Ford Granada, to a house to collect some money. They handed me £40,000. They then drove me back to the Black Horse, where I'd left my own car. We shook hands and parted.

I then got a call from Turkey. It was The Vulcan. He told me that Mehmet Ansen, a retired colonel, would be in London to collect the money I'd collected. This would be the first time I'd met him. I packed the money, got it ready and waited for the call. When Ansen called, he asked me to meet him up from the Ebury Court Hotel. I walked into the lobby and saw a man reading a Turkish newspaper. I approached him and asked if he was The Colonel. He said yes. We walked to my car, got in and drove to my mum and dad's house. He didn't get out of the car; neither did he say much. I do remember he did have a box of plates and bowls from Wedgwood. I returned to the car with a few bags full of counted money and gave the bags to him. I drove him back to the hotel and left him there. I called The Vulcan and told him he had the money. The next day, Ansen flew back to Turkey with the money. He had a diplomatic passport. He would collect money from England, Italy and sometimes Spain.

John called me and said he wasn't happy with one kilo of the two kilos of heroin I'd given him. So I told him I would be up the next day to collect it. I drove up the following day and met Eddie, collected the one kilo. I then phoned a contact I had who was known as The Banker. He was Curtis Warren's partner. I asked him if he wanted it. Even though he was a very big dealer, worth tens of millions of pounds, doing hundreds of kis of coke with Curtis and other things, he said that he did. That's just the way the drugs business is. Heroin is heroin, no matter how big or small a parcel it is, and dealers will buy whatever they can get their hands on, no matter if it's one kilo or a hundred. Especially if there's a drought. I met The Banker in a pub in Anfield and gave him the gear. He was happy. He was a man who didn't complain. He was easygoing, laid back. Instead of charging £20,000, I asked him for £16,000. That made his day. I said, 'Don't give me the money today. I'll be back with Kaya in a few days to collect it.' The Banker was a man I trusted more than John and Ben.

When Kaya came back to England, we met The Banker in a pub, at the Old Swan, with a view to doing business on a more permanent basis. We had a chat and told him we would be giving him a few kilos to start off with as we were expecting a shipment. Liverpool had a drought on then; there wasn't much gear around. We left The Banker and met John and Ben in the Black Horse. We told them that The Vulcan would be coming to England very soon so be ready for a meet and that we would not be talking in a pub. John suggested we meet in a pub and then go to his sister's house.

When The Vulcan arrived in England, myself and Kaya met him. We then took him to one of our safehouses in London and talked about what had been going on. He was happy with progress and said that we'd go to Liverpool as soon as possible.

We got to Liverpool and met John and Ben. It was night when we got to John's sister's house. John had made sure that his sister was not in at the time. John made tea and coffee and we all sat down.

We started talking about more heroin. Vulcan and Kaya trusted John but sometimes Ben would behave like a little boy. Most of the talk, because of this, was aimed at John. As we were talking, the doorbell rang and John went to answer it. It was Eddie with a bag in his hand. It was full of money, around £90,000. We took the bag and Eddie left. We told John that he would be getting all the gear when it was ready. John and Ben were very happy about this and very happy that The Vulcan was there talking to them about all this. Afterwards, John suggested taking us all for a meal but we said no as we had no time and had to get back to London. I later counted the money then booked a flight for The Vulcan back to Turkey.

Business carried on as usual – heroin and money just going up and down the M1 and M6 motorways. But Joey the Turk was becoming a liability and one day, after collecting money in Liverpool, he proved it. That night, I took him to my local pub, called the Jubilee. He started to show off and say things that he shouldn't have, playing the gangster and so on. Then, when we went to a nightclub afterwards – Oceans on Goswell Road – he walked up to the doorman like an idiot and said, 'I've got a gun on me, don't pat me down.' He was just behaving very stupidly. He didn't even have a gun on him and he didn't even have the guts to carry one. He was just being a prick. But stuff like that can get you nicked. Then we heard that Bulent Onay had been making threats. He was in prison on remand being interrogated by police, and now was threatening to grass up Joey the Turk and Manuk Ocecki for giving him the heroin. That was the final straw for the pair of them – we decided to get them off the firm. I drove them to Belgium, to the port of Ostend, to get them out of the way. I was glad to get rid of them.

I got back to London the next day and met with Kaya. He told me that one of his mates – whose first name meant 'bastard' when translated from Turkish to English – had 50,000 Ecstasy tablets and had asked us whether we could help him sell them for him as a favour. We met him at Queensway. We went for a walk and told him that we didn't sell tablets. But because we knew him, as a favour we would take them to Liverpool [to John and Ben] and see if our people there could do anything with them. He gave us six tablets. We were going to Liverpool anyway the next day to collect money. So we told him we would get back to him in a few days.

Me and Kaya set off for Liverpool the next day. When we got to the Black Horse pub, I phoned John to let him know that we had arrived. We waited around half an hour when John and Ben walked in with a carrier bag. We told them that we had some tablet samples and that 50,000 were available if they wanted. John took the tablets but said the price was too high and that he would get back to us about it. The meeting didn't last very long in the pub. John said that he had some Rolex 18 ct watches, covered in diamonds, if we were interested. We said we'd have a look. John then took us to his sister's house again. She was totally unaware of the crimes that were going on – totally innocent. He opened a big bag containing Rolex and Cartier boxes. We opened the Rolex boxes and started to look at them; they were covered in diamonds. John said they were worth £75,000 each but we could have them for £25,000 each. We took three and told him to deduct the money from the amount owed us. We then opened a Cartier box which contained a necklace, bracelet and earrings. I asked how much John wanted and he said £16,000. Again I asked him to deduct it from the outstanding money.

The money we collected was too bulky at times, so sometimes I would have it changed into dollars. I had a friend in [a West End travel agent's]. I'd met him in my local boozer. The guy never asked me where or how I got the money and I never told him. I used the alias Billy Moore. One day in April '93, I changed up $23,000. That was quite common.

One morning, I got a call from Kaya. He wanted to meet me at a mate's house. When I got there, there was another guy sitting with him called Cracker [not his real name]. This guy had six kilos of heroin and asked if I could help him sell it. I called John and asked him if he wanted it. He said yes. I said I would bring it up that day. I got the gear and drove up to Liverpool. It was night-time when I got there. I rang John and he told me Eddie was on his way to meet me. I met Eddie in a pub on Prescot Road. We then walked into the backstreets and parked our cars boot to boot. I gave him the gear and then I set off back to London. I got a call from John the next day telling me the heroin was no good, that it had too much cut in it. I told him it wasn't ours and that we were doing someone a favour. He insisted that he didn't want it as the quality was no good. I told him I would be back up the next day to collect it and then give it back to the guy who gave it to us.

I called Kaya and told him what had happened. I told him I was going to Liverpool to bring it back. I retrieved it, returned to London, informed the fella who we were doing a favour for that I was back and organised a meet. He took me to his house and said sorry for this and sorry for that. He offered me a bag of cocaine, which I declined. He then took me down the street and showed me a Porsche 959 car. He said I could have it for £16,000. I said, 'No thanks.' He then asked me if I would work for him. I told him to fuck off, that what he was doing was bad and that it was called 'back-dooring' [disloyalty and betrayal to Kaya by working for another dealer]. After that day, I never saw him again.

A few days later, me and Kaya arranged to meet John and Ben at Watford Gap service station to talk about a new shipment coming in. When we got there, they had another guy with them who was sorting out the transport. We talked for a while. Certain things were agreed. Then a plastic bag containing money was handed over and we all parted.

On one occasion when The Vulcan and Kaya were in England, the three of us went to see a guy called Vern [not his real name]. This guy had been sent to do a job in Belgium for us and was given £11,000 in cash. He hadn't done what needed to be done but had taken the money and gone instead on a skiing holiday. I was told to get a baseball bat and the three of us would pay him a visit. At the time, the guy had a clothes shop selling T-shirts, shirts, leather jackets and coats which he'd imported from Turkey. As soon as he saw us walk into his shop, he told his secretary to leave. All I wanted to do was do him in with the bat, but Kaya stopped me. We sat down and started talking to the man, who was scared shitless. He was told he would never work again and that we were taking the shop from him and his red Mercedes parked out front. He didn't say a word and just handed over the keys to the shop and the car. Kaya and The Vulcan gave me the keys and said they were mine to do with what I wanted. I didn't know what I would do with the shop because I didn't have time to run that sort of business, so I found the person Vern was renting it from. The owner told me Vern owed him over £6,000 in rent, so I just laughed and gave him the keys to his shop. The red Mercedes I used for a while then sold it for £8,000 and kept the money. I never saw Vern again or heard anything about him.

There was so much money that Kaya and me could take as much as we wanted. We just took it out of one of the bin bags from Liverpool – ten, twenty or thirty grand. We didn't have to ask anyone. The Vulcan didn't mind. The money wasn't important – it was about honour, loyalty and respect. That's why there was no formal system of payment. I'd just take the money and go and buy a car. Or go into the West End and blow £5,000 on clothes or thousands on jewellery and presents for the family.

———

Meanwhile, on the flip side of the coin in Liverpool, Paul Bennett was busy trying to 'wash' or legitimise the masses of cash the gang were raking in. Describing himself as a property developer, he invested in a portfolio of houses and flats, guided by a bent estate agent. But even this couldn't disguise the millions being generated, forcing Bennett into more bizarre schemes. He started asking an architecture student called Mark at Liverpool Poly, the brother of a pal, to get hard-up foreign students on his course to cash banker's drafts, pretending the money was for investment in property. In a single transaction, one Jordanian national put £30,000 through his account.

At the same time, Eddie Croker was busy running around processing the heroin supplied by Kaya and Ergun for distribution to middle-ranking dealers on the streets of Liverpool and beyond. On the surface, the former gardener maintained an air of respectability. His wife was a highly paid research scientist at Liverpool University, and he disguised his erratic movements by running a carpet-cleaning company, which he had set up in 1990, and buying and selling cars from the automart. The frequent changes of car made it more difficult to track heroin movements. After the gear was sold, it was his job to collect money and deliver it to the Turks under instructions from Haase. Croker invested his and the gang's profits in a string of properties. He bought three for £56,000 each at auction in one month alone. He gave one to his mum and dad in Tilston Road. Though lower down the chain of command than Ergun, his account – detailed in a statement he wrote two years later on 9 February 1995 – gives a fascinating insight into the non-Turkish part of the operation and into the world of drug dealing in modern Britain. The story, which has been edited, begins two weeks before Suleyman Ergun's induction into the firm in late 1992, shortly after Kaya and Haase had smuggled a massive parcel of heroin from Turkey via France. Part of this consignment was the 40 kilos later found at Bulent Onay's address, for which he was jailed.

EDDIE CROKER: In early December 1992, I was working with Paul Bennett and John Haase. Around 17 December, I was told by Paul Bennett to go to Scarsbrick Road in Liverpool 11. I was to go there to collect a consignment of heroin and stash it somewhere safe. I told Paul Bennett what vehicle I would be driving and went to the pre-arranged spot. I was met there by a male who recognised me by the car I was driving. He took two black bin liners from the boot of the car he was driving and transferred them to the boot of my car, which was a black Astra.

I then drove to a disused railway embankment, which is

nearby. On the embankment, I hid the two bin liners containing heroin in the bushes and the ground. About one week later, I was told by Paul Bennett to take 40 kilos of heroin from the black bin liners and take it to Pirrie Road in Liverpool 9, which is near my home address in Tilston Road. I was told I should meet John Haase and Paul Bennett there. I went to the stash on the embankment and took out 40 kilos of heroin. The heroin within the black bin liners was in quarter-kilo sealed bags and I put them in the boot of my car and drove the short distance to Pirrie Road.

It was about 8 p.m. When I arrived, John Haase and Paul Bennett were already there in a Ford Granada. Two other men who I had not met were in a red/purple Carlton. They turned out to be Bulent Onay and Yilmaz Kaya. Paul Bennett came over to me and asked where it was. I told him in the boot. Bulent Onay got out of the Carlton and came over. I opened the boot and Bulent Onay took one of the bags containing heroin from the boot, which he then transferred to either the back seat or the boot of the Carlton. He then came back to my car with Yilmaz Kaya and they both took the remaining bags, containing heroin, and placed them in the Carlton. Once this was completed, John Haase and Paul Bennett left in the Granada and Bulent Onay drove away with Yilmaz Kaya in the Carlton. I then went home.

The rest of the heroin, which could have been 10–15 kilos, was left in place on the railway embankment. After the New Year, in early January 1993, I was told by Paul Bennett to collect this heroin and take it to Scarsbrick Road, where I would be met by someone who I was to hand the heroin to. Again I collected it, went to Scarsbrick Road and handed it to a man I met there.

After this, I was told many times to go to various places and collect drugs. I would then have to either stash these or drive to hand them over to a third party. I did not always know the person I was meeting, but I would be told where to go by Paul Bennett, and the person meeting me would know what car I was in. At this time, I had a pager on which I would be contacted by Paul Bennett or John Haase. I would then phone them on a contact number for instructions.

Another job I did was to collect the money once the drugs were delivered. I would then take the money and leave it in my house or my mother's house in Liverpool until instructed where to take it. During the early part of 1993, I would normally take the money and hand it to Paul Bennett. This later changed and I was told that I had to count the money and go to the Black Horse pub, which is on Prescot Road in Liverpool.

I would meet 'the Turks' at the pub and give them the money. I went at short notice and they would usually be waiting for me. The two Turks I would meet were Yilmaz Kaya and Suleyman Ergun. Sometimes it was the two of them or just Ergun. I would hand the money across in plastic carrier bags. This money was solely from the sale of drugs.

But sometimes there wasn't enough money in the bags to satisfy the Turks. They had overheads like everyone. They had to buy opium in eastern Turkey and pay for a chemist to make the paste into heroin at one of the many hundreds of chemical-stinking makeshift labs in Istanbul. Sometimes the Turks got unhappy with the Scousers' sporadic payments – especially as they were preparing another big shipment like in the summer of 1993.

SULEYMAN ERGUN: Kaya went back to Turkey to oversee things there. Then I got a call from him while he was in Turkey telling me he would be coming over the following week. He asked me to contact John and get money from him. I spoke to John and told him what I needed and that Kaya would be coming. John asked me to meet a friend of his called Roy who lived down south. John said this guy called Roy would give me cash. I met Roy in a wine bar on Essex Road in north London called Cheers. He handed me a small bag with £5,000 in it. I said that was a piss-take. I took the money and called John again and told him that it wouldn't do; it was too small. So I arranged to go to Liverpool and collect more money the next day. When I got there, I met Eddie Croker in the Black Horse. He had £12,000 in a carrier bag. I told Eddie that this wasn't good enough also and to tell John that the money drops have to be bigger amounts. I told him that Kaya would be here very soon. Eddie was a laid-back person who was just doing what he was told. He said, 'OK, I'll tell John about it.'

Kaya arrived in England. I met him at the airport – think it was Gatwick. We drove straight to Liverpool. John and Ben didn't know we were on our way. I told Kaya what had been going on with the money drops. He wasn't very happy about it but said we would sort it out. We got to Liverpool and paged John. He rang my mobile straight away. I told him that me and Kaya were in Liverpool and that we wanted to see him and Ben. Again, we met at the Black Horse. We talked about the money and they apologised and said it wouldn't happen again. John asked me to go to a house and pick up some money while Ben and Kaya had a drink. John drove me to a house in Anfield. I think it was his own flat because he went through an alleyway and when he returned he had a carrier bag. He handed it to me. It had £140,000 in it. We drove back to the Black Horse and had a few more drinks and talked about more heroin being made. Kaya explained to John that as we were sitting here, it was being made in Turkey and that it would be around 100–120 kilos. Both Ben's and John's eyes lit up. They started to make all sorts of promises. We talked about the transport and the best way it could be done. Kaya said he would be returning to Turkey very soon and that he would be coming back with The Vulcan to finalise everything. We didn't really need The Vulcan but he liked to take a break from Turkey and come over for a bit of shopping.

Me and Kaya left the pub and drove back to London. When we got back to London, Kaya said, 'Let's count the money and stack it neatly.' I said no because I was so bored. Kaya laughed at me and said even he got tired separating the ripped and burnt notes. In Turkey, banks wouldn't change ripped or burnt notes. So he said, 'OK, you go and I will count it.' The money was counted and stacked neatly. The ripped and burnt notes were put aside to spend in England. It was funny because there would often be a few thousand in just ripped and burnt notes.

Kaya returned to Turkey and a little while later he and The Vulcan returned to England. I knew they were coming but didn't know the day. I was having a drink in the Jubilee pub when I got a call from Kaya saying that he and The Vulcan were at Euston station, which was just around the corner from the pub and from where I lived with my mum and dad. I told my mates I had to leave and drove to Euston and picked them up. Everything was running great. The gear in Turkey was ready, all vacuum-packed into one-kilo bags. We had a special machine over there, I think it was for packing food, that did the job. It sealed it so there was no, or at least not as much, smell. The next day, we planned to go to Liverpool.

When I got home, I made a call to Ben. He told me John was in Ibiza with his girlfriend but would be back in Liverpool for the meet. The next morning, the three of us set off for Liverpool. It was a very warm day. When we got to Liverpool, we met in the Black Horse pub as usual, had one drink then the five of us left – me, Kaya, Vulcan, Ben and John. We went to the sauna on Rocky Lane. We started talking. We told John and Ben there would be 111 kilos of heroin coming to France. We explained that we would get it to Paris but John would have to pick it up there and get it to England. We told them that we wanted them to sort out the transport from Paris to Liverpool. They didn't object and said OK.

Ben and John left me and Kaya and Vulcan in the sauna. They said they would be back with a girl for each of us. We declined, but they returned with a black girl for The Vulcan. While the girl and The Vulcan were upstairs, me and Kaya were working out who would do the switch in Paris and how it would all be worked out. The gear would be brought from Turkey to France on a coach of people going on holiday to the south of France. It was only the driver and one other man who would know there was heroin concealed on the coach under the floorboards.

Everything was worked out. The girl and The Vulcan returned from upstairs. She was told to leave. Then we sat down and agreed on what was to be done. We all shook hands on the deal. John and Ben promised £1 million in the first week in one drop. We would be giving them 100 kilos. They or we were to use 10 kilos of the 111-kilo load to pay our Turkish contacts for the transport from Turkey to Paris. An extra kilo would be used for wastage or emergency payments, such as rent for a safehouse. The remaining 100 kilos they were getting from us at £20,000 a kilo on tick – credit! Ben and John were very happy about this as they had never had a deal like this before. Not only was it very big but to them the heroin was basically being given to them free. They didn't have to lay out a penny. Once it was sold, they would have to pay us 100 kilos at £20,000, which equals £2 million. The only condition was they would have to give us half of that, £1 million, in the first week after delivery.

Me and Kaya then went to Turkey. That was on 15 May 1993. Kaya wasn't feeling well. I noticed this on the plane. I didn't know what was wrong with him but I think he took something to calm him down or make him sleep. He started to knock a few whiskies back like water and after a while passed out. When we landed in Turkey, we were picked up by Kaya's brother. We greeted each other then walked to a big black Mercedes. We got in and started to drive away. We had another car in front and one behind for security. We were in Istanbul. First we dropped Kaya off to his own house, because his wife was waiting. Me and his brother went for a drink and talked for ages. After the drinks and talk, we went to his family's house. I didn't want to stay in a hotel. His mother wouldn't let me anyway.

We'd planned that John Haase was going to come out to Turkey on this occasion. It was someone's idea so that we could make the final arrangements for the 111-kilo run to Paris. And also to bring him a bit closer into the organisation, to build a bit more trust and so he could have a bit of a holiday over there, comped by us to let him know that we respected him. But all the work had been done for Paris, so it wasn't really necessary. I didn't like this trip one bit because I thought it was too soon and there was something about John that I didn't trust. I had sensed a lot in John's eyes at meets in the Black Horse pub and what

117

I'd sensed didn't please me. Ben I'd sussed on our very first meet. He loved to talk and loved to boast. He'd say too much. If he was saying all this stuff to us, God knows what he was saying to other people. So I just wanted to take things step by step. But it was one of them. I had to go along with it out of respect for my seniors and be diplomatic, which was a great strength of mine. We had to make the best of it, especially security-wise. Haase was going to bring his girlfriend Debbie Dillon so that he would look like a man on holiday to Turkey with his girl. He was also coming in on a false passport. They were arriving on 17 July. The following morning, me and Vulcan drove to Kaya's house. John Haase was flying to Turkey, to Dalaman airport, which was far away from Istanbul, and I was to pick them up on arrival. Kaya gave me three bodyguards, a vest and a gun. I told him I didn't need anything and that I would be going on my own by plane. I wanted to be low-key. I didn't want to attract unwanted attention and could move a lot faster on my own. I booked a flight and departed for Dalaman airport the same day. That was because John and Debbie would be flying in the next day – in the afternoon.

I booked into a little hotel in Dalyan. Dalyan is a small tourist town 40 mins' drive from Dalaman airport. It was such a peaceful place; I felt so relaxed. I didn't want to go anywhere. It had lots of little narrow streets full of bars and cafés and restaurants. I'd have loved to live there but it wasn't to be because of work.

The next day, I went to Dalaman and waited for John and Debbie. The plane was on time. If I remember rightly, they flew in from Newcastle, well away from Liverpool. They had a few bags with them. We greeted each other then went to book our connections to Istanbul. The next flight was over four hours away. I paid for the tickets. I noticed John's passport was in the name of John Williams. We walked out of the airport and took a taxi to Dalyan. When we arrived, I took them to a little restaurant and had the table covered with everything, from chicken to fish salads to mezze to drinks, the lot. It was our hospitality. Everything from now on would be paid for by us.

After the meal, I took John and Debbie to a place I can only describe as paradise. That's exactly what John said it was. 'I could live here' is what John said. They were his very words. The water lapping at their feet. The reeds growing out of it. Birds and ducks, and right opposite, the mountains with caves carved into them. They were very historic and one of Turkey's wonders. We sat there for a few hours drinking raki. Debbie didn't want to go. None of us wanted to leave but graft comes first over play. [There is no suggestion that Debbie knew of Haase's involvement in drug dealing.] We got a taxi back to Dalaman airport and flew to Istanbul. Debbie was pissed and fell asleep as soon as we boarded. We landed in Istanbul about an hour later and was picked up by another of Kaya's younger brothers. We had a lot of security around us but made sure John didn't notice it. I didn't like the reason as to why John came over in the first place and I was determined to stop important things – like him meeting Kaya or The Vulcan over there – from going ahead. I also wasn't going to let John get too close, to see too much. John was supposed to see things I didn't want him to. That wasn't my intention, so part of the reason for the security was to cordon John off a bit. In my opinion, he was being trusted too much too soon and I didn't like it.

We got to the Istanbul Hilton and booked them into the best suite looking over the Bosphorus. John went into the room and I went and saw Kaya. I told him where John was and that I'd made sure he was staying in Istanbul for three days. I explained to Kaya that I didn't like what was going on and put a little doubt in his head as to what he was doing, to make him think again and think carefully. In my mind, I didn't want John and Kaya meeting over in Turkey. To do that, he would have to get in touch with me. I just wanted John to relax and leave the business to us. For the next three days, John had been trying to get in touch with me but I was in Tarsus, the city of my birth. I was there seeing my family. John didn't see Kaya and after three days left with Debbie for a holiday resort called Marmaris. I was so happy that nothing had gone ahead. It soon dawned on Kaya as well that too much was happening too soon. He was happy, as was The Vulcan, that we'd slowed things down a bit. I was the most trusted man and I wasn't about to let John and Ben know or see too much. I was meant to be doing my job properly or not at all.

After seeing my family, I flew back to Istanbul, stayed the night then flew back to London on my own. I remember when I got back, we had meetings with Haase to finalise transport. We had been Haase's single supplier for ages by then. There'd been a good relationship for 18 months. But I began not to trust Haase around then. It was just a feeling that came over me at Watford Gap, summer of 1993. It was six months after I started working with them and we had a meet at a Watford Gap service station to discuss transport. I just didn't like the look of him. I told Yilmaz, but I was a kid to him and I didn't have the clout to take it further; I forgot about it.

One afternoon, I got home and my girl, who incidentally was Kaya's sister, said Kaya had phoned from Turkey and left a message. I looked at the piece of paper. It had a French address on it. It was a hotel in Paris and I was to be there the next morning. So I got on the phone and booked a seat on the Seacat, the hovercraft over the Channel. I intended to drive there. I arrived in Calais around two o'clock in the early hours and drove straight to Paris. I remember the dustbin lorries picking up the rubbish off the streets and it was starting to get light. I didn't know my way around Paris so I asked the bin men if they could direct me to the hotel Kaya was staying in. This was a stroke of luck because I was about four or five streets away. I found it with no problems. Kaya was staying at the hotel under a moody name. When I got there, he was already in the lobby waiting for me. We shook hands, walked a short distance to the car and drove out of Paris. En route, he told me what was going on. There was 111 kilos on its way from Turkey. It was in a coach with a troupe of Turkish folk-singers travelling on holiday in the south of France. On the way, we were phoning Turkey to ask for progress reports as to the whereabouts of the coach, its number plate, colour, make and model. We were to make contact with the coach when it reached the Eiffel Tower.

We got to the tower early, had something to eat and walked about a bit. We phoned Turkey and got a time to meet: three o'clock. We walked around the shops to buy some extra-strong bags for the gear. We found a luggage shop and bought four strong sports bags. We put them in the car and went to meet the coach. The driver was drinking tea. We asked him if he had the gear ready because me and Kaya were ready to take it then. The driver thought we were mad, but sometimes it's better to do things in the open, unexpected, as though we were not doing anything wrong. We had a talk and decided to compromise and follow the driver to the south of France. So we set off in the BMW, following the coach but always staying three or four cars behind. It was hard because of the amount of people on it. Not all, but a few people had seen us when we pulled into a petrol station. I informed Kaya that I thought a few of them were on to us and that we'd have to pull back a bit more. We drove on. It was getting dark. It seemed like the coach had taken a few wrong turns. We were driving through a lot of small towns and villages.

The coach eventually stopped in a narrow road. Trees lined both sides. I pulled the car into a little lane. Me and Kaya took it in turns taking a piss and keeping an eye on the coach. Suddenly the coach started moving and we jumped into the car and slowly followed. It was mad because there was no other cars on the road except the coach and us. When we came to a roundabout, we came to a sudden stop. I thought, 'Fuck!' And put my foot down and shot past the coach. We got a few stares. Then I stopped the car and watched the coach for a few minutes. A few fellas had got out and were looking at a map. They were obviously lost and looking to find the way to go. We waited for a while then started to drive towards the coach. Some of the guys put their hands out to stop us but we shot past them. It was funny because they were swearing at me and Kaya in Turkish. We had English number plates and they didn't know we were Turkish.

After a few hours, the coach found its destination, which was San Sebastian in the deep south near the border with Spain. We met the driver and had a chat. He said he wouldn't be able to get the gear ready until the next day. For fuck's sake, it was four in the morning and we'd had no kip for two days and now we were being told to pick up the gear the next day at four in the morning! We didn't have anywhere to sleep so we made off to Paris again because all our stuff was in the hotel, which was the Holiday Inn. We made our way back from San Sebastian to Paris.

When we got to the hotel, we had a munch and got a few hours' kip. We got up, showered, dressed and set off again for San Sebastian. The journey back was about 500 km. We got there around two in the morning. We spoke to the driver and he said pull the car up to the coach at three in the morning. So we went down to the seafront and parked the car and waited till three in the morning. Then we made our way back towards the coach. We pulled up right next to it, opened the boot. The driver and two men had two massive sacks full of gear. We put them both in the boot of our car. Then the boot wouldn't stick. There was so much gear in there we couldn't shut it. Then we had to force it and slam it very hard.

We did it in the end. We gave the driver an extra drink of £1,500. He was getting paid in Turkey but as it had gone well he deserved it. We had 111 kilos of pure heroin in the boot. We drove down country lanes. As we were driving, I could hear and feel the wheels hitting and going over things. It felt like little stones so I put the full lights on. Fuck me! The road was covered in rabbits and hares. I pulled the car over and got a torch out to look over the car. The wheels were covered in rabbit skin and blood. We carried on driving. It was pitch black. No lights on the road and no chance of dodging these rabbits.

There was so much gear in the boot that the car began to smell of heroin. It stank but there was nothing we could do. If we got a pull, we would be fucked. At one point, we decided to test the quality of the gear. As we were driving along, Kaya took a small sample from one of the bags and we got a bit of foil and chased it. It was beautiful, pure high-quality 100 per cent heroin. The car was full of fumes; it was the middle of the night but we didn't give a fuck.

The job now was to get the gear back to England. We got back to Paris, got our stuff from the hotel and headed for the Channel coast. On the way, a few strange incidents happened. We were getting followed. I don't know how but the French had got on to us. Maybe it was a routine pull or a traffic offence or whatever, but someone was on to us. We didn't care – we just wanted to get away. I thought we were going to get nicked so we had to make a split-second decision. Do we give ourselves up or make a run for it? I put my foot down and got up to about 120 mph. I couldn't believe it. I was going into a high-speed car chase with 111 kilos of gear in the back. Whoever was following us mustn't have expected it because we gave them the slip and after a while no one seemed to be on us. I pulled over at the side of the road just in case. I had a gun on me so I got it to hand and made sure it was ready. The plan was simple – if the police pulled over and approached the car, I was going to open fire, kill as many as I could and make a run for it with Kaya and keep on firing at whoever was stupid enough to come after us. We had 111 kilos in the boot and no one was going to get their hands on it. That was going back to England no matter what, and anyone who stood in the way was getting it. I was mentally preparing myself for a shoot-out. I knew the French police carried guns, but if it came to it I'd have shot 20 to get away. What did it matter? I had 111 kilos in the back. If I got caught, I was going to jail for a long time anyway. The wait was only a couple of minutes but it seemed like ages. Nothing happened. I'd lost them. So I pulled out, made a few moody turn-offs and that, and everything calmed down. That's how determined we were to make sure nothing interfered with the runs. Needless to say, we got the gear safely back to England.

Kaya had made plans to switch the gear to Haase's transport in France before the coast. That all went smoothly and we transferred the heroin to them in Paris. Ten kilos were taken out along the way as payment to the various people who'd been involved. One kilo was stolen by a contact of ours in Paris. Haase's transport collected the remaining 100 kilos in France and both Kaya and me went our separate ways. He flew back from Paris. I drove back. Job done.

9

BANG ONTOP –
CUSTOMS CLOSE IN

The 100-kilo load was successfully smuggled into the UK, but unfortunately for the Turkish Connection and John Haase there was a problem. The parcel had been under constant surveillance by Her Majesty's Customs and Excise. Oh, dear! Every movement the gang had made had been tracked by the service's crack Lima 3 undercover anti-drug squad. Even worse for The Vulcan, Ergun, Kaya, Haase and Co., this was not the only occasion the gang had been watched – they had been under close-quarter surveillance for over a year as part of a wide-ranging investigation called Operation Floor. According to Customs documents, the observations had started in June 1992 and finished 13 months later in July 1993 – shortly after the 100-kilo load arrived in the UK. During this period, almost every significant event had been monitored. Flights to Turkey, trips to Liverpool, bin-bag cash handovers at the Black Horse pub, heroin deliveries, meetings, phone conversations, pager messages – the lot had been observed, taped and, what's worse, photographed. Perfectly framed, full-colour photographs of The Vulcan walking along the street in Liverpool without a care in the world alongside some of the most hardened criminals in the UK were amongst the images available in the booklets of surveillance shots. It looked like a drug dealers' convention – which actually it was – complete with happy snaps for the folks back home. Customs and Excise had a ring-side seat on the greatest criminal show ever to roll up into town – better than the Feds at Appalachian, better than the Sweeney at the Great Train Robbers' farm, because this crime was happening real-time in front of their very eyes. John Haase and the Turkish Connection may have been amongst the most prolific drug dealers in the world at that point, but they weren't good enough to beat the law.

Ergun would later kick himself. He should have trusted his *Star Wars*-style instinct and his eyes and ears on the three occasions his surveillance team had, in the parlance, 'showed out' – the times when he had spotted or 'got on to' the fact that he was being tracked and watched. Remember the occasion during an early visit to Liverpool when he had spotted a man in a blue Ford Sierra observing him? Remember when he had become suspicious of a couple drinking at the Black Horse pub, to the degree of feeling specifically uncomfortable about her handbag? Remember more recently the shadowy pursuers whom he had outrun in France? Ergun should have forgone his almost godlike reverence for his seniors and fought harder with Kaya and The Vulcan to go along with his instincts – to close down the operation for a bit.

Though the exact chronology is difficult to piece together because of the secrecy surrounding the operation, the following timetable is as accurate as can be. Haase got out of prison in early '92. Kaya and Haase started to trade heroin one or two months later. According to Suleyman Ergun, they started dealing together between February and April 1992. Customs began their operation some time after, scoring their first success at the end of the year with the arrest of Bulent Onay. (He was immediately replaced by Ergun.) Ergun believes, though, that by the time Customs got a grip on the gang they had probably missed several months' worth of traffic, which could have amounted to a lot of heroin. But they were on to them early enough to catch them red-handed at the height of their power over the 13 months between June 1992 and July 1993.

The tip-off which led police and Customs and Excise to launch an investigation into Haase and the Turkish Connection is still a mystery, over which there is some dispute. Sources in the Merseyside Police claim that their officers were the first to identify Haase as a drug dealer, which led to surveillance on him. The tip-off allegedly came from a woman spurned, one of Bennett's ex-girlfriends, who took revenge after being dumped. Ironically, she claimed Bennett had got rid of her after discovering that she was using heroin. Customs and Excise were then able to work back and pick up the Turks and begin to widen the probe to include The Vulcan. This version is backed up by a newspaper article from *The Independent* on Tuesday, 3 September 1996. Based on sources in the police and security services, the story reveals that 'Haase and Bennett were arrested in 1993 after [a female friend of Bennett's] began using heroin. The woman informed on him to a Merseyside Police detective-constable.'

The head of the 100-man heroin-investigation team at Customs and Excise who was in charge of the case has two different versions. At first, Assistant Chief Investigator Phil Connelly claimed that Customs and Excise teams had got a lead into Haase after picking up wire taps from the Turks in London. Then he claimed that the tip-off might have come from a female source in Liverpool. As with many of these complex operations, there were probably several sources of intelligence and possibly more than one mole within the Turks–Haase gang reporting back to Customs. One of the prime movers in the case was Customs Officer Paul Cook, who moved from London to Manchester, helping Connelly track Haase and Bennett. In total, two squads of Customs officers were assigned to the operation.

PHIL CONNELLY: To the best of my knowledge, we came across them [Haase and Bennett] in the operation. We were working with the Regional Crime Squad, who obviously did know. They were based in Birkenhead.

I was an assistant chief investigation officer between 1990 and 1997. I ran the heroin branch primarily based in Customs House in London. This involved the management of approximately seven teams incorporating in excess of 100 people. During this time, one of the people who worked for me was Paul Cook. He was initially based in London, where the Haase and Bennett investigation began. Cook then moved to Manchester and a decision was taken that, as case officer, he would retain the case there. Cook would coordinate a team of approximately five people and he would probably report to John Furnell.

I myself would have had a working knowledge of the case in general terms, as opposed to each and every nuance of the case.

During an investigation, if Customs and Excise know that the targets are in possession of a large amount of heroin, they are duty bound to swoop and take it off the streets. Obviously, there is a risk that other parts of the operation, particularly undercover surveillance, may be compromised, but it is more or less policy to stop gear reaching the marketplace if they can. And that is exactly the call they had to make in December 1992 when, six months into the investigation, officers discovered that a large importation had just gone off and Bulent Onay was sitting on top of nearly 40 kilos of gear. The investigation against Onay was called Operation Salina.

The wider probe into the Turks and Haase was officially a joint one between Customs and Excise and police officers of the regional crime squads. These newly formed syndicates had been set up by Home Secretary Michael Howard to specifically target big drug dealers, bringing together resources from different agencies. When he established the five syndicate groups attached to various regional crime squads in the autumn of 1992, the directives for their operations were directly in line with the government's tough war-on-drugs approach. Howard said, 'These syndicates would develop operations against persons suspected of being involved in criminal activities with an objective of securing evidence to effecting their arrests.' Howard wanted to see a robust, proactive law-enforcement body, with better collaboration with Customs and Excise. The investigators looking at Haase and the Turks' heroin gang consisted of officers from syndicate no. 3 and Customs and Excise. Syndicate no. 3 was attached to the South East Regional Crime Squad (SERCS), its headquarters based at Dulwich in south London. Customs and Excise offered up officers from its Lima 3 team at Customs House near Tower Bridge in London and from the National Investigation Service at a northern base at Aldyne House in Manchester.

Phil Connelly said, 'I think somebody at some stage decided that it was better to run it as a joint operation because at the beginning it was being done from London. We had a national responsibility.'

Five years later, more than 40 detectives from the SERCS team were investigated following allegations of criminal offences and serious breaches of police regulations. The officers are alleged to have stolen heroin, cannabis and money during raids, lost evidence causing the collapse of a big drugs trial, unlawfully used confidential police information, threatened witnesses and planted and falsified evidence. One of the allegations was related to Bulent Onay's case. A detective-sergeant was accused of stealing between 3.5 and 4 kilos of heroin from the 40-kilo parcel during Onay's arrest. This officer was later dismissed from the force on a number of disciplinary offences, though records do not show whether he was found guilty of this offence. Several SERCS officers were convicted and jailed for corruption, while the rest were cleared.

But in 1992 the operation was still running smoothly. At first, officers found it technically 'very difficult' to tap into the gang's analogue mobile phones. Phil Connelly said, 'There was phone surveillance. It cost a fortune to get it up and running.' Officers were initially using a scanner but they asked government scientists at a research facility at Sandwich in Hertfordshire to develop a system. They came up with the answer quickly. Officers were also specially trained to speak Turkish so the most could be made of the new gadgetry.

PHIL CONNELLY: If it was in Turkish, you used an interpreter. But we actually sent officers to Turkey to learn Turkish, where they went for months living with a Turkish family. They call it immersion. So they live with a Turkish family where they don't speak English all the time. The Haase case was a big case. I can't think of one like it before it. Before, it had been Turks working with Turks because Turks don't like working with Brits usually. Turks like keeping with their own. They're a nightmare to get into because they are close-knit. The ones involved in organised crime tend to stay at home all day sleeping and about midnight they'll go out and go to a gambling club till about four in the morning. You can imagine what that's like. First of all, the hours you've got to work. Secondly, the fact that you can't get anybody inside; you can't get an undercover officer in because the Turks will know if there's a strange fella around.

We got around that by being on the outside of it and looking at where they're going in the meantime. I think it was one of the best jobs we ever did because it was difficult; it was a very big operation. There were people moving an enormous amount of heroin. Ergun and Kaya were bringing in hundreds of kilos when everybody else was bringing in twos or tens.

Haase and Bennett seemed to be fairly uninfluential people. Bennett was no Al Capone or anything like that. But they were very bright. I met Bennett and you know when you're talking to somebody [bright]; you know when you're talking to an idiot or when you're talking to somebody who's sharp. You don't just have to speak with an Oxford accent to be very sharp. They were good. They were very surveillance conscious. They've got a picture. Really it was just the size of the operation that made them stand out.

I don't think that it came to mind that we were never going to nail them. It's just that you're never sure. Even when you do the job, you're usually not 100 per cent sure the heroin's there. On jobs before that, we've stopped Turks at Euston station and thought they were carrying heroin down from Liverpool to London, but it wasn't heroin at all, it was money.

Official documents give an insight into just how detailed the surveillance was on the gang and just how much Customs and Excise knew. Customs had learned a staggering amount about them. It was as though every member of the gang were keeping a diary of their day-to-day lives – or at least Customs were. The dates and times on the surveillance logs are mind-boggling. A few months after Haase and Kaya hooked up, Customs and Excise were on to them.

CHRONOLOGY

26/06/92: 1st meeting observed by Customs. The gang were talking about a load of heroin that had just come in. Manuk Ocecki was observed at his house with Kaya and Onay.

04/07/92: Onay starts to take the profits from this importation back to Turkey.

At 1243 Onay was seen taking a lightweight suitcase into [an address in north London]. Joey the Turk and Manuk Ocecki made various movements in and around [the house] and at 1608 Onay, carrying a heavy suitcase, and Joey and Manuk left the house.

At 1723 Onay was observed at Heathrow airport talking to an unidentified male of Mediterranean appearance. This man showed Onay a white carrier bag. Both men board a Turkish Airlines flight at departure gate no. 11. Onay's suitcase was examined and amongst the items of clothing were two large packages. Both packages were examined and found to contain sterling but the amount could not be confirmed.

06/07/92: 1146 Onay left flight no. TK979 and carrying a white plastic bag went through immigration, where he talked to the immigration officer briefly. He went to the baggage carousel and spoke to a Middle Eastern male. Both men walked over to the carousel. Onay used a payphone within the baggage arrivals area. When Onay emerged from the channels, he was pushing a trolley with a rigid brown suitcase on it. At one point, he stopped and rummaged around inside the case. Onay left on the underground with the suitcase.

08/07/92: Manuk Ocecki also takes money to Turkey – was also observed carrying approximately £100,000 to Istanbul on another trip.

20/07/92: Kaya flew to Milan from Heathrow (possibly to arrange a drug deal with the Italian Mafia).

14/08/92: The money keeps on flowing back to east – Onay checked in for a flight to Istanbul with one piece of luggage, a dark soft-sided suitcase. The suitcase was examined and found to contain two tape-wrapped packages amongst items of personal clothing. One of the packages was examined and found to contain bundles of used sterling notes.

08/09/92: Onay was picked up at Heathrow airport by an unidentified female and they left in a [Vauxhall] car.

15/10/92: Kaya travelled under the name of Sarkizian on Alitalia. His case contained bundles of used sterling notes.

04/11/92: Kaya flew Heathrow to Madrid with case containing £2,000 in ten-pound notes.

08/11/92: Onay was again met at Heathrow airport by the same female as 08/09/92 and they drove away in [the Vauxhall].

In mid-November, the gang were busy arranging another 90–100-kilo load – the run-up to Bulent Onay's arrest.

11/12/92: Onay returns from Turkey after taking money out and also finalising heroin to leave Turkey. Seen leaving Heathrow airport after returning to UK. He took a bus onto the Eastern Perimeter Road and then drove [the Vauxhall] east on the A4.

18/12/92: Haase and Bennett seen with Jim Thomas [Haase's childhood friend from Toxteth/Dingle] at immigration controls for inward coming vehicles at Dover. Haase and Bennett had been overseeing heroin coming across Channel from France.

Later, they met with Kaya and Joey the Turk in a Kentucky Fried Chicken shop in Islington for a post-importation meeting. Over the next three days, the bulk of the heroin goes to Liverpool.

21/12/92: The Turks go to Liverpool to pick up 40 kilos from Haase's people over the next few days.

1220 The day begins shortly after midday in London when the Turks meet before heading north on the motorway. Kaya, Joey the Turk and Manuk Ocecki were seen outside [the address in north London] and Onay drove up in [the Vauxhall]. Onay and Joey had an argument in the street and then Kaya and Joey drove off in a blue Rover and Onay and Manuk Ocecki got into the Vauxhall. The Vauxhall was seen at 1550 on the M62 headed west towards Liverpool. The Rover was seen in Liverpool at 1600 with three people inside. Joey the Turk was in the rear.

24/12/92: Onay was stopped and given a speeding ticket on the M6 travelling south at 0035 and gave his name as Erdal Devrenk of [address]. Later that day, Onay was arrested at [that address] and 36 kilos of heroin were found on the premises.

But after Onay was taken out and Ergun joined up, the heroin dealing and money-washing continued.

01/02/93: Kaya checked in for Alitalia flight and his case found to contain £6,000 in twenty-pound notes.

14/02/93: Kaya detained coming into Heathrow with a false passport in the name of Simon Cohen.

28/02/93: Haase and Bennett were at the meeting at Watford Gap service station with Ergun, Kaya and an unidentified male.

12/03/93: Kaya flew to Amsterdam from Heathrow.

18/03/93: Bennett carrying a large sports bag and Ergun were seen in Black Horse Lane. They were later seen at the Boomerang Club.

19/03/93: Haase and Bennett were observed with Kaya, Ergun and Topaz in Granada outside Sunlight Street.

23/03/93: Kaya was also observed with Topaz. Haase met with Kaya, Ergun and Topaz in Black Horse Lane. Photographs were taken by Customs Officer Brown.

24/03/93: Kaya goes back to Turkey. Observed by Customs and Excise officers boarding a flight to Istanbul from Heathrow. His luggage was covertly searched and found to contain several assorted boxes which were sealed with Sellotape. From touch, Customs officers believed that the boxes contained money.

25/03/93: Croker was observed in Black Horse Lane handing over a dark green plastic carrier bag which appeared to be full to Ergun.

27/03/93: The vehicles of Haase, Croker and Ergun were all seen in Queens Drive at the same time.

29/03/93: Croker was seen in his car parked [on] Tilston Road.

30/03/93: Croker was observed with Haase and Bennett [on] Hazelhurst Avenue.

20/04/93: Croker was observed entering the Black Horse pub with a carrier bag concealed in his coat but left five minutes later without it. Ergun left the pub shortly afterwards covering something with his jacket.

23/04/93: Croker met Neil Garrett in a cemetery on Lower Lane. A few hours later, Croker was seen going into his parents' house.

26/04/93: Croker met Kaya and Ergun in the Black Horse pub and a green bag was exchanged.

30/04/93: Croker met Ergun in the Mason's Arms on Sunbeam Road and was observed handing over a green holdall.

12/05/93: Haase and Roy Lewis were seen in the Chelsea Hotel, London. Later, Haase met Kaya and Ergun at Euston station and gave them a blue holdall and a plastic shopping bag before boarding a train.

14/05/93: Croker observed on Black Horse Lane handing over a dark plastic bag.

The next significant event tracked by Customs was the 111 kilos brought to France on the coach and then driven by Kaya and Ergun.

15/05/93: Kaya and Ergun travelled to Turkey to plan importation. His case in name of S. Cohen on flight to Istanbul examined. Found to contain currency notes, false passports and driver's licences. Kaya's photo in passport with the name Tecimener.

13/07/93: After the 100-kilo load is brought over the Channel safely, Kaya and Vulcan arrived together on flight from Paris.

14/07/93: Vulcan and Kaya observed when they left address in London at Windmill Gardens [again with Ergun].

16/07/93: They all travelled to Liverpool: Kaya, Vulcan [Ergun is also present]. Haase and Bennett met Kaya, Ergun and Topaz in Liverpool and they were seen entering the Boomerang Club.

If that wasn't enough, intelligence officers were gleaning massive amounts of info from wire taps – especially on Ergun's mobile – and were able to pinpoint each member's whereabouts at any particular point by triangulation of cell-phone masts and radio waves. One report stated:

> He [Ergun] owned a Vodaphone which had the number 0836730636. The printout for that Vodaphone has been obtained, which is highly revealing in the context of this case. Analysis shows that the user of the phone made extensive use of certain telephone facilities which help preserve the anonymity of the callers, such as pager and message-deposit facilities. The latter enables the caller to ring and receive a message that has been left rather like an answer phone. That is how Ergun got in touch with the Liverpool connection. He also used the paging system. This enabled him to call a pager, which would then get in touch with another phone. Ergun had the sophistication to use these devices and was the vital link-man between the Turkish and Liverpool connections. He was a Turk who, by reason of his upbringing in the UK, was a fluent English speaker able to act as an interpreter or translator.

10

BUSTED – HAASE AND THE TURKS ARE ARRESTED

In mid-July 1993, with the 100-kilo load fresh from France in their sights, Customs and Excise prepared to bust the ring. But there was a bonus win as well – their number-one target, The Vulcan, had flown into the UK. Unusually, The Vulcan had flown in at the same time as one of his importations was being smuggled in. Astonishingly, he even went to Liverpool to oversee the handover to Haase.

Surveillance logs tracked his movements (the first few entries of which we have already seen), as well as every move the gang made in the run-up to the 'knock'.

13/07/93: After the 100-kilo load is brought over the Channel by sea safely, Kaya and Vulcan arrived in UK together on flight from Paris.

14/07/93: Vulcan and Kaya observed at Windmill Gardens [again with Ergun]. At the time, the 100-kilo load was in transit to Liverpool.

16/07/93: Travelled to Liverpool – Kaya, Vulcan [Ergun is also present].

16/07/93: Haase and Bennett met Kaya, Ergun and Topaz [Vulcan] in Liverpool and they were seen entering the Boomerang Club to discuss the 100-kilo load. Kaya then made a quick shuttle trip back to Paris to make sure everything was OK over there.

19/07/93: When Kaya returned from Paris, shock development – arrived on flight from Paris with passport in the name of Dusanian and is deported to Istanbul.

21/07/93: A portion of the 100-kilo load is being cut up by Croker and Neil Garrett at Dane Street. Haase and Bennett were observed accepting a heavy plastic bag outside the Manor House pub from another man. Croker and Garrett were observed driving to various places in Liverpool. They were both seen outside Dane Street wearing surgical gloves.

26/07/93: Croker arrested in possession of uncut 50 kilos of heroin. Added together, the two quantities so far seized from the gang – Onay's in December and Croker's now – amounts to 85.7 kilos, with an estimated street-level value of £13,234,229. £27,980 in cash was recovered.

28/07/93: Haase and Bennett were arrested in Croydon. Kaya sneaks back into UK after deportation and is arrested at King's Cross station with false passport in the name of Garo Sarkizian.

Behind the perfunctory detail of the official documents, real-life criminals such as bagman Eddie Croker, underboss Suleyman Ergun and crazed megalomaniac John Haase had been living out extraordinary existences in a world which seemed ordinary to them.

———————

EDDIE CROKER: In July 1993, I was told by Paul Bennett and John Haase to expect to receive a large amount of heroin within a few days and that I should get somewhere safe to stash it. I would be told when and where to collect it. By this time, Paul Bennett and John Haase knew where I had been stashing the drugs – and they were not happy. They told me to speak to

Neil Garrett about finding a better place to store it. Neil had been with me to the Black Horse when I was delivering the money to the Turks or stashing drugs.

I spoke to Neil about finding a new place to stash the heroin. He told me he could get a place where we could go to separate the heroin into smaller amounts and a second place where it could be stored. On 21 July, he picked me up at my house in his car, which was a blue Previa, and went to an address near the Everton football ground in the backstreets.

We were met by Mark Drew. He said that we could use his house to take the drugs once we had them. We would pay him £400. After this, me and Neil went to an address in the Gilmoss estate in Liverpool, where we picked up a friend of Neil's called Dave.

We then drove to Cherry Lane, Liverpool, where I used to stash gloves and plastic bags. Then to the Chaser pub on Long Lane, where we met a man who passed the bags of heroin from his car to ours. I don't know the exact amount of heroin; it would be between 25 and 30 kilos. Then we drove back to Mark Drew's house. Then Mark told us we could not use his house as his wife was at home but that he'd got a friend's house a few streets away. He took us to the house and all four of us went inside with the bag of heroin. Myself, Neil and Dave took heroin into the kitchen and Mark stayed in the living room. Part of Mark's job was to answer the door if anyone called. Then I went out to meet John Haase and Paul Bennett in a street nearby to let them know everything was OK. I told them that Neil had organised a safehouse for the heroin.

Back in the house, we were splitting the heroin into smaller quantities. This took quite a long time. Then we moved the heroin into the Previa. Me, Neil and Dave then drove to my parents' house, where we left the bag of heroin in the car. Neil and Dave got a taxi to make sure everything was OK at the place where we were going to stash the heroin later.

A few days later, Paul Bennett told me that a second load of heroin was expected, which I would be told when and where to collect. The day before I was arrested, he told me to go to the same place as before at lunchtime and take delivery of the heroin. I was to go the next day. I tried to contact Neil so that we could do the same as previously but I could not get in touch with him. On the day I was arrested, I bought a cheap Toyota Carina and went to the same pub as before. I was again met by a man [Suleyman Ergun or one of his runners] who transferred the bags of heroin from his car to mine. From there, I went to my parents' home, into which I took the heroin. I was going to separate the heroin but before I could do this the house was raided by the police.

The final leg of Croker's journey in the car full of heroin had been tracked by a Customs plane.

PHIL CONNELLY: We were looking for a car. We actually got an aircraft to overfly the address to whom the car was named. That was in Liverpool. We got the aircraft to have a look. That's when the police did the bust. It was 99 per cent perspiration and 1 per cent inspiration. It was just a lot of hard work.

Croker was the first to get nicked, at his mum's house. The panic-stricken carpet cleaner immediately got on his toes. The front door was booted in and Detective-Sergeant Taylor of Merseyside Police rushed inside the Coronation Street-style terrace. He saw Croker was at the top of the stairs holding a large green bag. 'Stop, police!' he shouted. Croker hurled the large green bag at him and bolted off. He ran into the back bedroom and kicked in a window, crouched down and jumped out. But there was a copper waiting for him. So he pulled himself up to the ledge and jumped onto a shed. He was collared in the garden. The second load of heroin which he had stashed at his mum's house weighed approximately 50 kilos.

In a blue nylon holdall there were 26 plastic bags, 25 of which were full kilo bags. The remaining bag had a quarter-kilo of heroin inside. A green canvas holdall contained eight polythene bags in a torn green plastic bag. Each had a kilo inside. Another green canvas holdall contained 14 kilos. Another contained two kilos of heroin. It was all 50 to 60 per cent pure. Four kilos of 'bash' paracetamol was also found. Realising the game was up, Haase and Bennett went on the run.

PHIL CONNELLY: We, the Customs, didn't even bother going in on the knock [at Croker's house]. Haase and Bennett were just sensible enough to not be around when it went down. Of course, they didn't know it was going to happen. It's just general practice that a major drugs trafficker will have people working for him. Not only will he not be there, he probably won't even be in the country and won't come back until he knows that it's all OK. Hence, Haase and Bennett were not at the house.

For a few days, Haase and Bennett 'sat off' in a caravan in Wales to evade capture. They tipped off Ergun to stay away from Liverpool.

SULEYMAN ERGUN: In July, we were busy. What happened was that we had just delivered Haase 100 kilos of heroin. That was the gear Kaya and I had drove through France to Paris, where it was given to Haase's people. They had got it to England and then taken it to Liverpool, where it ended up. I went to Liverpool to make sure everything was OK. I met Eddie Croker. That was me at the handover.

This 100 kilos had been split into two or three loads. At least two were given to Eddie. The first one was the 25–30 kilos he mentioned. A few days later, I'd collected money off him for that and then he was given more heroin as well. That was about

50 kilos. He was a mule.

In all, this load of 100 kilos in total was the last one we ever gave to Haase before we all got nicked – 100 kilos on credit at £20,000 a kilo. So they owed us £2 million. The arrangement was that I was to collect a million pounds from them in the first one or two weeks.

I was on the way to collect the million in cash. Just before I got to Liverpool, I phoned them. Bennett came on the phone. Suddenly, he said to me, 'It's ontop. We're going to London.' So I turned back round and went to London. I didn't know what was going on but the prop-shaft on my car had gone. I got to London but I didn't know where Haase and Bennett were going or nothing.

I then finds out that Eddie Croker had just been nicked for the 50 kilos I had seen him with a few days earlier. I felt sorry for Eddie. He was a quiet fella. He wasn't streetwise. But there was no time to think about that – I had to think about me, the pressure was on. I gave the car to a friend of mine who works at BMW to get the prop-shaft fixed. I go home, get changed and all that. That night, I went out for a meal with a couple of mates, but obviously a bit para' [paranoid], a bit panicky and that. I get dropped off at home. There's a helicopter over my house. I hid in the bushes. It was right over my mum and dad's house in Somerstown in Camden. I hid in the bushes for 45 minutes, covered in mud. Got home. Changed. Get some money and get back out on the street.

I then met up with John Haase and his mate, this black fella called Roy who John had given us £5,000 off once. We went on a drive through Swiss Cottage. But I was getting a bad feeling, so I said, 'Listen, I'm getting out here.' I got out of the car and said, 'I'll phone you.'

The next day, I met them again and Roy took me to a safehouse in Crystal Palace where he was holding Haase and Bennett. They asked me for money. A bit of a liberty, wasn't it, since they owed us a million fucking quid or more? But I kind of understood, that for the moment all bets were off. Then I said, 'I'm going.' I got back down to Enfield. I lived there with my girl at the time. I'd left the keys on me key-ring, which I'd given to my mate at BMW with the car keys, so I couldn't get in the house. I went into a Bretons café on Windmill Hill. Had some sandwiches and that. I come out the sandwich shop and made a few phone calls to Turkey from a phone box near Enfield Chase railway station and another by a parade of shops on Link Side. I phoned Kaya and left a message for him not to come to England because it's ontop. I couldn't get through to him but I left a few messages with his brother and his wife.

As I'm walking through Enfield town, suddenly I hear a beep-beep sound. I looked round and it was a post-office van. A young fella who was walking behind me said, 'Fucking hell! He nearly killed me!' He was talking about nearly being run over by this post-office van which had gone beep beep. I just smiled at him and kept on walking. The next minute, he slammed the cuffs on me, spun me around and searched me for a gun. The cheeky fella who had said he'd nearly been run over was undercover Customs officer Mark Sprawson. The next second, I was lying on the floor with red dots all over me – from police guns.

That was it. I was nicked. All over in a few seconds. End of story. The beep beep was the signal to take me down. The whole place, including my flat, had been surrounded. And I hadn't known.

First they took me to Enfield town police station but then the police said the station wasn't secure enough to hold me. Because of Mr V and all that, they were scared in case a team was sent in to get me out. Then they took me to Edmonton police station. At about twelve or one o'clock in the morning, they put me in an Audi, Customs and Excise, and took me to Bromborough police station in Birkenhead on the Wirral. That was me getting nicked. What a fucking day!

I wasn't the only one. Haase and Bennett had been tracked from the Norfolk House Hotel, then Haase was nicked in a car with Bennett somewhere in Croydon, south London. They rammed him from behind and boxed him off with vans. When I got to Birkenhead, Bennett was in one of the cells, but on the board by the desk it said: 'Ergun. Bennett. Keep them apart.' That was so we didn't communicate. He was there. I heard him.

There was more bad news to come. Kaya was nicked in King's Cross station with a false passport in the name of Garo Sarkizian. He came to England a couple of days after I was nicked. He was in Italy. I couldn't tell you why he came here. I don't know if he got the messages but he come over here. I'm with his sister, aren't I? He probably wanted to get money – see how the thing's going. He's phoning my mobile.

Luckily, the Customs didn't find any evidence in the house. When my old man saw the Customs in my house, they asked him, 'Where does your son keep the money?' They think there is millions in the house.

My old man grabs him by the collar and throws him out and says, 'Do you think I'm going to grass on my son, you dirty bastard!'

Some of the others got nicked at different locations with a matter of minutes between us. The Colonel, Ansen, got nicked at the Ebury Court Hotel. He was a retired colonel. He was the one who was taking cash over to Turkey for us. I was charged straight away after the arrest.

Manuk Ocecki got away at first. But a few months later, on 2 September '93, he was arrested at Felixstowe coming off a P&O ferry by Customs Officer Shaun Edwards. He was strip-searched and his Fiat was searched. All they found was a black briefcase, in which were two passports, both in the name of Manuk Ocecki.

Then I was on remand for twenty-four months, just gone two years. Three months of it was JR'd [judge's remand] and then we got sentenced. There was still one outstanding matter: we had given Haase a hundred kilos. Fifty kilos had been seized. We wrote that off and didn't ask Haase for the money. That's the unwritten code in drug dealing. But there was another 50 kis still outstanding. Part of that was the 25 or 30 kilos Eddie Croker had put in the blue Previa which Neil Garrett and another kid called Dave were last seen with outside Eddie's mum's house. We assumed that Haase had sold the 50 kilos either before he got nicked or while he was on remand with us, with someone on the outside doing it for him. That meant there was another million pound outstanding – owed to us. We needed that money now. When you get nicked, you can't do anything out on the street, so wages stop coming in.

JOHN HAASE: In July 1993, I was arrested in London. I had fled there from Liverpool because I knew the police were after me. When we were arrested in London, the first man who was arrested was Eddie Croker. There was one big parcel of 100 kilos. Eddie Croker had picked up 50 kilos from this parcel. That was how it started. He'd gone to pick up our parcel just in from Turkey. He was the first man.

Croker should have phoned Bennett on that morning but never did. So we went to the street where Croker lived. It was blocked off by police cars and everything. He lived by the Crown pub. Bennett and me knew the shit had hit the fan, sort of thing, and two hours later Bennett and me were in Wales, where Bennett had a caravan on a site.

We made a lot of phone calls telling everyone we were in Wales and then left Wales and headed to London to meet the Turks to let them know it was ontop for everyone. The main deal was to meet the Turk and warn him. He didn't know it was ontop and that [the police] had everyone's cards marked. That was the worst thing . . . the police were all over them as well.

That night, Bennett and me stayed in a hotel in London. The next morning, we left the hotel about eleven o'clock and on the high street two white vans rammed us. A gang of armed police swamped us. They bashed in the windows and suddenly in a London street I was sat there with my arms held high and a load of machine guns at my head. There were machine guns smashed through the side windows of the car and we were arrested. It was the most frightening moment of my life and I thought, 'This is it, I'm dead.'

Eight of us were arrested in London and Liverpool. After we were arrested, we were taken to Liverpool and charged and put in Walton.

The Liverpool mob had been caught red-handed, with damning evidence including 50 kilos of heroin in the range of 51.5 per cent and 59.4 per cent purity and loads of cash. Though not an offence, when Croker was nicked he also had on him 2 kilos of paracetamol dilutant – known in the trade as 'bash'. At one of the gang's HQs in Rocky Lane, Liverpool, £164,715 in cash was found concealed under the bath surround, along with a diamond-studded necklace worth approximately £46,700. On their arrest, Haase had £2,208 and Bennett had £2,465.

All in all, Operation Floor had been a massive success – with just one reservation. All the major players had been caught, except for the biggest man of all: The Vulcan. Before the July importation, The Vulcan had slipped into the UK to make sure that everything was running smoothly and to give the go-ahead for more heroin to be smuggled in. However, he left the country before the shipment arrived, preventing Customs from picking him up during the coordinated raids. But, as experienced officers knew, the game wasn't over until it was over. More surprises were in store.

PART TWO

THE GUN/POWDER PLOT

11

THE CON

Haase, Bennett, the Turks and the rest of the gang were facing massive sentences. They had been caught bang at it, as a result of the greatest victory British Customs had ever had over an international drugs ring, at a time when the Tory hard right had vowed to destroy trafficking in the War on Drugs. They were going to make an example out of this one for everyone to see, to show everyone how great they were and how well they were doing. The government was going to throw the book at them, no two ways about it, and then throw the key away. No one was getting any breaks; no one was getting anything that wasn't coming to them. Haase and Co. were going to jail for a very long time. That was a fact.

Only a comic-book miracle was going to save them now. Pessimistic Haase did not believe in miracles. He was devastated. Deep down he knew he couldn't face another big stretch in the shovel. He also understood, however, as a modern drug dealer schooled in the dark arts of counter-surveillance, plea bargaining and generally playing the system, that there were always options. After all, the law was now a business. That was also a fact.

The best answer to the grave set of circumstances that faced him was the simplest one: turning grass. By ratting on the rest of the gang, including the Turks, and confessing first-hand in detail how their heroin operation worked, there was a good chance that he could buy himself some credit with the authorities and get a portion of his sentence knocked off as a reward. But there were limitations to this strategy. As the second-most-wanted prize behind The Vulcan – and considering Customs might not even need him onside because of the vast amount of evidence they had already accumulated – Haase would be bargaining from a weak position. He would be telling them things they already knew. For this, he would be risking a lot, including certain retribution from the Turks, for an outcome of which there was no guarantee. In addition, Haase knew that Customs almost certainly wouldn't let him go just like that. He'd have to serve at least some time in jail. As the uncompromising John Haase, though, he was demanding an unconditional instant 'walk out', and as far as Customs were concerned that was an outcome which they could not deliver.

The second option was to turn supergrass. The difference between a grass and a supergrass is that grasses only inform on the specific crimes with which they have been charged. Supergrasses blow the lid on everything that they know of, relevant and irrelevant to the case in hand. Haase would have to inform on everything he knew about the wider underworld over and beyond the Turkish Connection, any crimes or criminals he could think of, any organisation, friend or foe who was bang at it and of interest to the law. As a Liverpool Mafia godfather, that was potentially a lot of sensitive, valuable information. He could bring a lot of people down. But there was a problem: this option didn't sit well with his underworld code of silence. In addition, it would mean instant death or, at best, life on the witness-protection programme away from his beloved villainy when he ever got out of jail.

The third option was a win–win solution, but one that was almost impossible to achieve: to pretend to be a supergrass. That would involve stunting up a series of phoney crimes, fabricating evidence to make them look real and reporting the incidents to his handlers in a bid to simply *convince* them that he was an informant. If that could be done while he was in jail on remand, and they fell for it, he might be in a position at the trial to watch the sentence-meter go into reverse. The bigger the bogus crime, the more years would be scrubbed from his time. A good word goes into the trial judge's ear and bingo, you're back on the street, a hero to all concerned. This scam had been successfully used by villains to wriggle out of smaller cases in Scotland and London for a long time, but never on such a high-profile case. If it was done right and no one realised what was going on, everyone would be a winner. Haase would get out of jail early. To boot, he would be revered by the underworld for conning the government, his reputation intact for not really grassing anyone up. Customs and Excise and the police would not only get a result on the Turkish Connection, but on a whole raft of other 'big crimes', which would make them look good, leading to greater commendations, etc. and hopefully promotions and pay-rises for all concerned. It's a no-brainer.

There was only one problem: pulling it off. The phoney crimes would have to be big and spectacular – drugs, guns, murders, terrorist attacks, underworld hits, etc. – and have to look real. The bigger the lie, the more likely it is to be believed, to paraphrase Hitler. It would take another devious and practised liar, a criminal mastermind, no less, to organise such an audacious and preposterous scheme. Haase was certainly up to the job – even though his hands were tied to some extent, being behind bars in Manchester's Strangeways prison. That meant he would need a team on the outside to follow his orders to the letter, good communications with them and a war chest full of money to ensure that his Hollywood-style special effects were successfully put into action. The con would have to be good enough to conjure up an illusion of reality to a high degree, so much so that it would deceive the trained observers of the law.

Haase would also have to rely on the gullibility of his handlers, to an extent. How much would they want to believe it? How hungry were they for success? How desperate were they to repeat their recent achievements in smashing his gang? How much did they want to believe that they were dealing with a top villain? How much did they want to believe that he was capable of handing them top cases on a plate? Haase figured they would go for it. He knew the psychology. In general, he believed that certain middle-ranking investigators in Customs and the police had the same motivations as the villains they chased for a living. They were ambitious. They had big egos. They were impressed by reputations. At the end of the day, they were still boys at heart – in it for the adventure, fearful of the mundane and mediocre. They were like desperate reporters chasing a story – success at all costs. They sacrificed a lot in pursuit of the villains they hunted – family time, seeing their kids, weekends, wives, marriages, their well-being. It was an unhealthy, unbalanced lifestyle, and one that could be exploited by someone as cunning as Haase, who was seemingly offering short cuts to success. Haase knew that they would be pleased with themselves for netting as big a fish as him. He also knew that they would try to become his mate. Law-enforcement officers could be as guilty as villains in respecting the gangland hierarchies, in revering the big players. If he started talking, it was the icing on the cake – it would blow their minds for sure. They would put the double coup down to themselves, down to their own skill. That's just the way they were. Ego would prohibit them from suspecting that Haase was pulling a fast one.

A possible theory is that Haase chose option three and that the con was put into action with immediate effect. It makes sense that he hatched the plan within a few days of being arrested. His main worry would have been how he was going to fund the campaign, but that could be instantly sorted. His gang on the outside was still in possession of 50 kilos of heroin from the 100-kilo parcel that the Turks had given to him. Some of this was the 25–30-kilo load that Eddie Croker had been observed bashing by Customs officers the week before he was arrested. Astonishingly, this 50 kilos had slipped the Customs net during the arrest. As Haase's stand-in boss in his forced absence, Chris No-Neck had got it and was awaiting instructions from Haase on what to do with it. Haase knew he could sell it to fund his war chest.

The next problem would be choosing the right solicitor. Haase and Bennett's initial tactic seemed to be finding a brief who would actively participate in the scam – a respectable professional to front the con. The downside would mean they would have to confide their plot to the lawyer – a risky business – but the upside, if it paid off, would be that they would benefit from the injection of expert and specialised legal knowledge. It seems that they looked around for a bent lawyer to bring on board for the big win, and it didn't take long to pinpoint a possible conspirator. Colourful Kevin Dooley was Liverpool's number one mob lawyer. He was a local lad made good, able to talk to his shadowy clientele in a language they understood. The larger-than-life character was rumoured to have 'washed' millions of pounds of Curtis Warren's drug money – a suspicion which hung over him until he was struck off many years later and until his subsequent death. Dooley was so close to the city's top gangsters he was dubbed 'Alfonso' – a reference to his flashy suits, blingy jewellery and bullish manner. Like so many people who love hanging around the underworld, Dooley started to behave like the gangsters he represented, throwing his weight around, issuing ultimatums and giving the impression that he was untouchable. Some of his big clients loved it, including Premiership football players, big businesses and international terrorists. Other clients did not know about his shadowy links, including many of Liverpool Football Club's top players such as Robbie Fowler, and even Colonel Qaddafi's son. Business boomed, but Dooley refused to move his 50-strong staff from his dingy offices in Kirkby. The down-to-earth HQ gave him even more street credibility.

According to Dooley, Bennett made contact with him with a view to retaining his services. Though Dooley was wide, he wasn't stupid. As soon as the con was explained to him, he refused to have anything to do with it. The gun-planting scheme was a preposterous perversion of the course of justice with a one-in-a-hundred chance of working. He knocked it back, without further ado. To curry favour with the Merseyside Police, Dooley later claimed that he tipped off his senior contacts about Haase and Bennett's devious intentions. Meanwhile, the pair were furious that they had been forced to show their hand to Dooley without benefit. Later, Dooley claimed that they swore revenge, to get him back for not going along with their plan. No one said 'no' to John Haase. Dooley said that, as a result of his refusal to cooperate,

Haase and Bennett set out to destroy him, constantly trying to ruin his reputation in a smear campaign.

The pair decided to be more careful about what they told the next lawyer. They decided to choose someone straight and keep him in the dark. Solicitor Tony Nelson was a rising star on the criminal-law circuit. He was introduced to Haase by shaven-headed Liverpool hard-man The Enforcer, a security consultant who ran most of the nightclub doors in the city. This time, Haase and Bennett were more discreet. They did not tell the lawyer about their intention to stunt up phoney crimes in which they had a guiding hand. They simply told him that they wanted him to defend them against the drugs charges and they would like to cut a deal with Customs. On top of his normal brief, would he act as a conduit for their supergrass information, passing it on from them to Customs? According to senior police sources, it is unusual for a solicitor to act as a middleman between a supergrass and the authorities. But Nelson agreed and, unbeknown to him, it was time for Haase to put his plan into action.

Over the next 18 months on remand, Haase pulled off his massive con – mixed in with a heavy dose of alleged cash bribes – and got out of prison.

CHRONOLOGY

July 1993 – Haase and Bennett arrested in London and put on remand in prison.

October 1993 – mass gun-planting begins.

December 1994 – key gun planted at Strangeways – clincher for Royal Pardon.

February 1995 – Haase and Bennett plead guilty to heroin distribution to avoid an open court and jury.

June 1995 – mass gun-planting ends.

August 1995 – after the trial of other defendants, Haase and Bennett are sentenced to 18 years each.

Autumn 1995 – alleged bribery begins and continues into 1996 in order to cover up suspicions over gun-planting.

June 1996 – Royal Pardons granted to Haase and Bennett by Michael Howard.

July 1996 – both men are released.

The con comprised three phases. Firstly, Haase instructed his gang on the outside to buy hundreds of guns from the underworld. Stacks of deactivated weapons were sourced from official depots and rearmed. Plastic explosives were purchased from mercenaries. Haase's men on the outside, led by Chris No-Neck, then planted the guns in safehouses and abandoned cars. The key element in this phase was that Haase was given the glory of telling his Customs handlers the location of the specially made caches – obviously implying that they were owned by other gangsters who were about to use them in killings or terrorist outrages. He pretended they were IRA arms dumps and weapons for use by contract killers.

Convicted heroin dealer Ken Darcy was one of the foot-soldiers paid by Haase's gang to buy and plant Semtex plastic explosive. 'I got paid five grand for just two kilos of Semtex,' said Darcy. 'It was planted in a flat in Liverpool and later found by Customs or police.'

On another occasion, Haase's gang diluted three kilos of heroin to make six, so that it would make a better find for police and Customs. Darcy said, 'When the police found it, along with loads of E tablets, plus loads of guns, it gave them better credit.' Other phoney caches included 150 illegal firearms, 80 brand-new shotguns, Kalashnikov assault weapons, Armalite rifles, Thompson machine guns, Uzi sub-machine guns and 1,500 rounds of ammunition.

Former gangster Paul Ferris also admitted helping to supply between £20,000 and £50,000 worth of weapons to Haase. He said, 'They were planted in a car in Holyhead ferry terminal in North Wales and a lock-up in Liverpool, and Haase said they were IRA. Customs never found out the truth.'

Suleyman Ergun said, 'I was told three times about the gun-planting: before, during and after it happened. The first time, Bennett told me while we were in prison that they were going to buy up guns from all over Britain and plant them in Liverpool to make Customs think that they were informants. He told me he'd help get me free using phoney plants.'

Between October 1993 and June 1995, Haase and Bennett led police to 26 gun and drug caches containing 150 firearms and explosives. Phase two was the clincher for the Royal Pardon: the crown jewel of the phoney gun plants. It consisted of no more than a single pistol – but it was the location and the timing of this particular set-up that were so crucial. Haase dreamt up this stroke of genius two-thirds of the way through the gun-planting period, in December 1994. By that time, even after offering up a series of spectacular arms finds, getting out of prison immediately was not on the table. Customs and Excise were playing hardball with their remand prisoners. They were saying that they could get a bit of time off, but a walk out was out of the question. After all, no arrests had been made as a result of Haase's intelligence. Some wise old officers were also getting a touch suspicious. And at the end of the day, Haase was asking a lot – he was asking them to wipe the slate clean on 50 kilos of gear, and on one of the greatest arrest coups they had ever achieved.

Haase was getting frustrated, racking his brains to discover a way to raise his game. Then he stumbled on it – the Royal Prerogative of Mercy. Haase found out that only this Prerogative, otherwise known as a Royal Pardon, would guarantee instant freedom. He had also found out that this ancient decree dating back to the Norman era was exclusively used in modern times to reward model prisoners who had helped save prison officers' lives in one way or another. It was a quirk of history, rather than official policy, but that was the lie of the land. Haase thought that if he managed to have one of his moody guns smuggled into a prison with one hand and then conveniently grassed it up with the other, meanwhile gently blaming it on a fellow prisoner, that could be construed by the authorities as having prevented the potential killing of a prison officer, an IRA-style breakout or a hostage situation. In December, Haase arranged for a gun to be smuggled into Strangeways prison, Manchester, the weapon hidden in a sandwich toaster. Haase told his handlers about it. The authorities pounced and Haase got the credit. Bingo! Royal Pardon in the bag. The fact that the gun was wrongly blamed on another prisoner, Thomas Bourke, was of no consideration to Haase.

A report to trial judge David Lynch later praised Haase and Bennett for 'The prevention of a possible hostage situation. A prisoner convicted of two double murders was planning to escape by use of a gun. A loaded gun was recovered and the prison officer responsible for smuggling the weapon into the prison was identified.'

Haase was over the moon. Everything was going sweetly and if no one rocked the boat, he'd be out in no time. He just had to make sure that between that point and his official sentencing (in August '95) and the Royal Pardon hearings no one in authority cottoned on to his massive scam. He carried on as normal so as not to ring alarm bells, feeding his handlers info but gently winding down gun-planting. Unbeknown to him, some officials had begun to get suspicious that the finds were too good to be true. Haase then launched into his final phase. Claims by underworld sources suggest that officials and other mysterious figures were bribed to cover his tracks. Haase also wanted to grease the wheels of justice so that they would turn faster, in the hope of getting his Royal Pardon more quickly, before the whole house of cards came crashing down.

The bribes were allegedly paid from both the war chest and other funds on five occasions, split roughly into two groups: those that involved Michael Howard's relative Simon Bakerman and those that did not.

- Payment one: the insider pay-off. Haase claims that £100,000 was given to an insider connected to the case.
- Payments two and three: the London pay-offs. An alleged £1 million was taken by a drug-money courier called John 'Paddy' Scanlon from Haase's main lieutenant, Chris No-Neck, in Liverpool to a Turkish café in Paddington, west London. Another London bribe of just under £1 million was handed over to representatives of an influential VIP at a hotel in the capital.
- Payments four and five: the alleged Bakerman links. Haase claims he ordered No-Neck to pay the home secretary's cousin Simon Bakerman £400,000. Another payment of £920,000, with an alleged Bakerman link, was handed over in room 133 of the former Forte Crest Regent's Park Hotel in north London.

Scanlon claimed he received a call from a man codenamed The Bank Manager (Chris No-Neck), while the drug barons were on remand awaiting trial. He used a kid called The Bank Clerk to move the money between Haase's gang and himself: 'I was told it was a million. I got a phone call the morning of the drop telling me I had to be at the café in London by teatime. The drop-off was a café in west London. The man I handed it to was a fella I'd met there before. I just passed it to him and said here you are. I was paid £2,000 for it.'

The £920,000 Forte Crest drop was planned with military precision by a female associate of Haase's known as The Supervisor and The Enforcer, who acted as consigliore. The Enforcer has revealed that the cash was split into four loads of £250,000. He took one bag, and three couriers took the rest. All four were to pay themselves £20,000 from the cash. In the winter of 1995–96, each courier was told to go to the Forte Crest Regent's Park Hotel (now a Holiday Inn) at different times and take the bag to room 33 or 133. (The source claims the room contained the number 33, possibly changing from 33 to 133 after a refurbishment.) The Enforcer said, 'The detailed instructions were given to me by a female who was visiting Haase frequently in prison. The hotel room opposite was being watched by Haase's men and they were also outside the main entrance. There was a tray of food left outside the room. I was told the people we would be paying the bribe to would come and collect it when all the drops had been done. I was told that Bakerman was the link.'

The second London payment of a similar amount of money was arranged in much the same way. Further corroboration of the bribe allegations has come from Suleyman Ergun. In prison, Ergun later demanded the £1 million he claimed was still owed to him by Haase and Bennett for 50 kilos of heroin. He was told the money was going to be used to get them all out. Ergun explained, 'Bennett said the money was getting switched to big people that would help us all get out. Bennett was so happy he was clapping about it. So I put the debt on hold.'

12

INFORMERS

From January 1994, while on remand, Haase and Bennett were registered by Customs and Excise as official informers and all information received was recorded on contact sheets. The story of how they 'turned' gives a fascinating glimpse into the astonishing behind-the-scenes wheeling and dealing that underlies many court cases today. For several politicians, lawyers and journalists, the case signified the end of an era, the nail in the coffin for common-sense justice. Gone were the days when Dixon of Dock Green nicked a suspect who was banged to rights, and the investigation, court and jail sentence were just a formality, based on the fact that the criminal was clearly and irrefutably guilty. If there is a point in recent British history when the *Daily Mail* can look back and say, 'That was the point at which criminals began to have more power and more rights than their victims,' then this is it.

By the 1990s, even prior to the Haase and Bennett Royal Pardon negotiations, in drug-swamped Britain it seemed as though the legal system had lost the plot. Good guys and bad guys were a relic of the past. Now there were only players, refereed by highly paid lawyers. The big dealers were so powerful that they were able to negotiate with the authorities on an almost equal footing. In big cases, the police, Customs and judiciary had lost ground to the villains they were supposed to be punishing. Narco-superstars now led the charge, dictating unconditional terms like terrorists and using double-tricky mob lawyers to wriggle out of charges and to push their will through the corridors of power. Awestruck coppers and Customs investigators, who had watched far too much TV for their own good, kowtowed to their arrogant big-shot captives, talking to them in near reverential terms. What's more, it all seemed so legal. Streetwise solicitors held court in the plea-bargaining sessions with Customs officers, which were little more than drug-deal-style negotiations. But this time it wasn't the kilo price of heroin that was bartered, it was how many years the suspect was going to get off his sentence. Dealer goes high; Customs go low. Eventually they meet in the middle and everyone goes away happy. Even if you couldn't cut a deal before going to court, the system still worked in your favour.

Customs Officer Harry Ferguson, who was part of the team that had shadowed Haase for 18 months, revealed in his excellent book *Lima 3*:

> You went away, did some time on remand and then had your say in court. At the end of the trial, you still had a better than evens chance of getting away with it: your lawyer would get as much of the evidence excluded as possible and there was always the possibility of bribing or intimidating a member of the jury. Even if you were convicted, after doing half your sentence you went straight back to work. In fact, many were able to continue to run their smuggling activities from inside prison.

Today, many people might be tempted to ask why it was ever allowed to happen. Wasn't it enough that the dealers were clearly winning the war on drugs, flooding the streets with cut-price crack and smack? However, the criminals weren't the only ones to blame. Both sides shared responsibility for the ruination of the justice system in the early '90s. On the law-enforcement side, Customs, police and prosecution lawyers simply couldn't cope with the drugs boom. The new phenomenon had taken them by surprise. Large-scale, American-style undercover operations against traffickers were a relatively new approach to policing organised crime – and Haase's case was one of the first. They were difficult and costly to run. The evidence-gathering was often accompanied by new plea-bargaining tactics as the power shifted towards the villains. Plea-bargaining is an official system in the US, whereby defendants can negotiate with judges and prosecuting lawyers to reduce sentences using bargaining chips such as guilty pleas, confessions and supergrass information. Plea-bargaining has never played an official part in British courts, but in the '80s and '90s much more began to emerge from behind the scenes, especially in big, complicated drugs cases. In the US, such tactics brought successes in the war on drugs. However, emulating the system in the UK by introducing deal-making, often in a piecemeal and unregulated way, led to grave mistakes. The problems may have played a part in many of the big Customs cases which have collapsed in the past ten years. The bad publicity associated with these failures may also have influenced the government's decision to break up the Customs service into separate investigative and revenue-collecting divisions.

The villains played their part in this new phenomenon, the vast amounts of legal knowledge they had accumulated enabling them to play the system effectively. As soon as Haase was arrested in July '93, he had a strategy. In his eyes, the senior Customs officer in charge of his case was his equal – and Haase claims he simply summoned him in order to start negotiating the sentence he wanted.

JOHN HAASE: I was arrested in July 1993 in London, taken back to Liverpool and charged, after a day or two of investigations and interrogations, with conspiracy to supply Class A drugs. The solicitor I got at the time was Tony Nelson from Haworth and Gallagher Solicitors in Birkenhead. I was placed on remand, Category A, in Walton prison, Liverpool. Also with me was my co-accused, Paul Bennett, who is my nephew. All my other co-accuseds were in Walton prison. On my first visit from my solicitor, I asked him to get in touch with the head man of the Customs and Excise who was involved in my case. Mr Nelson said he would see what he could do and get back to me.

After about a week or so, Mr Nelson got back to me and said that a visit had been arranged at Walton prison to see this Customs and Excise officer – his name was Paul Cook. I had the impression he was in charge of everything. The visit took place in Walton prison with Mr Nelson and Paul Cook. When Mr Cook arrived, I asked him straight away, 'What's the chance of doing a deal?' He asked me what I meant. I said, 'Information in return for a reduced sentence.' He asked me what type of information. I said I could supply all types of information on drugs, guns, anything. He said he would have to go away and talk to people and get back to me. That was the end of the meeting.

Cook came to Walton prison again. Present was Mr Nelson. Someone else was with Paul Cook, who didn't introduce himself – I didn't know his name. Paul Cook started discussing the case again, saying, 'Depends what you can give us information-wise.'

I said, 'It depends on what's in it for me, what the deal's going to be.'

I then mentioned that I would like my nephew, Paul Bennett, brought into this. Cook said no at first. I said I would like him to be brought in because Bennett knew an awful lot more than me information-wise. At the time, I was brand new to the drugs game and Bennett had been in it for a long time. Though I had met them [the Turks] myself, he had been in it longer than me but a lot lower down. The meeting ended with them saying they would have to speak to people to see if Bennett could come along.

Later, at Walton prison, there was another meeting. Tony Nelson, Paul Cook were there and I think Bennett was brought in on that meeting as well. He was told that he could come as long as the information was good. While this had been going on, there were things going on on the outside. Meanwhile, in Liverpool [prison], Cook met with me and Bennett and Nelson and said the deal was depending on what we could give and how much we could give. He said the more the better. I got moved to Manchester prison then. I was only there about a week and then got moved to another prison, an Army prison, on high risk in isolation. After six weeks, I was taken off the high risk and taken to Hull prison, and Bennett was in Hull prison waiting for me.

Cook knew a lot of people. When I was in Hull, he was in the background. Imagine the scenario. Smash! Bang! I'm in London with the [police] guns [on me during the arrest] and I'm saying, 'Fucking hell! I'm gone here.' Imagine, I've just done 11 years for a robbery. And what am I looking at here, 20-odd years? Imagine how my brain's working. From day one, I was scheming.

Haase had more chips to bargain with – other things on the table as well as the phoney gun plants he could offer Customs Officer Cook in return for a reduced sentence. First, he could force or persuade the co-defendants in his case to go guilty – saving Customs the cost and hassle of a trial. He offered to get Kaya and Ergun to go guilty. Slyly, he had no intention of telling the Turks that he'd be benefiting from this plea. If the omerta-obsessed Turkish Connection found out Haase was turning them over, they would have killed him in prison. Lower-level people like Eddie Croker would be no problem – Haase could manipulate or simply bully them into submission.

As the terms of the deal got more complicated, so did Haase and Bennett's deceit. They decided that they would not give statements. They did not want to give any clues to their co-defendants, especially the Turks, that they were grassing. So they talked off the record to Cook, but cleverly invented a way of getting crucial information relating to the case on the record so that it could be used in the up-and-coming trial without being traced back to them. For instance, Haase claims that Cook and the prosecution were keen that at least one member of the Liverpool gang confessed in detail to receiving heroin from the Turks. The detail would fill in the gaps on the surveillance logs, making a watertight case. Haase and Bennett simply got Croker to 'front' the deal. They instructed Croker to make a statement on their behalf saying that he had been in possession of the heroin and that he meant to sell it.

Throughout the whole of the negotiations with Paul Cook and other Customs officers, Haase covered his back in case they reneged on the terms later and refused to slash his sentence – he secretly tape-recorded the meetings. He arranged for a mini-tape recorder to be smuggled into prison and strapped it to his body before entering the prison visitors' area.

One of the tapes (which I have obtained from an underworld source) contains a meeting between Haase and Bennett, their solicitor Tony Nelson and Customs Officer Paul Cook. Haase appears to begin by saying that he is trying to get to see Eddie Croker – presumably to influence what he will say in his statement – but is finding it difficult to bypass prison rules to fix a meet or even see him in the gym because it only admits one inmate at a time. Haase seems to be saying that they will have to use another witness if he can't get Croker to cooperate. But Cook seems to be asking Haase about Croker's first statement.

> HAASE: It depends on another witness. It's gonna take a lot of hard work to put in to see him [presumably to see Croker]. Put in an application. Got to get over to see him in the morning. Thursday morning, that's the only time I can see him, but you can only go to the gym one at a time here . . . there's always some stupid rule.

COOK: What about that first version of his statement?
. . . Exploiting the side text . . . the prosecution think
that . . .?

There then follows an astonishing bargaining session. The gist
of the deal is as follows: Nelson seems to have negotiated a
draft agreement with the prosecution. If Haase and Bennett
assist the prosecution – inform on the Turks *and* make a
statement against them *and* go in the witness box – then they
will get a whopping 60 per cent discount on their sentence.
The prosecution have told Nelson that the maximum sentence
Haase and Bennett will get will be fifteen years, from which
they can immediately deduct nine years in keeping with the 60
per cent discount and thus serve six years. The sentence could
be as low as ten, in which case a discount of six years could be
given, thus serving only four. The deal is based on Nelson's
skilful manoeuvre in getting Haase and Bennett only
prosecuted for the lesser charge of distributing in the UK, not
importation.

Nelson, Haase and Bennett then begin to play hardball with
Cook. Nelson states his desire for a total 100 per cent
reduction. Haase and Bennett talk up the risk of revenge for
grassing the Turks and demand to know exactly who in
Customs will know that they are informing – thus weighing up
the risk of leaks. Haase pushes the envelope further, wanting
60 per cent off for simply going against the Turks and an
additional portion off for information on guns (the fake
plants). Cook seemingly agrees that, 'Guns and everything else
will seriously knock it down.' (Obviously, Cook does not know
that the gun plants are fake.)

Nelson appears to refer to the gun plants (though he has no
knowledge that they are phoney) as a bonus that will help
reduce the sentence further and get Haase and Bennett
protection: 'If it is that valuable, then obviously you'll be
treated as a confidential informant and given some sort of
protection.'

Bennett seems to tease Cook, dangling the gun plants as

bait, but demanding 'walk out [instant freedom] in return': 'A walk out's more beneficial to me; there's no other solution . . . a walk out is a walk out and is open to more possible [better gun plants].'

Here is an abridged version of the tape:

JH: John Haase
PC: Paul Cook
TN: Tony Nelson
PB: Paul Bennett

TN: . . . Assist the prosecution [on] the actual facts . . . just say guilty for a start . . . that will assist your sentence . . . We can then reach an agreement . . . giving prosecuting evidence . . . 60 per cent off. The prosecution, they've got an overwhelming case against you. As I said to Paul [Cook] today, your three points [guilty/statement/witness box], put them together . . . we will give it to them . . . The prosecution will then underplay what they will describe as your activities in a certain way.

JH: Yes.

TN: Which will carry a lesser sentence than that which you will be available for at the moment. Recent case law for importation is 30 years. But they will have you down as distributors – bagmen in this country. For that sort of offence, the prosecution wouldn't be disagreeing with our Counsel in chambers.

PC: I've got the stated case law somewhere but in the rush up here I can't find it.

JH: Go on . . .

TN: Prosecution is telling us top line is fifteen years. Sixty per cent of fifteen is six, right? . . . Sorry, 60 per cent off is nine . . . But if the information was as valuable and as serious as we think it is – and having discussed it with some people [it seems it is] – then they may go back to the prosecution and say,

'Well, forget the discount.' Then we're back to between ten and twelve . . . so . . . we're looking at five going on six as a rough guideline. The longer the trial is, the better to find out how valuable the information is. Now, confidential information could be given, could be extraordinary . . . then if it is that valuable then obviously you'll be treated as a confidential informant and given some sort of protection . . .

PB: I'm not grassing. [Turning to Cook] You'd know and [to Nelson] you'd know . . . but who else?

PC: My boss.

PB: Your boss . . . who else? You two would know . . . The finger comes right from above.

TN: I've been pressing for a walk out, are you with me? I'm setting our starting point and our finishing point is a walk out on this, all right . . . What the prosecution says is what we've just said. But what the judge says . . .

PB: As we've said to you from the beginning . . . your views mean nothing to me . . . What your job is outside means nothing to me. But a walk out's more beneficial to me; there's no other solution . . . a walk out is a walk out and is open to more possible. Four years is no problem but a walk out is more beneficial to all parties.

PC: Yeah, but it is just not possible, with the best will in the world. I'm just explaining . . .

JH: Then why are you explaining that it would be more beneficial to you if we did [give evidence]? I'm gonna get a four before I even go upstairs. I'm gonna get a four whatever the charges. I'm happy with a four but it's gonna stink anyway.

PC: It's their way.

PB: But it's gonna stink . . . out of order, course it is.

JH: Beneficial later on . . . [to Bennett] told you what would happen later on, didn't I?

PC: It's not the case of a 'want' thing – it's the case of the legal machinery . . .

PB: Interesting legal machinery – you said 60 per cent off for everything, putting us down for one thing. Now you put us down on something else, serving [distribution]. It would have worked out better if we done that, whatever.

PC: I'm just explaining. It could be four; it could be six. No one knows.

PB: It'll still stink. That's out of order. [To Haase] I told you what would be beneficial, didn't I? We're interested in the legal machinery – the 60 per cent . . .

[Cook talks about The Vulcan]

PC: If you do walk out with a four or six, you would have to have pleaded guilty and give evidence – against the Turks.

PB: I don't want that – Croker will do that. Will [Croker] do that?

[Bennett talks about Croker giving evidence after they have talked to him]

TN: I dunno, but he'll have to do some sort of . . .

PB: He'll do that.

JH: He will do that. When we've finished dealing with him next week, then we'll go and get a statement off Croker.

PC: We want that so . . . But priority is Kaya. You said you would go against Kaya to get extra years off.

JH: That'll be before Croker . . .

PC: You can speak about that.

JH [to Tony Nelson]: I would go in the witness box . . . and I testify against this one or that one . . . everything else. [But] then I'm getting a deal for nothing, aren't I? . . . Just going into the witness box is enough for a four or a six . . .

TN: I appreciate that.

JH: [What about] all the other things – the guns and everything else . . .?

PC: It's gonna help. Guns and everything else is going to seriously knock it down, isn't it?

JH: Not if I've gotta go in the witness box. How's that a proper deal if I've got to get in the box? If I go in the witness box, the idea is I've got a deal going on . . . the idea is that's your gain. You're gonna go down . . . what are you gonna do?

PB: Buttons . . .

PC: Yeah, it should be prepared. What's wrong in that?

JH: Witness box, that should be 60 per cent right away.

PC: I agree, but what you are saying is you've pleaded guilty full stop. Yeah – if you have to give a statement, you can't just give a statement expressing views. You can't give a statement unless you say what's in your statement. Can't just give evidence and then refuse to [back it up]. That's not going to shorten your sentence upstairs, you have to say [it].

PB: Croker against Kaya and Onay. Croker can say those things personally.

PC: He would have to say what you could say. Fifty or forty-nine kilos in his house. He's got to say where he got them picked up from – who off – from you?

JH: Yes.

[At this point, they talk about getting Bennett to accept a bigger charge than Haase]

PB: Have they [the prosecution] given you mine [my statement]?

PC: They're ignoring your statement.

PB: So we're . . .?

PC: No, we can obviously discuss what we're giving them . . . carrying [trafficking] . . .

PB: Carrying?

JH: No.

PC: That you . . . the drugs . . . deliver . . .

JH: Him, pleading guilty in court. I don't know. What's gonna come up in court? Why prosecute one and not the other? . . .

PB: Yeah, you can say the person who sent me is the . . . but it'll burst into news . . . this that and the other . . .

[There is a conversation about docks/Customs officers and 'people who'd mess around with politicians and everything else']

PC: Downstairs in the house . . . that's shaky evidence. If Kaya is pleading guilty . . . then he'll be part of defence evidence . . .

JH: Well, I'm not giving them everything . . . what they want – everything – I'm not giving them.

PB: No slip-ups . . . with Kaya.

TN: That's assuming Kaya goes not guilty.

PC: I think he will.

TN: If he goes not guilty, then the statements wouldn't be used.

[They talk about finding out how the other co-ds are going to plead]

JH: What we're going to have to do is debrief in the next few weeks. Then we must go down and arrange the court cases between the lot of us . . .

TN: Obviously, get their solicitors involved. Better I speak to their briefs.

JH: Inform them that we want to see the lot of them . . . in Liverpool . . .

TN: Can't stop you . . .

JH: That's what we're gonna have to do . . . arrange the court cases between the lot of us.

TN: It would be better for your statement if that was the case.

JH: Get in touch with them all and find out.

PC: The sentence would alter . . . if so, if that was then taken into consideration . . .

TN: What we want if we go down that route is for the judge to think JH and PB have shown remorse. Remorse, (a); the evidence, (b); the initial conviction [Onay] . . . (c); and on the information we're giving them . . . (d).

JH: Quite a lot . . . just on the transport alone and other things. Talk to the prosecution about the evidence . . . It was like when you was in last week; they think they know me. They're not getting all that. No way! They won't get what they want.

PB: As soon as [this is over], after this, I'm out, I'm away [reference to moving abroad]. So I've got to be footloose, as well as everything else. That may mean nothing to you but. Even though I'm innocent [of grassing, because I haven't yet given my agreement] . . . talking about people knowing – we know who they are . . . top people . . . – wouldn't mess around in politics and everything else. [This may be a reference to Simon Bakerman and the risk of him finding out they are informers.] You worry about who's involved, don't you? Do they know my picture?

PC: If I can just come back to the 60 per cent. The Appeal Court is quite right on this – that takes into account all three aspects.

TN: Guilty plea, information, statement. We've never spoken of less than five years, have we?

JH: We have.

TN: The prosecution haven't.

[They talk about getting away from Liverpool if they fulfil all three criteria]

JH: It's not worth all that.

[JH then talks about people they can give information on, and guns and where they are coming from. They talk about the Turks and punishment for grasses and Haase says that the Turks are sticking together. He is clearly worried about punishment in Turkey. Bennett says that he will continue to inform until there is a leak and the underworld finds out that he is a grass.]

PB: All I'm saying is, I'll say something, until someone knows it's me.

This tape is unique because it is one of the only recordings of a secret plea-bargaining meeting. Prison officers later discovered the illegal recorder – possibly during a meeting at Strangeways police station – and confiscated the device along with several of the tapes. Haase explained to the prison governor, contemptuously and with a snide reference to Customs, 'Well, you can't really trust these bastards, can you?' Customs officers went ballistic, fearing their potentially compromising conversations had been recorded. They threatened to call off the deal. Haase convinced them that there were no other copies. He was lying. Copies had already been smuggled out of prison and buried. Not realising they had been duped, the officers resumed the plea-bargaining talks.

Despite the complicated discussions, several clear outcomes emerged. Haase and Bennett were considering grassing up the Turks in person if enough time was scrubbed off their sentences. At this stage in the negotiations, Customs were not completely on board, so to effect a compromise Haase and Bennett agreed to inform on the Turks vicariously – by 'persuading' Eddie Croker to do their dirty work for them and make a statement against the Turks. For the prosecution, this wasn't as good as Haase and Bennett ratting on their co-defendants in their own words, but it was a start. Later, Haase and Bennett agreed to help further by trying to convince Ergun and Kaya to go guilty in a series of specially set-up prison meetings. For this, they were given credit in Paul Cook's secret report to the judge.

13

GUN-PLANTING

Using a bank of 18 stolen mobile phones, Haase and Bennett began coordinating the biggest con to date on the British judicial system. The pair were in prison on remand, so legally they could only communicate with underbosses on the outside such as Chris No-Neck during official visits. The stolen mobile phones were therefore essential to the military-style operation. They were smuggled into prison by a corrupt prison officer and paid for from a roll of fresh £50 notes which Haase carried around the wings. He was able to fiddle free airtime on the phones by keying in a special code when the contract credit hit max. That way, Haase was able to spend hours talking to his henchmen, carefully detailing where gun caches were to be stashed.

Mobile phones are strictly prohibited within prison, and inmates used them in secret in their cells. Bennett became frustrated. He needed to answer calls immediately, to thoroughly stay on top of the gun plants and to ensure split-second timing wherever he was in the prison – in the gym, in the toilets, in his mates' cells. He quickly devised an ingenious method. He stashed the phone in a Michael Jackson-style ghetto blaster which he carried on his shoulder like a breakdancer, the speaker containing the mobile phone next to his ear. When the phone rang, he was able to hear it. There was a secret panel in the plastic casing through which he could answer the phone and talk. If he was being watched and couldn't take the call, sometimes he would disappear back to his cell to call the person back.

On the outside, The Bank Manager Chris No-Neck was in charge of putting Haase's instructions into action. He was busy selling the missing 50 kilos of heroin and soon raised £1.25 million for the war chest to spend on gun-planting and alleged bribes. That's why he was known as The Bank Manager to some members of the gang; he had his hands on the purse strings. He stashed most of the money close by in the house of a straight-goer – a gangly teenager who had no connection to crime. He was dubbed The Bank Clerk, as it was his job to run around the city dropping off money from the main war chest to pay for underworld services rendered.

The first proper gun plant occurred in October 1993, when Customs recovered four machine guns, two moderator silencers, one stun gun, one revolver and one hundred and sixty rounds of nine-millimetre ammunition as a result of Haase and Bennett's information. But the scheme did not move into top gear until after Christmas in February 1994 and continued until June '95. Haase and Bennett were staging bogus plants for a full 21 months, and no one in authority realised enough to raise the alarm.

Haase arranged to buy many of the guns himself. After all, he was in the perfect place – prison. He put out the word to his friends within the penal system that he would buy anything and everything that could fire a bullet, and soon gangsters from London, Scotland, Sheffield and Manchester were queuing up with batches of Kalashnikovs, shotguns and pistols. Once they had shaken hands on a price, it was a simple case of getting his people in Liverpool to talk to their people, wherever they were, do the meets and pick up the parcels.

In Liverpool, a notorious gangster called Tommy Gilday was also supplying the gang with guns. Two of the city's most violent crime families – sworn enemies of Haase – also agreed to forget their differences and help Haase if the price was right. The real names of the other hand-picked gun-planters are known to the author, but cannot be revealed for legal reasons. They include two brothers who are protection racketeers and restaurant owners, another gangster called George, a villain called Ray, The Iceman and Curtis Warren's former right-hand man Johnny Phillips. Phillips later died in mysterious circumstances, allegedly killed by a professional hitman team called The Cleaners. Ironically, he had fallen out in an unrelated feud with one of the crime families involved in the gun-planting.

One phoney cache consisted of 80 brand-new Italian shotguns. The deal to buy them was helped along by gangster James Turner, a Park Road hoodlum who had helped Haase in his feud with the Ungi/Fitzgibbon crew. He said, 'I know where the guns came from. I got offered them. Came off a wagon, brand new. But he got them. I said, "John [Haase], do you want these?"' Chris No-Neck bought them on behalf of John Haase and they were planted in a McDonald's car park. Astonishingly, a nationally-known crime boss from London had sussed a way of sourcing a large amount of recycled guns from a police depository. These were guns that had been used in crimes and then confiscated by police, probably deactivated at an official proof house and then stored in a secure facility. Somehow, the London gangster was able to smuggle them out or buy them at auction, reactivate them and sell them to Haase. Another gangster in Scotland, who owned a workshop and had connections to Glasgow's top hit-men, began to supply very high quality guns.

The gun plants were so convincing that even MI5 thought they were real secret stashes. To get more credit, Haase pretended that he could help seize IRA guns, ammo and explosives destined for use in atrocities on the mainland. Haase was so devious that he knew this stash would get the authorities 'drooling'.

The IRA was the government's number one priority. A few months before Haase was arrested, on 24 April 1993, an IRA bomb at Bishopsgate devastated the City of London's financial centre, killing one and injuring more than forty people. The renewed campaign shocked the nation. Now the IRA was threatening other prestige targets, including the then newly built skyscraper at Canary Wharf in the capital's Docklands and, more worryingly, the under-construction Channel Tunnel. Canary Wharf was eventually bombed three years later in 1996 and a ceasefire was hastily declared before the Channel Tunnel was hit. The tunnel was one of the main British motivations behind peace.

Haase's ruse was nothing short of criminal genius. First, he bought £20,000–£50,000 worth of weapons from associates of Glasgow godfather Paul Ferris and a Manchester-based Scot called Rab, the heroin dealer once supplied by the Turks. Then Haase arranged for a car full of guns to be dumped near a British ferry bound for Ireland. To make it sing, Haase had his men go to the Republic and get Irish newspapers that were left on the back seat on return to the UK, and even cigarette stumps from pubs in Dublin, to make it seem that Irishmen had been driving the car. Haase tipped off his handlers, and an M15 observation team watched the car for three days to catch the phantom IRA operatives picking up the guns. Of course, no one turned up, but the authorities trumpeted the seizure as a great coup in the fight against the terrorists. This equalled Brownie points for Haase. Ferris said, 'They were planted in a car in Holyhead ferry terminal in North Wales and a lock-up in Liverpool, and Haase said they were IRA. Customs never found out the truth.'

Haase's devious operation was nearly exposed after a close brush with the law. Some of the guns were transported from Manchester to Liverpool by two stunning women (one known as The Supervisor) who were close to Haase. The idea was that a couple of dolly birds, who looked like they had been on a shopping trip to Manchester, were unlikely to get a pull off the police. But the ladies' sports car was stopped almost immediately for speeding. The boot was crammed full of assault rifles and hand grenades. The scantily clad girls did their best to distract the traffic cop away from the boot, flashing their legs and cleavage. It worked. He let them go with a ticking off without searching the car.

In another extraordinary incident, the operation nearly came crashing down amid fears for public safety. According to uncorroborated underworld sources, Haase's men claimed they planted a cache of Semtex and several small arms in a car near a pub called Black George's on Park Road in Liverpool 8. The pub was run by the Ungi family, and Haase hoped the find would throw some guilt by association on them, at least enough for a bit of harassment. But the plan backfired when the car was stolen by joyriders before the police could seize it. A massive police operation was mounted to find the car and eventually it was spotted by a patrol car being driven at high speed by a teenager and his pals through the streets of Walton. The joyriders were awestruck when they were suddenly roadblocked by nearly 20 police, an armed-response unit and a bomb-disposal unit. The Semtex was found in the boot untouched. The kids hadn't even noticed it and were never told. There was a collective sigh of relief. This anecdote has not been confirmed by Merseyside Police and the validity of the information cannot be verified.

Other seizures included 7,534 Ecstasy tablets, 5 kilos of amphetamine, 58 litres of methadone, the recovery of 100 LSD tablets, the locating of a skunk (cannabis) factory, 200 cannabis plants and a machine gun – all planted by Haase.

But there was only one problem – no one had been arrested, and the lack of bodies was now raising suspicions. Despite nineteen 'raids', there was not one single arrest. Police invariably arrived at the location of a tip-off to find a deserted safehouse or an abandoned car with a holdall full of guns in the boot. All fingerprints had, of course, been wiped clean. All of the vehicles had mysteriously been purchased for cash a few days earlier by untraceable men, who, despite numerous appeals in the press, never came forward.

So Haase set to work in finding a criminal who would knowingly sacrifice himself for cash. In January 1995, nearly a year after the phoney gun-planting had begun and at the point when some Customs officers were becoming suspicious and demanding 'bodies' to back up the Scouser's intelligence, Haase was saved from the brink. A low-level drug runner called Billy the Hamster agreed to hide three handguns in a toolbox in his house which would then be reported to the police by Haase. He would take the rap, go to jail and get a big bung for his trouble. On the day of the bust, the Hamster was arrested on suspicion while his house was searched. But then things went badly wrong. According to underworld sources, farcically, the first police rummage team failed to find the guns. And by the time of the next search, the search-warrant period had allegedly expired. The guns were found, but the evidence was inadmissible, and by this time Billy had had second thoughts about getting himself mixed up in such a hare-brained scheme, refusing to give a statement to back up Haase's plan. He was mysteriously released from custody and not charged. He then tried to blackmail Haase for £5,000, threatening to blow the lid on the gun-planting scam, but was quickly silenced and bashed up by Chris No-Neck.

In another attempt to show that 'real bodies' were behind the crimes that Haase was 'uncovering', Haase invented a story that The Vulcan had put a hit out on the family of Customs Officer Paul Cook. A total fabrication, but Cook and his family went into the witness-protection programme. (Customs had to take this seriously; a Liverpool Mafia heroin gang had put a contract out on several Customs officers in 1992, even firebombing one of their houses. For many Customs officers, this had been a big motivation for taking out Haase, as he was a Liverpool Mafia boss.) Haase then got the glory when he said that he used his underworld power to get the contract called off. This may have been an early attempt to meet the conditions of winning a Royal Pardon – by helping to prevent danger to a law officer.

In fact, the only people that Haase had 'grassed up' up to that point were corrupt law officials – a crooked prison officer, a corrupt CPS manager, a rogue solicitor and a bent copper.

This super-selective targeting of 'enemy' fall guys clocked up extra Brownie points on the street. The villains were happy that Haase hadn't actually grassed any villains up. The breakout was a triple-whammy success – the most audacious escape plan since Steve McQueen went over the wall on a liberated German motorbike. Haase became an instant underworld legend.

———————————

JOHN HAASE: On the outside, Bennett and me had been working overtime. When Bennett and me got nicked, we had over 50 kilos of brown [heroin], which is worth £1,150,000. Chris No-Neck, who was an associate of ours, had control of this heroin. This heroin was sold and we used some of the money to purchase weapons which were later planted so that the police and Customs and Excise could find them. Bennett already had a couple of hundred thousand pounds of cash and so did I, so we had plenty of money.

Tommy Gilday got a lot of guns for us, but no favours were done. We paid for everything – machine guns, AKs, hand pistols. When we were first getting the machine guns, they were £2k each, but later on, when we were getting them in tens, the price was reduced. One of our main contacts was a Londoner. A lot of our stuff was guns. This was a member of the underworld. I met him in prison when the guy was in prison doing an 18-year sentence for armed robbery. I can confirm that some of the guns that I bought had originated from a police depository – that is, they had been confiscated by the police in previous crimes, but then had been released back onto the streets for resale.

A lot of them were coming in from eastern Europe, especially the AKs. I was getting them in the end for £750 from my London contact. There were loads of people involved in getting us guns. People from Sheffield, Manchester – that's the one where they found the car in a car park with machine guns in it.

We got a couple of garages, a couple of flats, eight to ten

vehicles, cars and vans. One of the vans we parked in Bootle on the McDonald's [car park] with 80 shotguns in it. All this information I used to pass to Mr Nelson. All the guns were spot on. I was getting them and telling people where to put them so that I could inform Customs and Excise of where they could be found. It was a con all the way, but for some reason they were delighted to get the guns off the street.

The police wanted to get involved after the first couple of things had been found. Tony Nelson asked me could the police come and see me. I said, 'No, I'm only dealing with the Customs.' The Customs wanted information about anything but for some reason they were delighted – they couldn't get enough of it.

These little stashes get the deals going. For instance, there was bomb-making stuff in Lower Breck Road [in Liverpool]. Someone went out of town for me. This was because I met this guy on remand in Manchester prison. I was talking to him, got a bit friendly with him and asked him if he had any guns up there. He said, 'I've got loads, what do you want?'

I said, 'Whatever you can get me.'

When I was in Manchester with Bennett, we had mobile phones with us so I could speak to anyone at any time. We were co-coordinating the operations and the planting of the guns using mobile phones. I also had one in Hull. On one occasion when guns were brought back from out of town to Liverpool, there was a problem. Coming down the East Lancs Road, back towards Liverpool at about eleven o'clock at night, the two women got stopped by a police car. The car had all kinds of firearms in it – machine guns, rifles, etc. A police officer came to the car, asked the lady if everything was all right. She said 'fine', showed him her driving stuff and the officer waved them on their way – a normal stopping. But the guns were never discovered.

In the Southend, in Liverpool 8, we had a stash of guns in there, in an empty flat. One of Bennett's people was told to go round and put a couple more in. They never went themselves and sent someone else round to put the extra guns inside. The story I got told afterwards was that they didn't put the right number in the alarm. The alarm went off, they couldn't shut it down so they ran away. Later, the police arrived and found the guns – so we lost them.

The next one was one of the big ones they were all drooling at. Someone went to Ireland and got an address over there. They got some newspapers and went to pubs over there and got cigarette stumps and all bits and pieces [from ashtrays in the Irish pubs]. A car we bought in Liverpool was booked onto the Holyhead ferry. That was booked through a travel agency in Alderhay [astonishingly through the same travel agency that Haase had used to book drug runs to Ireland. A simple check may have exposed the link]. Booked on to go to Ireland. Thousands of pounds of ammunition, rifles, etc. were put in the car and that was parked in Holyhead car park. The newspapers and cigarette stumps were also put in the car and the keys were left on the back wheel. The car was full of rifles and thousands of rounds of ammunition and many weapons. We told the Customs about it. MI5 sat off and observed the car for three days before they hit it. That cache was planted by me and Bennett to give the impression that there was an IRA connection. This was a total fabrication. You can imagine the Brownie points Cook was getting and that's why the police wanted to get involved. [During this time] I made a tape recording of me in a [prison visiting] room with Paul Bennett, Tony Nelson and Paul Cook. I taped them in prison. The next time, I got nicked for having an unauthorised tape-recording machine.

They can't be that thick, but they are, believe it or not. How can I be in prison and know information like that? And every time it's spot on. Every time I told them, they got something. Without knowing what's going on, I knew it was there. Lower Breck Road: I knew it was there. Loads of guns. That was ours. There was bomb-making stuff in the Lower Breck Road one. That come from London, that. Nothing got robbed before the police found it.

So far they've [Customs] got no bodies. But I said to Bennett one day, 'These are going to get suspicious here, because they haven't got a body yet.' Me and Bennett are in custody, so it was left to Chris No-Neck to get a body. Billy the Hamster was nicked with some guns in January '95. I'd like to know myself what happened because even though he was nicked, he never went to court. Chris No-Neck, Bennett and me know him – he runs drugs around for people. Chris No-Neck got this chap, Billy, to accept to have a toolbox in his house with three guns in it. Loaded hand pistols, they were. The information was passed on to Paul Cook. The police raided this man's home and found the firearms. He got charged, but never went to court. All's I know is that he got on the phone to No-Neck after he'd been arrested for the guns and asked No-Neck for £5k. I thought he'd got a bit cheeky and said he'd do something. No-Neck met him/bumped into him, bashed him up and that was the end of the episode. But still Billy the Hamster never went to court. The reason I know this is because when I got the legal papers this time, for my last case in 1999–2001, I saw the papers in the court and they said that he never went to prison.

Remember all the trouble over Cheers? I gave them information – pure 100 per cent luck on my side. We planted a car full of guns near Cheers and two days later David Ungi was shot. That gave the impression to the Customs and Excise that I had the inside track on gangland shootings. Like I said, it was pure luck on my side over Cheers, the information with David Ungi. Said there was a car parked up with guns in and that.

We started the rumour that The Vulcan, the Turkish heroin dealer, was going to put a hit on Cook's family, because they [Customs] tried to get the Turks to testify against The Vulcan, who was the main man they wanted. But the police said that the Turks were too terrified to give evidence, so me and Bennett said there was a hit on Cook's family and he went to the witness-protection programme. This added credibility to our con because the Customs said that if you're going to be a grass, you've got to grass someone up. That was us who started the rumour about the hit on Cook, not Curtis Warren, as people thought. To give it more credibility.

The Vulcan was a dangerous man. He was the main man but they couldn't get him. I think he's done a couple of murders over here. . . . Customs wanted Bennett. And they said they'd let me walk if I gave them evidence against The Vulcan. I said, 'What's it worth, because he's dangerous, him.'

And they went to the judge. They said, 'Mr Haase does not give evidence against The Vulcan because we can understand that the man is too dangerous.'

I wouldn't have done anyway, because he's a good friend of mine. Even Kaya is [my friend]. Been to Istanbul and that. Met his mum and dad.

For him [Cook], it was credibility. If I said I could get The Vulcan, it looked good for him, didn't it? I said he'd been to my house, The Vulcan. He knows where I live. The man's got plenty of money. Especially him wanting protection for him and his family. If you're going to be a supergrass, who are you grassing? You aren't grassing anyone. That's why we put the body in. That's what they wanted. . . .

What you've heard there is about a tenth of what went down. Don't forget that this is nearly three years this is going on. We was on remand for over two years. That's why Cook kept delaying it. Kept putting it back all the time.

In a bid to ratchet up the terrorist link, Haase promised Customs they would supply information about a container of weapons on board a ship heading for Liverpool, according to uncorroborated sources. The ship was already in Liverpool docks, the container doors booby-trapped with bags of Semtex. The bomb-disposal experts blew the doors off, revealing 50 weapons and some heroin. Then Ken Darcy was roped in by No-Neck to get more Semtex explosive and heroin to add variety to the Customs finds. According to Peter Kilfoyle MP, some of the weapons came from a West Midlands police repository and some equipment registered in North Wales had come through the repository in Liverpool.

KEN DARCY: Just come out of jail [in 1991] from a three-and-a-half-year sentence for half an ounce of cocaine. Come home. Had to move house because the busies took the house, whatever. Knew Chris No-Neck for a long time, through mates. All in all, I've known him for 20-odd years. Done this and that with him. So I come out of jail and done a bit of this and that to get by.

Anyway, all these drugs and guns [were being planted] around the city and I ended up getting involved with that. John Haase and Paul Bennett were away. Gets a phone call from Chris No-Neck. There was simply too much for him to do. Half the stuff [the guns and explosives] he couldn't get, so I come in and got what he needed.

No-Neck had a lot of the firm's money – all of the firm [Haase/Bennett/Croker] had been nicked bar him. So he was left with all the money, the contacts, control over everything. He was acting on behalf of John Haase and Paul Bennett. All along, they knew they weren't going to be away for a long time. It was a scam from day one. Everyone knew that Haase and Bennett were going to get out of jail quickly. They were throwing people in [informing]. There was also the gun plants, the gun in the prison. That's what got them out.

No-Neck would have cups of tea with me, telling me he had planted guns and alarms had gone off and that. That was in the Southend [of Liverpool] where the alarm went off on the house. These two boys had put the guns in, but the alarm goes off. So the find was made by ordinary busies. So John Haase couldn't ring up the Customs and tell 'em about it. There was a bit of trouble over that. The boys got a hiding over that. That's the point when I said to No-Neck, 'I'll help you now. Make a list of what you want.'

He's up the wall planting guns every which where. Buying this, buying that. That's when he asks me about Semtex, when I got Semtex, firearms for him, and I did about four drops here there and everywhere.

I knew one was in Bootle strand. I knew one was in a house in town. I just supplied the firearms, Semtex, bullets . . . I knew a couple of the locations. Got [the Semtex] off these mercenaries from out of town through a mate of mine. I done a favour a few days before for him. Then I called the favour back. Got the Semtex, planted it on Haydock racecourse till it was time to bring it home, back to Norris Green. A man I'll call Soldier Boy came and collected it. It was gone then and put wherever it was supposed to go, and then it was found. Only one in Semtex. I got paid five grand for just two kilos. Soldier Boy come and took it from me.

I asked no questions. When the police found the guns, it usually was in the papers – big news. But it was never mentioned that Semtex was found. That was very strange; it was never mentioned in the paper. It was to be organised in a plant to make it look like a terrorist link. I asked him [No-Neck] about that. He said, 'Don't worry about that. It is not a problem.' It was very strange, seeing as they were going on about bazookas, guns and that.

I done about four plants over a couple of months. Only for a certain amount of time, before Haase and Bennett came out of prison. They was on remand. They'd been using fucking no-marks, idiots, before then.

There were other people high up in the city who were saying, 'I can get you this or I can get you that.' At the time, they [Haase's gang on the outside] had endless amounts of drugs. Some of it was shit, but they were bashing it for more than it was. From 3 ki to 6 ki. That was done so it could be planted and it would make a bigger find for the Customs. The busies aren't arsed because they're getting it off the streets. Tablets were also used in the phoney plants. But at the end of the day, the gear was shite, so it was worth giving in rather than selling. That's the way they were looking at it. I did guns but one lot was a drugs plant. The drugs were got by me calling in lots of favours.

I knew all the fellas No-Neck was using [to buy and plant guns]. There were a lot of people. Money bought some, but there were also friends. Everyone in the underworld wanted to geg in on it to get credit for it [from powerful Haase when he got out]. I had lads coming from Preston, Leyland, Manchester,

Wales with six or seven guns. I ended up buying some in town.

It didn't matter if it was any good. It was just for plants so the Customs could find them. Buy anything: hand grenade, stun guns, bombs. Some of the guns were from Davy Crockett days [old-fashioned] . . . but at the end of the day, a gun is a gun. As far as the Customs and police are concerned, it's off the street. They're happy.

A lad from Manchester, a football hooligan, he had ten in a suitcase. The quicker you stashed them, the better it was for Haase. The money was no problem. Some young kid [The Bank Clerk] would drop the money off to me to pay for the guns. I'd phone him and say, 'I need five grand.' The five would be brought round in the hour.

Billy the Hamster – how did he get off with all them guns in the box? He said the warrant expired. I'm not having that. The busies came with the warrant and searched the house. There's a big steel box with guns in and they never found it. Chris No-Neck rang John Haase and told him the busies haven't found it. He was fuming. The busies went round the next day, found the box, but he got off with it because the warrant had expired.

I did a few of them. I was still carrying on doing a bit of graft at the same time. Then one day I get a phone call telling me they [Haase and Bennett] are out. Then Chris No-Neck comes round to me and says, 'They're out.'

And I said, 'Fuck off!'

A couple of weeks later, John Haase comes round to see me. Shakes my hand . . . says, 'Thanks a lot.' Nice fella. No one got nicked. No one got hurt.

For Chris No-Neck, the massive logistics in organising the fake plants – buying huge amounts of weapons and shipping them all over the UK undercover – proved to be a nightmare. Plus there was the added hassle of dealing with unscrupulous gangsters who wanted to make a profit. On one occasion, two black gangsters from Toxteth – known as The Iceman and The Security Boss – were given money to buy guns to plant for

Haase. Instead, they bought a cache using Haase's money and then sold it for a profit. All-out war was prevented when The Iceman and The Security Boss got hold of a second cache and put it Haase's way.

But there were reliable gangsters including Tommy Gilday who provided many guns. It was No-Neck's job to liaise with Gilday, get him money and make sure that the guns were handed over to a runner and then planted without Gilday knowing what was going on. The cell structure ensured secrecy. No-Neck was obsessed with getting the detail right. Sometimes, No-Neck would observe gun handovers from afar with binoculars, disguised as a lycra-clad professional cyclist.

CHRIS NO-NECK: I helped John and Ben get out of prison because Ben was my best mate before John come out in '92. I had been grafting with Ben until then – but they fucked me off when John got out. They said they never wanted me in on their graft. Now, if I had been in on the graft in the first place, they and the Turks wouldn't have got nicked. The reason they got nicked was simple – because John had the same crew that worked with me and Ben for five years before John took over. Why didn't they break the pattern up? Where's the common sense in that? So it was their own fault – but I agreed to help because of Ben. He was the first proper friend to me. I would have died for him.

Doing the stashes was very stressful. It was severe pressure for three years, but I handled it. I went the gym a lot to box and started running – it was that training got me through it. That's why I ended up doing the London Marathon. I did quite a lot of gun plants. It was heavy. That's why I've gone grey. At the end of the day, what I did for them got them out of prison. And I did it because I cared about Ben – not for money, cos I got nothing out of it. I asked them for sixty quid [sixty thousand pounds] later but I got fuck all. But it didn't matter. Ben was an old mate.

They have never told me their innermost darkest secrets – so at first I had to make sure they weren't properly grassing. I'm not a gringo, I'm a grafter. Never crossed the line for anyone. Never grassed for nobody. But John said he was fucking the system. I said I'd do it for my bit. Not for John, but for Ben.

It was simple – I created crimes for Ben. Then I relayed the information, via a phone box, to a mobile phone [which Bennett had in prison]. That information was then passed on to his solicitor, who then talked to whoever it may be [Customs]. The people I know [the gun-planters] went through me. I done it. I knew what I got myself into.

The things were placed in certain places. I wouldn't pass any information over to John until I knew they [the gun-planters] were well out the way. They are clear, get off now. I got 200 brand-new shotguns from Southampton, in boxes. Two hundred quid a go, a mate of mine offers me. About eight grand in total. I said, 'Yeah, give us them.' Got a mate of mine to pick them up. Got a mate to go disguised, go to Birkenhead in a Rascal van, put them all in a van and parked them outside a McDonald's in Bootle. We left them there for two days to see if anyone was watching. Then I phoned John up and said, 'That's there now, blah, blah, blah.' I did another one where I got a fella's car full of guns and dispersed them wherever. In effect, we were creating crimes. No crimes done but it looked like they were. It was a good scam. Haase has got more audacity than Saddam Hussein. And he's got some front, hasn't he? Fucking kite [face] on him as well.

Tommy Gilday used to come to my house every day. Loved me, he did. I bought things [guns] off him. Not that I bought them, but Haase and Bennett would give me the money and I bought them. When I was doing the plants, Gilday couldn't fathom what was going on. He used to get me a few things but I'd plant them and that. So he didn't know about that stage. One exchange took place between Gilday and one of my lads. To make sure it went well, I was on a railway in Tuebrook with a pair of binoculars on my mountain bike, all the official gear, right. I looked a right plonker, but I did it. Proper Tour de Liverpool, it was. I goes up the embankment and I had my binoculars because I had set it up for the lad to go and pick those things up from Gilday. Gilday turned up in a red Audi. I focused in on him so I knew exactly what he was wearing, right, during the meet.

When I went to see him afterwards, I said, 'Everything sound?'

He said, 'Yeah, yeah. Can I use your toilet?'

Then I said, 'Didn't you have a loud, bright red T-shirt on, a stripy one, in your red Audi?'

That made him go right para'. He said 'How did you know that?'

'Because,' I said, 'I was watching you.'

And he said, 'I had someone watching your mate as well.'

Gilday was a hard-case but I clued him up that I wasn't stupid. He realised I was astute. Then he respected me for everything. In my house after that, he told me everything. Tommy's both sides of the fence. Classic saying was 'that's put to bed'.

John also put a fake contract out on Cook. One day, John and Ben asked me to go to the Crown Court. They had told Cook beforehand that there was a contract out on him but they was going to stop the contract. Now, if I showed my face in the Crown Court that day, that would give Cook the signal that they had called off the contract on him. That was the shit they were giving him. But it was a lie. A fabrication. Like a lot of things I done for him. I created crimes that never existed. Because people owed favours, whatever. That was the way their freedom was sorted.

One time, I went to visit Ben in Strangeways [to talk about organising more plants face to face]. I never used to visit Haase. He was always on the next table with his bird. You could see his grey hair and that. Ben said, 'I know these lads who have done a bit of graft.'

I said, 'Who?'

He said, 'The Security Boss and that. Sort it. Get on with them.'

That meant I had to buy guns off them for planting.

So I phoned up The Security Boss and The Iceman and said, 'You want to see me?' I went down there [to Toxteth] to meet them, and him and The Iceman are there. They wanted money. So I went and got some dough off lads I know and came back to them and said, 'There's our dough for our part of the bargain.'

Listen to this what happened afterwards: they get the graft in but they hold on to the guns, to sell the guns. They wanted to use my people on another second trip. But I thought, 'That's our dough they've used. They've got the fucking parcel there.' So I goes down the Southend [Toxteth] on me own. I asked them for the money but they wouldn't give me a penny. And these lads had a reputation, especially the one they call The Iceman. I said, 'Listen, this is nothing to do with John Haase or Ben. This is my name here. I can't walk away. This is my name, my mates, my dough.'

They said, 'You're gonna get the dough.'

But it escalated into a little underworld feud. I wasn't going to rest until there was closure on this – because I didn't want to lose face. I wanted either the guns or the money back. Later there was like a gangsters' meeting in Gilday's house. Curtis [Warren] was there. I said, 'You know your mate [The Security Boss], I'm going to cap [shoot] him.'

He said, 'You're not going to cap him.'

I said, 'I'm not scared of you, mate. I'm on me own.'

On your own is the best because at the end of the day, you live or die by your own bat. They have millions of pounds between them but I didn't give a fuck. I'm not a back-stabber. I said to Curtis, 'I don't fear you. You could have me scrubbed. But you wouldn't do it yourself.' Then I left. Then Gilday comes knocking on me door. He tells me that they like me, that I'm all right. That's because I'd stood up to them. I said, 'I don't give a fuck whether they like me or not. They don't know me. I shouldn't have to go down there for the money, Tommy. I shouldn't have to do that.'

Then Curtis phoned up, said, 'I'll get your dough back.'

But nothing happened, so I went in the jug to see Haase and

Bennett, right. Sat down with Ben. Then he started backtracking, saying that I shouldn't have done business with them. He goes, 'I wouldn't have done it with them.'

'What?' I said. 'It was you who put them on me. You introduced them to me! Now you're backtracking.'

I knew I wasn't getting any sense out of them, so I just decided to sort it myself. I goes back down the Southend, right. Had a meet with The Security Boss and The Iceman. Two of them in the car. I jump in the back of the car. They come in with caps on, plugging [intimidating] me. But I wasn't wobbling. They thought everyone else would, but I wouldn't. Stood me ground. Then I said, 'Listen, lads, I can't let this go. I'll die for this. And I will do because I am not having my mates calling me a fucking rat.' I got the money back in the end. And I thought, 'You'll never ever do this to me again.'

After that, I felt that Haase and Ben had used me. But I was loyal so I carried on. They never trusted me 100 per cent. If they had been thrown in [my friends], they would have hated me. I wasn't a very nice character at the time. I've got a photograph in ours that me bird gave to me. It was a photograph when I was doing the clubs. It was me with a pair of glasses on. I had a side part. I scared myself. It was fucking horrible. But I never let all that – the lifestyle – get inside. I've no doubt that the police knew [we were planting guns]. Sometimes, some of the lads I was using wobbled under the pressure. For instance, there was a nice lad. I asked him to do something for me [to plant guns]. But once it went off [and the guns were discovered] his arse went to blancmange. He got worried because of the exposure. There was a little bit of telly and newspapers. Every fortnight, the stories [about the gun plants] would be in the paper. [Because the police loved to talk it up.] So I went down to his house and asked, 'What's your problem?'

He goes, 'I never knew this would happen.'

I said, 'No one knows you. No one knows you done it. What have you got to worry about? The only person who knows whether you've done something is you. That's the way it is going to stay unless you do otherwise. You fuck it up and you are finished. Never give anyone your word if you are going to betray them.'

While he was inside, people started taking liberties with Haase, thinking that he was never getting out of jail. Some lad was banging a bird he was protective of. [The Supervisor] I warned the kid off. The lad is going, 'Yeah, yeah.'

I said, 'You'd better stop it now because you're not making a cunt out of me. He [Haase] is in there; you're out here.' I knew the lad. I said, 'Stay away or I'll fucking do you.' Not for him but because of me. . . . I said, 'I'll rip you apart now.' Then, Haase was my mate. You're not going to let anyone shit on your mate.

This woman started bending under the pressure. I've stopped this bird OD-ing three times, on the Charlie, in front of the kids. Her auld fella's sitting there at four o'clock in the morning. He rings me and says, 'She's popping pills, blah, blah, blah.'

I gets in me car, go down there. She's slobbering. I said to her dad, 'Just knock her out! Knock her out right now.'

He was wide-eyed. He said, 'What?'

I said, 'Knock her out! Give her a fucking hiding!' You don't do that [drugs] in front of the fucking kids. I told the auld fella and her. But they turned Turk on me. They didn't want to know.

At the end of the day, what I done for them [Haase and Bennett] meant they walked out of prison in '96 because of me. That was me, right. I never got paid for it. They wouldn't give me fuck all [for planting the guns]. The money used for it all was really the Turks' cash – from the missing gear. But they didn't give a fuck about the Turks. They used their money.

Ben wanted me to meet the Customs. He asked me to meet certain people. But I didn't want to meet them. No way was I going to sit down with Cook, that motherfucker. Then Merseyside Police wanted to see Haase and Ben but they were fucked off by the Cussies. They were obligated to protect them.

SULEYMAN ERGUN: I knew they were planting guns because Bennett told me on the exercise yard when we were on remand in Walton in about November 1993. Kaya and Manuk were also there. We were demanding the million pounds they owed us for the 50 kilos. But he said – and this was actually before he did it – that he was gonna plant Semtex, guns and heroin to get out and that they were gonna use it to get us out as well. It was a good plan, but I knew the bit about us was bullshit. He was only going to get Haase and himself free. He told me that Chris No-Neck was gonna be in charge, it would be in Liverpool and that they had already done one dummy run. There was also a bird called The Supervisor who was in charge. She was the one who came into prison all the time to see him. Haase was always on the phone to No-Neck for hours. On the dummy run, Haase said that they had told the Customs about some guns in a few boxes and that the police swooped on them straight away but there was nothing there. By that time, I had become wary of them. I didn't trust Haase so I just pretended to go along with them.

Ben later told me about planting the guns on the boat. It was supposed to have come from Venezuela, but it never actually left Liverpool docks. John Haase was the brains behind everything.

Because we kept asking about our million quid, they got themselves shipped out from Walton to Strangeways. John didn't get nicked in his cell with that vodka, Scotch, pot, the Es and the phone for nothing. That was a set-up so they could move.

Months later, a special visit was arranged for me to go to see Haase in Strangeways in the solicitor's visiting room. I got a special taxi cab from my prison in Liverpool. By then, they had done a good few plants. They had a message from a mate on the outside. It was from The Banker [Curtis Warren's boss] offering help. But I kindly refused – I didn't need it. Haase just said about the gun plants that 'we're gonna do more'. All the plants were a massive fucking hoax. Then they started blagging me that they were gonna help me with it. But they were just trying to play me. They had set the meeting up to persuade me to plead guilty. I later found out that they were doing that on behalf of Customs as a condition of the deal to get out. They said I was looking at 15 or 20 years. I told them that I didn't give a shit – I was gonna go not guilty. Then they told me that they planted 80 shotguns in one go.

They told me who planted them for No-Neck. It was a lad who was on remand with us but he got out. He was all right. He did a few plants for them.

No-Neck did everything. Years later, he told me that he did the planting – that's when I fell out with him. Then Eddie Croker told me about five kilos of Semtex they had planted. Eddie also told me that they were planting heroin. Haase had promised Eddie that he would get out as well. Eddie knew it was bull but he kept quiet because he was shit scared of Haase.

In Full Sutton, Ben was bouncing around the wings like a kid. I was getting packets and packets of trips. He was taking them and bouncing around the wings like a kid.

We knew John would fuck us over, so me and Kaya decided to do our own plants. But instead of guns, we were going to plant massive stashes of heroin in holes in a forest and then grass them up. Ten or twenty kilos at a time. But we called it off because we knew that because they had done the guns, it just wouldn't work. We didn't have a relationship with Customs.

Over a three-month period between February and May 1994, seven huge arms caches were 'discovered' by police. On 4 February, a stash included a Kalashnikov, an Uzi and seven Czech machine guns. One haul unearthed on Monday, 14 February 1994 – the biggest ever on Merseyside – included 80 brand-new Italian Armi Technique 12-bore shotguns worth £30,000 retail still in their boxes. The shotguns were the parcel bought by No-Neck with the help of James Turner and were stashed in a red Daihatsu in Bootle. They had been part of a consignment of 89 that had been stolen from a lorry while the driver was asleep near Oxford six days earlier. Another stash gave up ten sub-machine guns, five silencers, three magazines and two hundred and twenty-nine rounds of ammunition. The first find, in February, yielded thirteen automatic weapons. On 31 March, buried wartime rifles were dug up in Formby. Four discoveries in April turned up pistols and a machine gun in Fazakerley, AK-47s in West Derby, a Czech pistol in Stanley Park and, among other weapons, an elephant gun in Ellesmere Port. In June, six Uzis were recovered.

The finds were sold to the public as a major coup in the fight against organised crime. Confidently, investigating officers immediately ruled out a terrorist link and said the guns were definitely heading for the criminal underworld. It was just the success that Merseyside Police had desperately been looking for. The city was reeling from a recent spate of gangland shootings. The success of Curtis Warren's drug operation was causing friction between those favoured distributors who were growing rich on his business and those gangsters who were being kept out of the loop. The rivalry would eventually lead to the shooting of David Ungi on 1 May 1995, though there was no evidence to suggest that he was involved in drug dealing.

Big photo-calls were staged by the police in which serious-looking officers posed with the staggering array of weapons they had taken off the streets. The press conferences were reminiscent of the RUC displaying captured IRA weapons in Northern Ireland. It was unprecedented on the mainland. Experts, like celebrity cop John Stalker, were wheeled in to ominously explain how Merseyside had become a 'staging post for gun-runners', but that the good news was the police were getting on top of it. A police spokesman said, 'The information is proving spot on. We are trying to improve intelligence – this shows it is working.'

14

THE STRANGEWAYS GUN PLANT

Even though the gun-planting was going spectacularly well, instant freedom wasn't guaranteed, because of bureaucracy. Customs couldn't free a prisoner like John Haase just like that – no matter how valuable and cooperative he was apparently being with them. They were also playing hardball. Suspicious investigators were now asking for bodies to tag on to Haase's hoax crimes. They wanted faces and names, arrests and convictions, and were pushing their informant to the limit.

But Haase wasn't playing. He was desperate to find a way of getting out *immediately*. He then, quite incredibly, stumbled on the idea of getting a Royal Pardon. Only the home secretary has the right to exercise this little-used legal instrument in modern times, and it has been granted only five times since 1996. The Royal Prerogative is the only opportunity outside the appeal system, government guidelines and judges' rules by which criminals can be freed from prison. No official procedure exists to win a pardon – each applicant is assessed on a largely *ad hoc* case-by-case basis. In fact, Royal Pardons are so rare that most lawyers don't even know how to get one. Haase did, though, so he allegedly set about dreaming up a hoax crime that he could stunt up in prison while on remand that would give the impression that he was saving prison officers' lives – the key factor in getting a pardon. A tall order, but time was running out. The outlandish scheme begged the question – just how did a drug dealer know exactly which boxes to tick to get a Royal Pardon? The answer is that he was probably told by a corrupt mob lawyer he knew nicknamed The Devil. The Devil got his nickname because of his thoroughly disgraceful and underhand dealings with gangsters, combined with an unimaginable disregard for justice. The Devil had nothing to do with Haase's official representative, Tony Nelson, but he was acting as unofficial consigliore on the gun-planting scheme, offering tips on how to get maximum benefit and how to present it to Customs. His crookedness was so thoroughly ingrained that The Devil often scared his gangster clients.

Two-thirds of the way through Haase's gun-planting operation, in the winter of 1994, Haase began plotting the phoney plant that would get that elusive Royal Pardon in the bag. A gun needed to be smuggled into the recently privatised Strangeways prison and planted inside to make it look like a crazed inmate was planning a shoot-'em-up, IRA-style breakout. Or, failing that, other types of weapons could be used to make it look like a riot was in the offing in which officers would be attacked and taken hostage. Or, more conspiratorially, some kind of poison could be planted to make it look like rogue prisoners were planning to lace the guards' tea urn with cyanide. Haase tried all three. Such a ruse would not only fulfil the conditions of a Royal Pardon, but if the hoax crime could be pinned on a defenceless, disreputable prisoner, no matter how loosely, it would also provide his Customs handlers with a body. Successfully duping Customs into arresting and trying a suspect would make Haase's gun plants look at least half-real.

As usual, the methodical mastermind that was Haase did a dummy run to see how the practicalities would work. He decided to persuade a fellow prisoner to get caught with a bag of heroin in jail in much the same way as Billy the Hamster had agreed to get caught with a toolbox full of guns in his house. Possession of a bag of heroin was a lesser offence but one which would at least show how the prison authorities dealt with plants – whether they were as foolable as the police and Customs, and whether Haase would get the credit under this type of regime. Never one to miss an opportunity, Haase could also use this relatively harmless plant to 'throw in' (give Customs) a body to help his cause to boot. But the plan went disastrously wrong when the inmate 'double-bubbled' Haase with a heavy dose of prison cunning – he doubled-crossed him by keeping the heroin himself so there was nothing for the prison warders to find.

SULEYMAN ERGUN: I didn't hear about the Strangeways gun plant until after it happened. But it wasn't the first time Haase had tried to moody up plants in there – the gun was just the first one that worked. Firstly, he tried to get some heroin smuggled in so he could inform on a pre-arranged plant in a radio, which was owned by a con I knew who had agreed to take the rap. This Welsh fella agreed to get caught with Haase's heroin for £1,000 so Haase would get the credit. But in the end the geezer backed down and had John over as well. He took delivery of the radio with the gear in it, but just before Haase 'informed' on him, he took the heroin out of the radio. He removed the heroin just before the screws raided his cell. So the screws found fuck all. The Welsh fella got all the gear, fucked Haase off and Haase was made to feel foolish.

Even though the dummy run had failed, Haase was undeterred. He begged his pal The Enforcer, a loyal ally on the outside, to get a gun and some cyanide smuggled into Strangeways. He was also trying to persuade The Enforcer to pretend to be an informant, to butter up Customs Officer Paul Cook with false promises of intelligence. By this time, the gang had nicknamed Cook Eliot Ness, after the real-life Prohibition-era gang-buster made famous in the film *The Untouchables*. The movie remake was popular at the time. The name was partly to make fun of Cook's image as a big-time lawman, partly because he was seen as untouchable in the close-knit team he worked in – the gangsters were impressed by his power to do deals – and partly because he was untouchable under the witness-protection programme after Haase's bogus assassination threat.

———————

THE ENFORCER: Haase was arrested in July 1993. I still saw him and visited him at Manchester and Hull prison and elsewhere, having been passed [background-checked] by the police. On one occasion, he said that he needed to bring a gun up to Manchester. I asked why. He replied, 'Never mind. You want me to get out, don't you?' I asked for time to think. His girlfriend was with me but was getting refreshments when he asked this.

Some time later, I went for dinner with a lawyer Haase knew [The Devil] and he asked if I was doing that favour for John. I said, 'What favour?'

He said, 'He wants you to take a gun up to Manchester.'

I told him to fuck off.

Prior to this, I had been at court in Liverpool and this lawyer had said, 'Guess who is here? Eliot.'

It turned out that this was Paul Cook from Customs and Excise. The lawyer said he would take me to see him, but when I did I was to say to him, 'Don't be worrying, Mr Cook. Anything you want off me, John or any of his friends, you'll get much more than you've already got.' I do not remember whether guns were being found by then.

The next time I saw John after the gun incident, he asked me to get some cyanide, suggesting that [handwriting unclear] I had no involvement in guns or anything else.

———————

When The Enforcer refused to get Haase a gun or cyanide,

Haase ordered other members of his gang in Liverpool to put a gun on standby until a method was found to smuggle it into the prison. A serving officer in Merseyside Police has stated that the gun was taken in on 14 November 1994, but this is probably the date on which Haase launched his secret operation. The Scousers bought a sandwich toaster and hid the gun inside, resealing the box carefully and wrapping it in brown paper.

Then Haase allegedly turned to another remand prisoner, Kenny Price (not his real name), to help him. Kenny was on remand accused of threatening to shoot a policeman and was part of a gang in Moss Side run by a notorious underworld family. The family's godfather and a lower-ranking member were also in the prison at the same time. Through this family, Kenny had made contact with a bent auxiliary prison officer called Colin Baxter (not his real name), who worked in Strangeways. The naive officer, who had only worked at the prison for eight months and had very little training, agreed to smuggle in booze for Kenny. Then he started to smuggle in sealed parcels, not knowing that they contained drugs and mobile phones. For this, he was paid paltry sums, often between £50 and £80 a time, and promised the gift of a second-hand car as a Christmas bonus, which was coming up fast.

This was the system that Haase allegedly used to smuggle in a gun to Strangeways prison. In mid-December, Haase asked Kenny if he would get a sandwich toaster that had been bought for him by a friend in Liverpool smuggled inside. Kenny told his contact on the outside, the Moss Side gang-boss, to expect a parcel to be delivered to them by a Scouser at the Brown Bull pub. The Moss Side gang-boss received the sandwich toaster wrapped up in brown paper but did not open it. The toaster was then given to a younger member of the crew called The Kid, who later met the bent warder. The Kid gave the bent warder the parcel and told him that it was for Kenny. In the same drop, the warder was also given a mobile phone to smuggle in for another prisoner. Little did the Moss Side gang-boss and The Kid know that Haase had secretly arranged for a gun and nine bullets to be hidden inside the sandwich toaster.

MOSS SIDE GANG-BOSS: Basically how it started, Kenny wanted a bit of booze taking in. We dropped a few bottles off here, a few bottles there. The next thing is, a parcel has to be dropped off [to Kenny inside Strangeways]. It's supposed to be a Scouse kid that dropped it off for us. We were told that there was a sandwich toaster in it but it was sealed. Then it was delivered to The Kid. But obviously we don't want to be meeting anybody, seeing anything. There's only a sandwich toaster in it, so we said to The Kid, 'Don't worry about it; no problem.' So then it gets dropped off to the prison warder. When the prison warder picks it up, does all the routine drops, The Kid gives him his £50 or £80, whatever. We don't hear nothing about it, don't know nothing about what's gone on. Then all of a sudden there is a gun scare. The top and bottom of it is we did not know anything about any guns.

On Friday, 25 November 1994, Colin took the packages into Strangeways prison. He knocked off his shift at 3.45 p.m. but he told his supervisor that he was going to the gym. He was carrying a sports bag. He then diverted to A wing, using a cover story that he had to sort out some canteen queries. Fifteen minutes later, he was spotted by a colleague acting suspiciously near a toilet on A wing over the course of the next 45 minutes and reported to his superiors. When quizzed by his boss, Principal Officer David Halliwell, three days later on Monday, 28 November 1994, Baxter stuck to his story that he had gone to A wing to sort out canteen queries. Halliwell was sceptical but had to let him go for the time being. The heat was temporarily off.

Meanwhile, Kenny told Haase that the parcel had safely been smuggled into A wing. Haase arranged for the gun then to be removed from the sandwich toaster and stashed in a secret hiding place in the small prisoners' toilet recessed into the wall on the landing. Inside the WC, there was a stainless-steel cupboard which housed pipes under a washbasin. The gun was wrapped in a black bin bag and put in there. The gun was a Czech-made, .25-calibre self-loading pistol. The magazine inside it contained eight live rounds. In the bag, there was another bullet, but it did not fit the gun.

Haase phoned his handler Paul Cook and told him that a gun had been smuggled into Strangeways and was being stored somewhere on A wing. He explained how a prison officer had brought the weapon into the prison and gave details of his outside contact and a mobile telephone number for this contact (who was not convicted). To give the episode greater credence, Haase put some probably carefully calculated spin on it. He intimated that the gun had been smuggled in for a fellow remand prisoner called Thomas Bourke, who was on trial for the horrific murder of two MOT inspectors.

———

PHIL CONNELLY: Cook told me that he had received a telephone call from Haase in Strangeways at 1200 hours on Thursday, 1 December. (Cook made reference to the logs and I am aware that the logs of that telephone call exist today.) Cook then said that he passed this information to a security officer in Strangeways with whom he had become friendly whilst visiting Haase and Bennett. Cook then said he was aware that the security officer contacted Greater Manchester Police. Cook said that Haase called him and the conversation was quite short, in terms of, 'There's a bloke on A wing for the MOT murders. A prison officer has smuggled a gun in for him.' And Haase described the prison officer. Cook confirmed that he had not ever been interviewed by the police in relation to this.

———

Garage owner Thomas Bourke, who made a fortune selling cut-price exhausts and was now on remand in Strangeways, allegedly killed the two MOT inspectors because they were probing his business. The civil servants had banned Bourke from issuing MOTs at one of his four garages in south Manchester. Family men Simon Bruno, 28, and Alan Singleton, 56, were shot dead at one of Bourke's garages in Stockport on 22 November 1993. It was alleged that self-made Bourke donned a grotesque Halloween mask and black overalls before bursting into his own office and shooting the men at point-blank range with a shotgun. Bourke then allegedly went for a cup of tea with his strict-Catholic mother. But three of his employees made damning statements against him: one saying that he saw Bourke taking off the mask after the killing, another saying that he had witnessed Bourke making a confession and burning his overalls, and a third saying that he had seen Bourke lying in wait.

Whatever the truth, one year after the murder, Bourke was halfway through his trial at Manchester Crown Court and things seemed to be looking up for him – issues of mistaken identity were causing observers to predict that there was a better-than-evens chance of a not guilty. The trial had been plagued by problems and stopped twice already – once because two members of the jury knew the wife of one of the victims and once because of a serious problem with the police statements. Now there were issues over mistaken identity. But however optimistic Bourke was, unknown to him, while he was busy in court beating the case, back at Strangeways Haase was pinning the gun on him and saying that he had it smuggled into the prison in a desperate bid to break out. The rumour was that Bourke was a crazed gun freak who was going to take prison officers hostage if he was found guilty and use them to escape.

Three days after quizzing Colin, on Thursday, 1 December 1994, Principal Officer Halliwell found out the real reason why Colin had been hanging around A wing. Halliwell was tipped off about the gun by an 'outside source', either Customs directly or by Manchester Police, acting on behalf of Cook. Later, Halliwell went direct to a source inside the prison. He mistakenly took the informant's word that the gun was destined for Bourke, despite there being no evidence of a link. Meanwhile, the gun find (the first for many years) was about to explode all over the papers, making it likely that Haase and Bennett would be exposed as the informants. Information was being leaked by a fellow prisoner. Cons' suspicions fell on Haase, but he had to front it out so no one found out that he was the real bad guy. To make sure the authorities looked the other way, the pair filled out a questionnaire relating to the events for Greater Manchester Police, who were the investigating body.

DAVID HALLIWELL: I received information from an outside source that there was a gun within the prison. My source informed me that the gun was located on A wing inner, the same side as where Bourke was located. Bourke was the prisoner for whom the gun had been brought in. At the same time, my source informed me that the same officer had brought a mobile telephone into A wing for another prisoner. I was also informed that a prisoner called Kenny on A wing was also involved with the same officer, bringing alcohol and drugs into the prison for him, via a contact called Terry at the Brown Bull pub in Salford. The pub was located near Granada Studios.

A complete lock-down of the prison took place. Preparation to search A wing completely, using all available staff, including arms-and-explosives dogs, commenced at 1900 hours. The search was completed at 2130 hours and was negative. During the morning of Friday, 2 December 1994, a search was made of the visits area, reception, kitchen and the officers' mess, which was again negative. I then contacted my source within the prison, who stated that the gun was definitely on A wing inner. The reason that we had not found it was because Bourke, the category A prisoner concerned with the gun, had been seen messing about with steel panelling, both in his cell and in the toilet and shower areas.

The dogs indicated that there was something on A2 in the recess area, at the same time that work staff and Senior Officer

Platt, who had been searching the recess area A3, found a package. The police were called in and the package was later identified as a gun.

My source also informed me that Colin, whilst meeting friends of Kenny at the Brown Bull, had shown an interest in a cabriolet car driven by one of Kenny's friends. They had indicated that Colin could have it for Christmas. He said that they were not really giving Colin anything, as it was a shed and only worth a couple of grand.

The source also stated that Baxter had in the past been seen to take telephone cards valued at £4 each onto A wing and pass them to two prisoners, Colin and another man. At 0800 hours on Tuesday, 6 December 1994, Colin was told that he was being suspended.

The effect of the gun was simple: it robbed Thomas Bourke of a fair trial and his lawyers say that he was convicted of double murder on shaky evidence. The scandal exploded at a critical point near the end of his trial. On the day that Customs had sounded the gun alert, Bourke's QC had just finished summing up. Instead of carrying on the trial the next day and summing up himself, the judge postponed it until Monday, and suspected gun-planter Bourke was whisked back to Strangeways and placed in a segregation unit not knowing what was going on. When he returned to court on Monday, he'd gone from being an average con to Public Enemy Number One. The gun inside Strangeways was all over the papers and TV (the media strongly hinting at who the intended recipient may have been without actually naming him) and the jury had been at home all weekend soaking it up.

When the court case reopened on Monday, Manchester city centre was dramatically closed off and Bourke was protected by a fleet of armed police cars. When the jury retired, they were guarded by an armed policeman. The kitchen staff were not even allowed to serve the members of the jury with meals. The meals were brought up in a lift and taken in by the police. The police, court ushers and the jury had a floor of the hotel to themselves. Consciously or unconsciously, the jury were getting an impression of Bourke as a guilty, dangerous man, whether he was or he wasn't. Legally, this phenomenon is known as prejudice and is against the law. Not surprisingly, they found him guilty, after nine hours and fifty-two minutes of deliberation. He was lifed off immediately.

Mr Justice Sachs said, 'On a scale of human depravity, this must rate high. It was an utterly callous and brutal execution of decent public servants. You are a most dangerous man from whom society must be protected for a very long time.'

THOMAS BOURKE: On Thursday, 1 December 1994, upon completion of the summing up of my leading counsel, Mr Richard Ferguson QC, Judge Sachs announced that he would not sum up until the following Monday. He gave the jury leave to return home and come back on the following Monday morning. On the Thursday evening, when I got back to HMP Strangeways, I was placed in the segregation unit. On the following day, Friday, 2 December 1994, I found out the reason for this – that the prison was closed down because a firearm and ammunition had been found, and the police were searching in case there were further similar items. I spent the whole of the following weekend in the segregation unit, and when I was about to return to court on the following Monday, I was amazed to find that I had a massive armed-police escort, and that the roads into the town centre had been closed off to permit the escort to pass through to the court. I was at no time charged in relation to the firearms or ammunition.

Quite clearly, there were no reporting restrictions about the firearm and ammunition. The story was in the press and on national radio, to which the jury had had access during the previous weekend. Following Judge Sachs's summing up on Monday, 5 December 1994, the jury retired for the afternoon and went on throughout that night, the whole of the next day, Tuesday, and returned to their hotel that Tuesday evening. The deliberations of the jury continued until about midday on the next day, Wednesday, when they returned to present their verdict, which, by a majority of ten to two, found me guilty of both murders. This was on 7 December 1994.

Whilst the jury in my trial were in their hotel, they were under armed guard after the gun had been found at Strangeways prison. It is more than reasonable for me to presume that, in addition to the jurists having had access to the press, such activities at the hotel supported their 'knowledge' that the gun clearly related to me.

For Haase, there was only one small problem: to the underworld, stitching up Thomas Bourke would be considered evidence that John Haase was a grass. The revelation would ruin the 'no bodies' image of his gun-planting scheme, destroy his street credibility and possibly put his life in danger. Bourke was a popular inmate in the prison system, known as the Milky Bar Kid because his hair and glasses gave him a resemblance to the famous chocolate-ad icon. If Haase's dark secret got out, there could be hell to pay. Haase immediately began spinning against the rumours, discrediting Bourke's sisters, who were fighting for justice for him, as 'madwomen'. Instead of keeping schtum, Haase bragged about the plant, claiming that the Bourke connection was not deliberate but an unfortunate mistake. Haase sneeringly told this version of events to eccentric Manc godfather Domenyk Noonan, who wasn't having any of it.

DOMENYK NOONAN (OR DOMENYK LATTLAY-FOTTFOY): I was serving a 14-year prison sentence at HMP Whitemoor. During my stay, I met John Haase, whom I had met in HMP Leeds and HMP Full Sutton. During my stay in HMP Leeds, John and myself became good friends. We would exercise daily while being held in the segregation unit.

During the mid-'90s, I learned that a gun was found in HMP

Manchester and the rumour [through the prison grapevine] was that John Haase was involved. Later, I encountered John Haase at HMP Whitemoor and asked him if he was involved in it. He stated clearly to me that he had arranged for the gun to be brought in at HMP Manchester via a prison officer and that he hid it behind wall panels in the toilets on A wing. I asked if the prison officer was aware the gun was inside the sandwich toaster and he replied, 'If he had, do you think he would have brought it in?' and then laughed.

He went on to say that a lad [Thomas Bourke, known as the Milky Bar Kid] was accused of getting it in. He said everything went 'pear-shaped', which meant not according to plan. He told me that he informed Customs it was inside the prison. He said that he had mentioned the lad's name as being involved. He explained that because they never caught the lad with the gun, they could never charge him with it, because there was no proof. My impression was he had set someone up to get a deal for a lesser sentence.

He told me that he had done deals with the police and Customs on recovering guns and drugs and no one ever got arrested. He said it was a well-planned operation which worked fairly good to get a pardon. He more or less said he 'fucked the system', but it is unfortunate that the lad's [. . .] trial was wrecked.

Following Thomas Bourke's conviction, there was a flurry of activity at Strangeways. Colin was suspended from duty on 6 December, the day before Bourke was convicted. He told the local paper, 'I did not take a gun into prison. I've been framed.' Two weeks later, he quit the job after he confessed to not declaring minor convictions when he applied for the job. He later pleaded guilty at Manchester Magistrates' Court to bringing in the sandwich toaster without knowing there was a gun inside, as well as bringing in a mobile phone and a bottle of Bacardi.

But his lawyer rapped the prison for putting their youngest officer – then just 21 – on the wing housing the most dangerous inmates, with little training. The lawyer said that

Colin had come under the influence of hardened criminals. 'This kid was just chicken fodder.'

Kenny had suddenly been shipped out of the prison, fuelling speculation among cons that he was somehow linked to the gun. Initially, the rumours suggested that Kenny had unknowingly helped to smuggle the gun into the prison. Then the story changed to Kenny somehow helping Haase to stage the plant and getting credit for helping Haase to inform on the guilty conspirators. This later rumour seemed to hold more water, especially after it emerged that Kenny was not in any trouble and in fact had started to receive better treatment – mysterious rewards often being granted to informers for helping the authorities. For instance, his trial for wounding and attempted murder was stopped after an audience was arranged with the trial judge. Rumours abounded that Haase and Bennett had given evidence at this secret meeting. Had Haase and Bennett told the judge how Kenny had helped foil the gun plot? Had Kenny played a key role in telling the authorities about the Strangeways gun and was now getting payback?

This scenario seemed to be confirmed in a report in the *Manchester Evening News* that said an unnamed inmate had turned informer and was hoping for a reduced sentence at a trial he was facing at Manchester Crown Court. It all pointed to Kenny.

Astonishingly, his trial was then moved to Carlisle, some say giving him a better chance of getting off. He did, and soon Kenny was back on the street. Bourke's sister Jo Holt, who was gathering evidence that her brother was turned over, confronted Kenny at his home.

———————————

JO HOLT: I asked [Kenny] about the gun. He was extremely nervous and said he did not know anything about the gun, in fact he had been moved out of Strangeways straight away, but he said he would try to help me and he would try to find out as much as he possibly could. About a week later, I went back to see him at his home. Kenny introduced me to the Moss Side gang-boss. They both blamed the gang-boss's cousin for the gun being smuggled into Strangeways prison. Eventually, I spoke with the cousin, who denied being responsible, and I believed him. Later, I was at home when, at about 8.10 p.m., the phone rang. It was the Moss Side gang-boss. The man told me that his good name was being threatened and that it was going to be in the press about the gun in Strangeways prison and his involvement. He told me that if his name appeared in the papers, then I would see what his family would do. I took this to be a threat and told him so. He put the receiver down and I dialled 1471 and phoned him back. He answered my call. I told him I would not be threatened and he said he felt threatened by having his name in the newspapers. He told me I would see what his family would do and he hung up.

As word spread around the underworld, even hardened gangsters were appalled at Haase's stitch-up. In his book written with James Morton, London kingpin Mad Frankie Fraser reveals how he branded Haase a grass and refused to go near the lag-mate with whom he'd done time:

> He [Haase] rang me up. I said, 'No. On your bike.'
>
> He said, 'You calling me a grass?'
>
> I said, 'Yes, I am.' It broke my heart because I liked him so much. 'I'm not having nothing to do with you.'
>
> While Haase was on remand for 18 months, a gun was found in the top-security wing and there was a suggestion in the press that it had been brought in for a man who'd done a couple of tax inspectors in Stockport. That wasn't the case. Anyway, not too long ago, a London brief got in touch with me to say would I get hold of Johnny Haase and get him to come clean and say he'd been in collusion with the law over bringing it into the nick. I said I wouldn't even think of talking to him. First, it would be a waste of time, and second, the next thing you'd find yourself up on a conspiracy to pervert, with a man like that.

15

THE TAX MEN

Haase and Bennett's power to defraud a Royal Pardon from the system was down to one asset – money. This was the stuff which kept the whole show on the road – buying guns, planting them, wages for the lads, bribes. Without the loot, the whole charade would have come to nothing. So where exactly was the money coming from?

On top of the £200,000 each in cash the pair had lying around, they had the 50 kilos of heroin which had been supplied by the Turks before the bust. Because of the bust, the £1 million sale price for the 50 kilos due to the Turks had not been met. The 50 kilos was worth various amounts depending on how it was sold. If they got rid of it quickly by the kilo, they could easily get £25,000 a kilo. That meant a total of £1.25 million. That was all theirs. Haase and Bennett could bump the Turks for the £1 million cost by blagging them that they were spending it on gun plants and bribes that would benefit them.

If Haase and Bennett had the time to sell it in smaller amounts, say ounces, then that would generate millions and millions. To accomplish this plan, the gang would need the luxury of time – which they had. Sold in street wraps, Customs estimated that the parcel would generate up to £18 million. It was unlikely that Haase would do it that way, but feasible.

Either way, Haase's gang were awash with cash. And word began to spread. Suddenly, other gangsters decided that, with the main men in prison, they were free to try to steal the cash or the 50 kilos from Haase's henchmen, who were outside. After all, who were they going to tell – the police? The war chest was quickly becoming as much of a scary liability as an asset for Haase's men who were put in charge of hiding it. The drugs they possessed brought with them the risk of 'have-offs' and 'tie-ups' – being robbed by other gangs. Liverpool's second generation of drug dealers had spawned a ruthless new phenomenon – specialist gangs of kidnappers and torturers who preyed on drug dealers, 'taxing' them of their super-profits. They often burst into rooms where deals were going down or drugs were stored, masked and armed with assault rifles, to relieve dealers of their 'tackle' and tens of thousands of pounds in cash.

There were now two massive but secret operations bubbling under the surface of Liverpool's underworld and waiting to explode: the gun-planting and the hunt for Haase's heroin. The two opposing forces were on a collision course that would only lead to disaster. None of it would ever have happened if Customs had not allowed the first 50 kilos to slip through the net. So just how did it happen?

In mid-July 1993, before the big arrests, Haase's men had taken possession of the 50 kilos. This originated as follows:

1. 17 May–2 June 1993: 110 (+1) kilos of heroin are prepared in Turkey. Ten kilos are given to Turkish couriers in France as payment for transport from Turkey to Paris. The 100-kilo load is switched from the Turks to two of Haase's men in Paris. The Scousers are now responsible for taking it back to the UK.

2. 8–13 July: 100 kilos of heroin arrive in the UK on the Calais–Dover ferry. They are stored in Purchase Street, Camden Town, London.

3. 14 July: Turkish Connection meets Bennett in Upper Street, Islington, to discuss payment for 100 kilos, which are now winging their way to Liverpool.

4. 16 July: heroin arrives in Liverpool. Turks meet Scousers in the Black Horse pub in Prescot Road, Liverpool. At this point, 17 kilos are shaved off the load, possibly without Haase's knowledge. This was done by either Neil Garrett, Chris No-Neck or a man called John, who, with his brother, was a protection racketeer. Some sources say it was never seen again and others say the 17 kilos possibly came back into Haase's possession at a later date and were put into his war chest.

5. 17–20 July: the remaining 83 kilos are split into two parcels for cutting and distribution. The larger, 50-kilo parcel is given to Croker. The remaining 33 kilos are given to Garrett. The 33 kilos are transported in a blue Honda Previa for dilution and splitting into dealable amounts. This is the heroin that will make up the bulk of the war chest.

6. 26 July: Croker arrested and 50 kilos seized.

Customs officers tracked the movements of the heroin on 21 July 1993 – the day on which they lost the second load. The surveillance log reads:

> 21 July: Gloves and bags to cut up heroin collected from Cherry Lane, Liverpool. Heroin picked up by Eddie Croker from Chaser pub, Liverpool. Heroin taken to Dane Street in heavy canvas bag to be cut. Garrett arrives at Croker's house. Both seen travelling in Croker's blue Previa via various places, including Asda supermarket, then to [the safehouse] at Dane Street. Croker and Garrett both go into [the house at] Dane Street. Drew seen to emerge. Garrett is wearing surgical gloves. So is Croker. Croker seen to put a large green holdall into the Previa and another white man called Dave puts a black one in it. Previa leaves and is seen later parked outside Croker's parents' house with holdall inside. At 1650, Croker gets out of car but the mystery white man Dave remains inside with the heroin. It is then driven off to a secret stash which had been checked out earlier. [One of the bags possibly contained the

> mystery 17 kilos and the other contained the 33 kilos
> Croker later admitted to.]

Later, when the heroin-stuffed blue Previa was moved, surveillance officers lost the car as it turned right at a busy junction. This split-second mistake on a shabby, anonymous terraced street in backwater Liverpool allowed the heroin to fall back into Haase's hands – and he used it to create one of the biggest judicial scandals in recent legal history.

John Haase would later accuse Chris No-Neck of shaving off 17 kilos of his consignment. No-Neck blamed it on Neil Garrett, denouncing him as a grass. Suspicions were raised after Neil was cleared of all charges, even though he featured heavily in Customs' evidence – one time wearing compromising surgical gloves. Rumours abounded that he had secretly given evidence. Everyone was blaming each other because, at the end of the day, it was The Vulcan's gear they had 'shadied'.

CHRIS NO-NECK: I've never ever touched anything that didn't belong to me. Respect. I didn't have a clue even where it [the heroin] was. They had me digging. I wish I had stolen it now because of what they did for me. But I had integrity. I had respect.

Neil Garrett was a grass. How can a man come out of a house with rubber gloves on, a bag of gear and not get nicked? Months later, he's driving around in a brand new Jag and a blue metallic Mercedes. Do I need to say anything more? That's where the missing gear went.

I knew Garrett was a grass. He blew Haase up. I know this because get this: one day I was driving down Queen's Drive with Haase just after he got out of prison. Neil Garrett pulls up, says to Haase, 'You want to see me?' Meaning, 'Do you think I'm a grass?'

Haase goes, 'No.'

That's when I knew that the Customs had said to Haase, 'You

have got to leave Garrett alone because he is part of our operations.' That's when I fucking knew.

I'd like to meet The Vulcan and say to him, 'Look into my eyes. I didn't take your gear. You can't take that away from me.' He might scrub me. But there's nothing in my closet but my clobber. Haase and Ben are making me out to be a patsy. They are going to blame the most innocent person out of it all. They know I don't walk around with anyone. I may get plugged but I'm not going to walk away. My position is I've been on my own for a long time.

SULEYMAN ERGUN: I asked John Haase on remand where the 17 kilos was and the other 33 kilos. He just said, 'Ask Garrett where it is.' Neil Garrett took the 17 and cut it to pieces. Neil Garrett benefited. But the whole 50 ki is down to Haase and Ben. When The Vulcan gets out of prison, he will put it down to them. He will want revenge. That will, I'm afraid, be the end of the story.

It didn't matter who had the heroin or money. A notorious gang of tax men known as The Hyenas, because they attacked drug dealers like a pack of animals, laughing hysterically while they tortured them, were determined to track it down and steal it. The leader of the tax-man gang was the scarily violent George Bromley. Another was called Flannagan and another possibly Tommy. The gang would never have taken liberties while Haase was on the outside – but it was a different story when he was facing a long stretch.

The tax men targeted three of Haase's men who they thought had the money: Chris No-Neck, Neil Garrett and Haase's money-washer The Estate Agent. The Estate Agent had invested much of Haase's drug profits in property. The tax men were convinced that Haase trusted him enough to give him the money. The tax men also zeroed in on Haase's and Bennett's girlfriends and families.

Their plan was simple: torture the targets until they gave up the money or drugs and threaten to kidnap Bennett's baby child. The tax men broke into Neil Garrett's house and pressed his back with a red-hot electric iron while his wife and children looked on. They tried to kidnap No-Neck at his door posing as policemen.

CHRIS NO-NECK: It was hard, lad. A fucking nightmare. People tried to wrap me up. Three fellas came to me. They thought I had Haase and Ben's money. I knew who they were when they came, right. Me door was ajar. They come in: 'CID, blah, blah, blah.' They tried to get me in the living room. Trying to knock me out. They had a telly aerial round me neck trying to stun me and knock me out. I thought, 'The only way to get out of this is to get out towards that hallway.' So what they done was try to put a trap over me head. They had a car over the road with a boot open, right. They were gonna try and put me in it. Three heavy lads, right. So I let them think I was going with them, right. So when I comes out me front door, there's this brick wall, right. Got two of them in a headlock and back-flipped. Done all me ribs in. Was in ossie [hospital] for six days. I screamed like fuck and they shit themselves. That attracted the neighbours. They stunk of ale. Fucking cowards. Bit of Dutch courage to come and take me on.

I went in to see Ben, had a little shiner, few marks and that. You know what: Haase and Ben didn't even want to deal with it. One of those that did it went to prison but he's out now. I'll walk into him one day, right. Eight o'clock in the morning. When they've just woken up and that, right.

Chris No-Neck planned the gun-planting operation down to the last detail so as not to leave any clues. The priority was to find criminals to stash the guns who wouldn't talk about it to anyone – so No-Neck only hired trusted, long-standing partners-in-crime. However, even within the inner circle, betrayal was never far away, criminals being criminals. One of the main threats to No-Neck came from the money-launderer The Estate Agent. The Estate Agent had been appointed by Haase and Bennett to invest their heroin profits in property before their arrest. He also owned and managed property bought with drugs money for Chris No-Neck.

Following Haase and Bennett's arrest, The Estate Agent planned to rip Haase, Bennett and No-Neck off by selling all of their property and keeping the money. According to underworld sources, he knew that No-Neck was the only one who stood in his way, because he was not in prison, so he plotted to have No-Neck killed. The alleged hit-man was called John.

The Estate Agent tried to get No-Neck to employ John as a gun-planter to give the hit-man an opportunity to get close to his target.

CHRIS NO-NECK: When I took that job on [of gun-planting], I was hiring and firing [the criminals who did the plants] so I knew the history of everyone we used – where they come from. The rule was, 'If I don't know you, tara!'

But The Estate Agent tried to set me up. The Estate Agent tried to get me ironed [assassinated]. I didn't trust him but he had some of Haase's dough [tied up in property]. He introduced me to a fella called John with a view to helping us, getting the guns and that. This John was a super-duper hard-case. A fucking man-eater. Fucking horrible, he was. I met this John in Stanley Park car park with The Estate Agent. The Estate Agent starts going on about all these things and all that [secret things which he should not have discussed in front of John]. I said to The Estate Agent immediately, 'No disrespect, mate. I know who you are and where you're coming from. But I don't know you [John]. And I don't talk shop out of school.' So I turned to John, shook his hand and said, 'Me and you are finished.'

Now, Ben couldn't see that The Estate Agent was not to be

trusted. He wanted to work with The Estate Agent. So I had to put my feeling aside and get on with it. But all's that The Estate Agent wanted to do was pick my brains. He knew that we as a firm were already up there [a top criminal organisation] so he wanted our secrets. He was trying to get all the info off me. He was saying, 'Did you do that?'

I said, 'I'm telling you fuck all, mate. Between you and me, I don't like you. You've never done a fucking tap. You have never robbed a handbag. And you expect me to tell you everything I know? You can fuck off!'

So eventually I goes up to see Ben [in prison], right. Ben goes, 'You're out of order. You should have told John this and that.'

I said, 'I'm your mate, not his. You want to play with him, you see how far you get.'

In the end, I was right. He stole all of my property [and according to underworld sources he fled to the US with £1 million of Haase and Bennett's money as well]. The bottom line was that I had to be on my guard all the time during the gun-planting. I had to meet fellas all the time and weigh them up like a shrink, mate. I had to analyse fellas. I was meeting people and I was thinking all the time whether I could trust them. I would let them talk to me and I could decipher whether that fella was kosher or a complete waste of time. All that crap with The Estate Agent and the tax men was going on while we were doing the planting.

JOHN HAASE: Just after we got nicked, three fellas came to No-Neck for tax purposes. Never got him, though. Fought for his life. He had a right fight, didn't he? Ended up in hospital. He ended up with broken ribs. It was in the *Echo* and everything. One of the tax men is dead now, little shit.

Haase referred to the tax men's attacks in his taped plea-bargaining session with Bennett, Paul Cook and Tony

Nelson. They talk about an attack on a victim in their gang, possibly Neil Garrett or The Estate Agent. At one point, Haase is even blamed for being behind the attacks to get revenge on Neil Garrett and The Estate Agent for dipping into his war chest.

JH [to TN]: News on anything? Any of our friends? The victim or anything?

PB: [The victim is in hospital] with iron marks all over him.

TN [defending Haase and Bennett to Cook]: Nothing to do with us . . . nothing at all to do with us . . .

PB: They went round his house and went for his kids.

JH: They're gonna say I asked him [the tax men to do it].

TN: No.

JH: Are they the same people who threatened quite a lot of people? [To Bennett] You?

PB: My kids . . . that's what they said . . .

TN: That's disturbing . . .

PB: That's what the victim said. He's in hospital . . .

PC: With burn marks . . .?

JH: Someone said they'd seen him in the hospital and he's got iron marks all up his back, over his private parts.

PC: When the victim came to see you, he said you did it. [You were behind the attacks.]

JH: No!

PB: No! Anything else?

PC or TN: Kidnapping on Saturday night. The victim's flat's burnt . . .

JH: It may transpire that the victim's wife knew more. They got to the victim's wife. They never got the target himself.

PB: They wanted money and stuff. The men said, 'We know you've got money in your purse. You lying fuckers!'

217

> PB: One of our girlfriends, at three o'clock in the morning, she gets a phone call – half an hour before the attack happened – get out the house!
>
> JH: One person had been branded [with a red-hot iron], and another basically been threatened.
>
> PC: Was it [the threat] genuine?
>
> JH: Don't know.
>
> PB: We haven't seen the burn marks . . .
>
> PB: All the time he's in hospital, he's got bruises, cuts, this, that and the other, hands all bruised, burns all over. The attackers were smoking cigars, everything.
>
> JH: They are trying to do me.

The tax men never managed to get the money. But sources suggest that Haase later got revenge on most of the gang – either directly or by proxy. Bromley was assassinated, possibly on the orders of Curtis Warren's boss, The Banker, over a feud with his son. Ironically, Paul Bennett would draw cold comfort from this – the triggerman employed to do the job was his own white-supremacist assassin, linked to six killings. Flannagan was later attacked by Haase and No-Neck. Haase allegedly cut his throat. Another villain called Tommy, who had plotted to kidnap No-Neck's wife in a bid to get drug money, possibly the war-chest cash, was shot four times in the arm and now suffers complete loss of feeling there.

16

THE TRIAL AND
THE REPORT

On 10 February 1995, as one of the conditions of the secret deal with Customs, John Haase and Paul Bennett pleaded guilty at Liverpool Crown Court to conspiracy to supply heroin between 17 December 1992 and 28 July 1993. It was a good decision. Customs had agreed that a second, more serious charge of importing would not be brought against them as their part of the bargain. Pleading guilty was common sense, as the importation evidence against them was overwhelming. It resulted from journeys taken by Haase's gang to Paris to collect heroin from the Turks for importation back to the UK. There was never a chance in hell of beating the case – hence the motivation to do a deal. Pleading guilty also meant they did not have to stand trial, preventing close scrutiny of their shady bargains.

Smuggling supremo Yilmaz Kaya was in the same boat, up the same treacherous creek, but unfortunately he did not have the Customs and Excise-issue paddle that had been so conveniently supplied to Haase and Bennett. He had no way of navigating the tide of negative evidence against him. One Customs surveillance officer joked that his face was more photographed (by them) than Princess Di's and he had more false passports than Lord Lucan. To boot, he had fallen for Haase and Bennett's blag that they would use some of the gun-planting credit to help him. That was his only hope and it didn't come true. In desperation, and after taking sly advice from Haase to do so, Kaya pleaded guilty to being involved in a conspiracy to import heroin into the UK in the hope of getting a reduced sentence. For rolling over, for saving the taxpayer the cost of an expensive trial, Kaya was rewarded – a second charge of distributing in the UK was not brought. In the spirit of cooperation, he admitted sending between £500,000 and £600,000 of drug profits back to the main men in Turkey, giving the Crown the future opportunity to seize assets.

Following the lead from these main players, all of the lower-ranking members pleaded guilty before the case went to trial. Eddie Croker blew everyone up in a big statement in a bid to get a lesser sentence, again under pressure from Haase, as well as secretly being assured by Haase and Bennett that they were going to help him get out of prison. He pleaded guilty to possession with intent to supply.

Bagman Mehmet Ansen, The Colonel, tried to squirm out of the evidence, changing his story so many times that it was embarrassing. At the end of the day, he was hung by his diary, which listed every money drop with The Vulcan's name next to it. Oh, dear! On one page, there was even a drug-related diagram of a chemical molecule, so suspicious it raised the alarm during a random search by a German Customs officer. Initially, the bumbling Ansen denied any knowledge of carrying money out of the country. Then he said that he had taken money out of the country only once, for a man whom he could not identify, that he had met only once, in a London restaurant. He said the money was the proceeds of gambling. In his third interview, Ansen was more forthcoming. He gave an account of his dealings with Yilmaz Kaya. In interviews four and five, he went into more detail, including the role played by The Vulcan and the occasions that he had met this man in

Europe. He also agreed that references in his diary to 'Mr V' were references to The Vulcan. With no hope, Ansen pleaded guilty to three offences of transferring proceeds of drug trafficking out of the country on 29 November 1992, 17 February 1993 and 24 March 1993.

Distributor Bulent Onay was collared with a wardrobe full of flashy Turkish clothes – and 36 kilos of heroin. He was the gang member arrested very early on in December 1992. He had had to wait on remand to go on trial with the rest of the gang. Even so, evidence-wise it was end of story. He pleaded guilty to two offences of transferring the proceeds of drug trafficking and to one offence of possession of the heroin with intent to supply.

Bagman Manuk Ocecki pleaded guilty to one sample offence of removing the cash proceeds of drug trafficking from the jurisdiction on 8 July 1992.

Safehouse supplier Mark Drew admitted he had been asked by pal Neil Garrett to find premises for an illegal purpose, but thought it wise not to ask questions. He later smelt an odour that he associated with drugs, though he himself never saw them. He was supposed to be paid £200.

But underboss Suleyman Ergun was having none of it. He was a fighter. 'Me? Go guilty? Fack off.' That was his standard reply in his sharp Cockney accent to anyone who tried to persuade him to do otherwise – including Haase, Bennett and his own lawyer. As far as he was concerned, he was a prisoner of war – the war on drugs. End of story. It was his duty not to cooperate with the enemy, no matter how hopeless his position. Ergun was facing two charges: one for importing and one for distribution.

In his defence statements, Ergun limply tried to pass himself off as a chauffeur, saying that he was simply Kaya's driver who had been paid between £100 and £200 each time he did a trip to Liverpool or given free, all-expenses holidays if he went abroad with his boss. Little did he know that Croker had already admitted handing him between £500,000 and £2.5 million inside black bin bags at various meetings in Liverpool.

Ergun's statements were littered with 'no comment' and 'no reply', but on the odd occasion he tried to mount a defence, his explanations were rubbish. He said that he took the job with Kaya after the textiles business, Dressmodel, that he was a director of closed down.

His trial kicked off in the summer of 1995, nearly two years after the arrests. The prosecution went to town on him. Reams of photos and compromising logs littered the trial. He was described as a major figure in the conspiracy – the link man between the Turks and the Liverpool connection. In the conspiracy to supply, it looked bad because of his strong and frequent links by mobile phone and in the 23 drug-related visits he made to Liverpool in the first six months of 1993.

The court was told, 'When Ergun was arrested, his home was searched and documents which were found showed that he owned a Vodaphone which had the number 0836730636. Analysis shows that the user of the phone made extensive use of certain telephone facilities which help preserve the anonymity of the callers, such as pager and message-deposit facilities. The Crown allege that is how Ergun got in touch with the Liverpool connection. He also used the paging system. Ergun had the sophistication to use these devices and was the vital link man between the Turkish and Liverpool connections. He was a Turk who, by reason of his upbringing in the UK, was a fluent English speaker able to act as an interpreter or translator.'

———

SULEYMAN ERGUN: Everyone else – Haase, Bennett, Kaya, Croker – pleaded guilty, so they never went to trial. I pleaded not guilty because I'm not a grass and the grasses that were Haase and Bennett weren't gonna trick me into pleading guilty. I kept my mouth shut – didn't make no statements, nothing. My trial lasted ten days. The verdict was guilty on both charges. I got 14 years for conspiracy to supply and 14 years for conspiracy to import, to run concurrent – that means at the same time. So I would have to serve 14 years in nick.

Then I got nine months for not complying with an asset-confiscation order.

Haase and Bennett had their mitigation separate, behind closed doors, both of them. Secretive – that meant they were doing a deal. That set the alarm bells ringing but I didn't say anything. Keep your enemies close. It wasn't concrete but there was enough suspicion.

After the guilty pleas had been entered and Suleyman's trial finished with a conviction, Judge David Lynch retired for reports and mitigation before sentencing. This was the crucial moment at which all of the credit that Haase and Bennett had built up with the gun plants would come into play. Customs officers decided to write a secret report to the judge detailing all of the 'help' given to them by Haase and Bennett in the hope that he would show leniency in his sentencing. The secret report was written by Haase's handler Paul Cook, signed off by his boss Assistant Chief Investigator Phil Connelly, and presented to the judge in private chambers.

The bombshell report was leaked well after the trial, after Scottish hard-man Ian McAteer was convicted of shooting a man. He accused Paul Bennett of grassing him up and applied for all secret-informant reports related to him to be released.

The report reveals just how much the authorities had fallen for Haase and Bennett's con, listing all of the phoney arms seizures, including the Strangeways gun, as a success and praising the gangsters. Where the word GAP appears in the following extracts, sensitive information and names have been scrubbed out by the prison authorities prior to release:

> With regard to these defendants in September 1993 they indicated, through their solicitor Mr Tony Nelson, that they wished to cooperate with the prosecution.
>
> This cooperation was to be in the form of a guilty plea, to conspiracy to supply heroin and the giving of information relating to the criminal fraternity.

In relation to the guilty plea the prosecution case against these defendants was, and still is, that they were one of the initial recipients of heroin once it was imported into the UK. The prosecution would suggest that the evidence in this case would have resulted in a conviction but accept it is evidence of association which could justify a lengthy and expensive trial. The defendants pleaded guilty to the offence on 10 February 1995 at Liverpool Crown Court. It must be said that a guilty plea would have been offered at a much earlier stage; due to the quantity and quality of the information supplied by these defendants a plea was delayed in order for such information to continue unabated. As from October 1993, the defendants commenced the flow of information to the prosecution. The information given in my opinion falls into several categories.

A. Information which produced an instant positive result and led to the authorities making an arrest, recovering stolen property, seizing drugs or firearms and ammunition. The latter being the most significant from their information. Over 150 illegal firearms were recovered and included Kalashnikov assault weapons, Armalite rifles, Thompson machine guns, Bren guns, Uzi sub-machine guns and over 1,500 rounds of ammunition. GAP An awesome array of lethal weapons, illustrating the demand for firearms amongst the criminal element of society. A major contribution in light of the recent shootings in Liverpool. They also gave information which resulted in the recovery of two handguns (one loaded), a meat cleaver and a claw hammer from a motor vehicle parked GAP the information warned of the developing war between the owners of that establishment and GAP.

This was a mistake. The establishment was a bar called Cheers. The rights to buy and use it were used as pretext for a battle between the Ungi family and Curtis Warren's right-hand man

224

Johnny Phillips, which resulted in the death of businessman David Ungi. Haase's men had planted guns near the pub purely by accident – but Customs gave him the credit for cooling the war.

> Other significant results were the seizure of:
> 1. 7,534 Ecstasy (MDMA) tabs and 5 kilograms of amphetamine;
> 2. 58 litres of methadone. The recovery of 100 LSD tabs. The locating of a skunk factory (where cannabis resin is made into concentrated cannabis oil). 200 cannabis plants and a machine gun GAP A seizure of heroin and a seizure of cocaine, the recovery of £20,000 worth of antiques and an OBE medal.

This batch included the heroin which Darcy helped to plant.

> B. Information which prevented serious offences from being committed. The prevention of a possible hostage situation. A prisoner convicted of two murders was planning to escape by use of a gun. A loaded handgun was recovered and the prison officer responsible for smuggling the weapon into the prison was identified.

This outrageous passage referred to the Strangeways gun plant, unfairly referring to Thomas Bourke, who was never convicted of getting the Czech-made pistol onto the wings. However, this passage, littered with false assumptions, was the key information that would eventually win Haase and Bennett a Royal Pardon. The salient features of 'prevention of a possible hostage situation' and 'planning to escape by use of a gun' were all that was needed.

> C. Information which led to major operations being instigated. Operation 'FLEET' was commenced by Customs and Excise based upon their detailed information. It involves the major import of Class A

drugs and the method of transportation being used to avoid discovery. A large-scale operation has been mounted by the South East Regional Crime Squad to investigate the supply of forged Bank of England notes and illegal firearms, based on their information.

D. Information which has assisted major operations already in existence. They assisted Manchester Customs and Excise in identifying four members of an organisation responsible for the importation of 150 kilograms of cannabis previously seized for which one person stood charged.

They assisted in identifying individuals and supplying contact telephone numbers in relation to a major operation currently under investigation by Manchester investigation division. They assisted NCIS South East in connection with a major arms dealer.

E. GAP during the search of premises at GAP at which a skunk factory and a machine gun were located GAP.

They supplied information relating to a major drugs target having a contact within the CPS Liverpool. They identified a GAP solicitor who is criminally linked to numerous drug dealers.

This solicitor was Kevin Dooley. Dooley later claimed that Haase and Bennett deliberately smeared his name after he refused to 'front' their gun-planting charade. As a result of this information, Merseyside Police planted a bug in the ceiling of Dooley's Kirkby office. He was later struck off by the Law Society.

They identified a serving police officer who was assisting the criminal fraternity.

They have supplied an extensive list of drug importers and dealers GAP they supplied the name of an individual who obtains arms from GAP.

F. The statement made by Mr Croker and the evidence he gave at the trial of the co-defendant Ergun was given after extensive encouragement by these defendants.

This proved what the Turks suspected – Haase was getting credit for getting his co-defendants to cooperate.

1. Firearm Seizures

The number of firearms and ammunition seized is indeed of frightening proportions. The questions as to why no substantial arrests were made in connection with these matters can be answered by the fact that while names responsible were given by the defendants the need to take the weapons off the street was seen as the main priority. Situations did not arise where extensive observations could be undertaken involving the necessary participation of armed response personnel and vehicles which, even under controlled conditions, are difficult to use in a covert manner.

The above paragraph put a brave face on the fact that there were few arrests and no convictions as a result of gun finds, stating that it was not possible to wait for criminals to return to the cars and safehouses where the guns were stashed and arrest them. The security and operational reasons may be true, but the fact remains that there were no arrests because most of the plants were staged – and no one was ever going to return to the plants.

These defendants at personal risk offered to introduce an undercover officer to a contact within the arms-supply organisation. After consultations it was decided that such an operation could run into legal difficulties on the ground of entrapment and was declined. The defendants as detailed warned GAP.

They then gave immediate information regarding the names of those involved in the murder which have proved to be accurate, information regarding GAP which allowed the police to anticipate events and seize a cache of weapons, which would otherwise have been available for use.

With hindsight and manpower, had a concentrated operation commenced on the names they were giving as supplying weapons GAP then the current GAP situation GAP may have been controlled to a greater extent. The priority has now changed but is fighting against the tide. These defendants have pledged to continue the flow of information after sentence, and I would expect their information to be of great value to the police in these difficult times.

These words of a promise of future information would come back to haunt Customs officers, as the information supplied by Haase in the future did not seem to amount to much. But even worse, Haase reverted to serious crime, seriously compromising his value as an informant.

2. With reference to the recovery of stolen property at Hull which included an OBE medal, the defendants put themselves at the risk of reprisals by imparting this information from those who committed the offence. All the proceeds of the robbery were retrieved and given back to the rightful owner. The identity of the robber was supplied but independent evidence could not be obtained to justify any charges.

3. With reference to the information of GAP the defendants took great risks in this matter, in that the person involved was a fellow prisoner who had given the information. This particular individual was a dangerous criminal and the case related to serious wounding and attempted murder. An audience was arranged with the trial judge who, after listening to evidence under oath, stopped the trial. As a result GAP re-trial ordered to be heard GAP.

The above paragraph possibly refers to the trial of Kenny, the Strangeways inmate who smuggled in the sandwich toaster in which the gun was found.

> 4. In GAP the defendants again at great personal risk supplied information that there was a loaded firearm concealed within Strangeways for the use of a fellow prisoner standing trial for a double murder. They explained how a prison officer had brought the weapon into the prison and gave details of his outside contact and a mobile telephone number for this contact. The loaded gun was found and the prison officer identified. The case was widely reported to the press on the grounds of the information being imparted by a fellow prisoner. Suspicion fell on these defendants who, notwithstanding, completed a questionnaire relating to the events for Greater Manchester Police, who were the investigating body.

This second reference to the Strangeways gun plant proved many details connected with the mystery, particularly that they deliberately linked the gun to Bourke. It was no accident, as they tried to make out later.

> Arrests made and details of goods seized
> February 1994 – 2 arrests at GAP both charged with drug offences. 199 skunk cannabis plants.
> January 1995 – 1 male arrested GAP charged with firearm offences, 3 handguns seized.

This January 1995 entry refers to Haase's failed attempt to bribe Billy the Hamster to get himself convicted with three guns. Significantly, he was never convicted.

> Drugs Seized
> April 1994 – GAP 1 kilogram of heroin seized.
> April 1994 – GAP 4 oz of cocaine seized.

March 1995 – GAP 5 kilograms of amphetamine, 7,534 Ecstasy tablets seized.

March 1995 – GAP 58 litres of methadone seized.

Weapons Seized

10.93: 3 GAP machine guns, 2 moderator silencers, 1 GAP machine gun, 1 stun gun, 1 GAP revolver, 160 .9 mm ammunition

02.94: 80 shotguns

03.94: 4 GAP, 3 GAP sub-machine guns, several rounds of ammunition

03.94: 4 automatic weapons and ammunition

05.94: 6 GAP sub-machine guns, 3 GAP machine guns, 1 GAP sub-machine gun, 5 silencers, ammunition

08.94: 1 GAP semi-automatic handgun, ammunition

09.94: 3 GAP sub-machine guns, 1 GAP sub-machine gun, 1 sub-machine gun, 175 rounds of ammunition

10.94: 1 sawn-off shotgun, 1 semi-automatic, ammunition

11.94: 2 rifles, 2 revolvers, 4 shotguns, 700 rounds ammunition

12.94: 5 GAP sub-machine guns, 900 rounds ammunition

01.95: 3 handguns

01.95: 7 GAP automatic pistols, 1 GAP sub-machine gun, ammunition

03.95: 2 handguns

03.95: 1 handgun, body armour, 30 rounds ammunition

04.95: 2 handguns

05.95: 2 handguns, ammunition

05.95: 4 GAP sub-machine guns, silencers, ammunition

06.95: 1 loaded GAP machine gun, 18 rounds ammunition

06.95: 1 GAP sub-machine gun, 2 semi-automatic pistols, ammunition

Significantly, there was no mention of the seized explosives or the heavy machine-gun allegedly supplied with the help of

Paul Ferris, presumably for reasons of national security, since they were falsely linked by Haase and Bennett to the IRA.

> Other Recoveries
> 05.95: £20,000 worth of forged postal orders
> The number of arrests made do not do justice to the quantity of information given by these defendants.

Again, the report plays down the low body count, praises the quantity but does not question the quality – because much of the intelligence was fictitious.

> Over a period of 20 months they have continued to supply information relating to serious offences concerning firearms and or drugs. This information has not related to minor players but by its very nature has concerned GAP.

The report implies that Haase and Bennett targeted major players concerned with serious offences. The report fails to mention that the crimes were phantom crimes committed by phantom criminals.

> This is the avenue [down which] this Department has sought information from the defendants. I have no doubt that had information been looked for on minor offences/offenders that a lengthy list of arrests would be before the Court.
>
> It is a rare occurrence when the authorities have such a vein of information on quality criminals, more so when that information can, by other means, be shown to be genuine and 100 per cent accurate, as in this case.
>
> Major investigations have been instigated as a result of information given which by their very nature have not reached a conclusion.
>
> Resource difficulties have restricted the use of information given by these defendants but should not

detract from its ultimate importance. A plethora of intelligence has been gained and introduced into the authorities system, the value of which should not be underestimated, nor true worth shown at this precise time, in terms of results.

Conclusion

No rewards have been paid to either defendant in respect of any information given, seizures made and property recovered.

They have, without doubt, put themselves and their families at high risk of reprisals by their course of action, both on the quality of criminals and the type of information they have imparted. By the fact that they were incarcerated throughout this period, they have had to seek information themselves from individuals outside, so spreading the risk of discovery.

The report fails to mention that many of the 'individuals outside' colluded in the gun hoax and were not a threat to Haase and Bennett. The main 'risk of discovery' was from being caught in conning the authorities.

Although they eventually chose not to give evidence against a co-accused who recently stood trial, the threats made against one who gave a draft statement in the case were such as to deter even the strongest will when made against family members and have to be weighed against those risks already taken by defendants.

It is my considered opinion that such is the impact of this case on the defendants that, for differing reasons, it is highly unlikely that they would revert to a life of crime upon their ultimate release.

These words would also come back to haunt Customs and Excise.

I consider that their continuing value to the police with regard to the recent increase in the use of firearms GAP has a great deal to offer as does the intelligence they can impart relating to serious drug importations.

They cooperated fully in regard to their DTOA [confiscation orders under the Drug Trafficking Offences Act], another indication of their willingness to assist and intent not to revert to a life of crime.

Signed: Paul Cook

9 August 1995

Cook first sent the report to his boss Phil Connelly. But there was a problem. Connelly was faced with a shocking dilemma. Astonishingly, he had rumbled Haase and Bennett's con. Bingo! For the first time throughout the whole con, a senior investigator had seen common sense. The cool-headed Northerner had figured it all out. He had realised that there was something very fishy about their gun plants. Though he had no direct proof, he strongly suspected that Haase and Bennett were behind them. In his own words, 'they were too good to be true'. In fact, his suspicions had been aroused way back, about *one year* before the trial, just six months after Haase and Bennett had started informing. His suspicions deepened because of the low number of arrests. He said, 'I was told that was because they [the police] were too impatient to make the job [get the guns seized]. Might have been two [arrests] but nobody was ever going to pick a fight [with the police about it].'

Now he was faced with a decision. Should he sign off this document suspecting what he did, knowing full well that it might lead to credit for Haase and Bennett, or should he put the kibosh on the whole wretched affair? This was the question he had been faced with when he first suspected that they may have been colluding in the gun plants. But at that time, in the summer of 1994, he had been forced to look at it through purely lawman's eyes. At the end of the day, the operation was removing scores of dangerous weapons from the street, directly from the underworld, no less, which otherwise may have been used in crimes. In the summer of 1994, Liverpool was in the middle of a massive gun war and terrorists were plotting to

233

blow up prestige targets all over the UK. Even if the finds were based on skewed, self-serving intelligence, they were de facto reducing the amount of weapons on Britain's streets. No one could argue with that. And protecting the public, like that of any lawman, was Phil Connelly's primary purpose. Connelly reasoned that the operation was an 'efficient' way of removing guns from the street. So he decided not to rock the boat and carry on the flow of information. There were also other strong arguments. In his report, Cook was correct in pointing out that there was not always time to mount a big investigation around each find to hunt down the owners. At the end of the day, if there were any issues about catching those responsible, it was the job of Merseyside Police, the investigating body, to see to them.

PHIL CONNELLY: The majority of reports from Cook would be by telephone. Cook was in Manchester; John Furnell and I were based in London. The fact that Haase/Bennett were giving information was within my knowledge. It would not have required my approval, although I am sure that Cook registered them as informants. I was aware throughout that Haase/Bennett through their solicitor, Tony Nelson, were giving information about arms caches which were being found in Liverpool and Manchester.

It was my decision to continue with the seizures even after it became likely that they could not have such information without being a part of it. I was aware that Haase and Bennett had access to mobile phones whilst in prison.

Consequently, I was asked to sign a letter prepared by Cook to indicate the extent of assistance given by Haase/Bennett and to be placed before the trial judge. This was in line with normal Customs procedure. The subject of Haase/Bennett would often be discussed between myself and Cook.

I was not over-aware of the suggestion that large amounts of money were changing hands. I was told that Haase/Bennett were trying to influence other co-defendants to plead guilty. I am now employed by the United Nations as a chief technical adviser to the African Seaports Project. Paul Cook is still with Her Majesty's Customs and Excise. We remain in touch.

———————————

The report was handed to Judge David Lynch. His job was to pass sentence on Haase and Bennett. Based purely on their crimes and the fact that they had been caught red-handed, they should have been given something close to the maximum penalty, which, in comparable cases, was 15 to 20 years. But the credit earned from the gun plants would then have to be subtracted. In return for their services, Haase and Bennett wanted *all* of their sentences to be cancelled. But there were two problems. First, bound by law, the judge was not powerful enough to annul the whole tariff. Second, if the sentence was quashed so suddenly after the trial, it would become obvious to the Turks and the rest of the underworld that they had turned informants. The Turks, whom Haase and Bennett had promised to help free in return for guilty pleas, would know that they had been thoroughly betrayed. Mr V would not be happy. And Haase's and Bennett's lives would be in danger. To boot, there was a risk that the whole deal would be exposed to public scrutiny.

Faced with wholly exceptional circumstances, Judge David Lynch put the sentencing decision in the hands of a higher authority. He referred the case to the Home Office. Judge Lynch probably understood that Haase and Bennett both qualified for a Royal Pardon based on the Strangeways incident and the home secretary was the only authority who could exercise that right. Lynch wrote a letter to the home secretary and probably enclosed a copy of Paul Cook's secret report. (The exact contents of the judge's letter and the discussions that took place have not been made public, and this account is speculation based on interviews with several sources.) For the time being, the credit would not be given. If the Home Office decided to implement a sentence reduction later, then it would happen after the trial finished, outside the realms of the court.

While the Home Office deliberated, Judge Lynch went about sentencing Haase and Bennett in the normal way, along with all of the other defendants. On 22 August 1995, the eight-man heroin gang was jailed for a total of 110 years. Haase, then 46, was sentenced to an unprecedentedly severe 18 years, as was Paul Bennett, then 31. They had £840,000 in cash confiscated. Croker, then 31, was jailed for 14 years and had £110,000 confiscated. Judge David Lynch said, 'It is rare that the courts deal with people so high up the ladder. It must be marked by a heavy sentence.' The five Turks also received hefty sentences. Suleyman Ergun, then 26, got 14 years and 9 months. Yilmaz Kaya, then 29, got 20 years and had £200,000 confiscated. Mehmet Ansen, then 54, got 8 years. Bulent Onay, then 39, got 14 years. Manuk Ocecki, then 37, got 4 years. In addition, Mark Drew, for his small part in the operation, got three years.

On the face of it, it was a major coup for Customs and Excise, who were still reeling from the fallout from the collapsed Curtis Warren case three years earlier. A senior Customs investigator who worked on the case – but was unaware of the secret deal to free Haase – could barely contain his jubilation: 'We were delighted with the result. For us, it was a turning point in the fight against the big players. We had managed to bring down a complicated international gang successfully. And we were confident we could do it again. The sentences were deservedly harsh – without time off for good behaviour. And we were confident that Haase would get as little as possible off because he is notoriously uncooperative – he was expected to be released in 2013. We couldn't have wished for better. He was a dangerous man best kept off the streets.'

That was the public face that Customs wanted to portray. But behind the scenes, the dilemmas were still there. At the Home Office, one of Michael Howard's civil servants summoned Customs boss Phil Connelly to discuss Haase and Bennett's case. He was asked a simple question, along the lines of 'Would the police have been able to recover the amount of weapons that they did without the help of Haase and Bennett?' In true civil-servant style, Connelly was obliged to give a simple one-word answer, preventing him from explaining or adding meaning. He said, 'No.' The civil servant did not ask whether Connelly thought the plants were phoney. And Connelly did not volunteer his suspicions.

PHIL CONNELLY: I am aware that the judge sent the letter to the Home Office or I myself delivered the letter. I know the letter went there as I was summoned to see one of Michael Howard's civil servants . . . I think they wanted to see someone rather than just words on a page.

Haase's devious con was casting a dark, complicated shadow over the case. Though most Customs officers didn't know it yet, much of their hard work was already being undone at a rapid rate, as Haase and Bennett sped along the road to freedom seemingly unhindered. However, there was one glimmer of hope, one stroke of luck which seemed to prove briefly that right was on their side. In a million-to-one shot, The Vulcan was suddenly captured. He was nabbed in Holland during a routine arrest. No one could believe their luck.

The Vulcan had not been seen in the UK since the summer of 1993 when he had flown in to pave the way for the 100-kilo importation that led to Haase's arrest, before quickly flying out again. However, greed had got the better of him, and despite the destruction of his Liverpool arm he had continued to smuggle heroin. Determined Customs officers, though, circulated his details to drug liaison officers (DLOs) all over Europe in the hope that they might pick up his trail again, knowing that the cocky Turk was back in business.

Almost immediately after his north London and Liverpool cells had been taken out, in late summer 1993, The Vulcan switched control of his UK operation into the hands of the Brixton Connection, a south London-based Turkish ring employing some of the residue of Kaya's gang. For instance, the on-the-run Manuk Ocecki, who had escaped capture in the main raids, was tasked to liaise with a Dutch smuggler on consignments being brought in at Felixstowe docks by lorry. The Vulcan did not dare come back into the UK himself for fear of being arrested, so he decided to run everything remotely, inevitably leading to a decrease in control and an increased risk of mistakes.

The first misfortune struck less than two months after Haase was arrested. Manuk and the Dutchman were picked up in September 1993 by the same Lima 3 Customs team that had nailed the Liverpool mob. The under-pressure Vulcan immediately flew to Holland to regroup once again. Over the next two years, he would be forced to spend a lot of time in the 'flat place' – and Amsterdam rather than London became his EU HQ.

In 1995, his false papers aroused the suspicion of a Dutch copper, and he was arrested. A sharp-eyed DLO at the Hague informed the British Limas of the good news and The Vulcan was brought back to the UK at once. Customs were over the moon, but almost immediately The Vulcan began fighting the legal process. While on remand in Walton Prison with Ergun, he claimed that the authorities had got the wrong man and demanded a formal identification. Everything hinged on this. If it failed, he would walk free.

A formal ID parade was arranged at a Liverpool police station so that Customs officers could pick him out. The six officers who had observed him at close quarters during Operation Floor were asked to identify him under strict conditions. By this time, the Vulcan had hired the best lawyers, and one of the six officers failed to give a positive identification. It was enough for his lawyers to make a case and, unbelievably, The Vulcan was set free at once.

The only response that shell-shocked Customs officer Harry Ferguson could muster was, 'You're joking.' Once again, he and his colleagues were probably thinking that perhaps they were on the losing side.

17

BRIBE ALLEGATIONS ONE (THE INSIDER PAY-OFF), TWO AND THREE (THE LONDON PAYMENTS)

Following the trial, it has been alleged that Haase made a number of huge payments to help influence his bid for freedom. He and Bennett were still in prison awaiting news of the request for leniency and the Home Office was deliberating whether to grant them a Royal Pardon. All was seemingly going well – but cracks were beginning to appear. Other Customs and police officers were beginning to raise suspicions about the validity of Haase's intelligence. Underworld gossips, who could barely contain their delight at being involved in a scam to hoodwink the system, were breaking the code of silence to tell startled pals of the fantastic scheme. The family of the Strangeways gun victim Thomas Bourke were investigating a potential miscarriage of justice – and significantly had already linked the scandal to a deliberate ploy by Haase. Deadly rumours that Haase and Bennett were grasses were flying round the penal system. And it wouldn't be long before the Turks would realise that they had been betrayed and that their million quid had been spent exclusively on benefiting Haase and Bennett and no one else. Who would want to explain this to Mr V? All in all, the immediate future did not look rosy.

The pair were keeping too many balls in the air and at any moment it looked as though it could come ontop big-time. The longer it went on, the more likely it was that the supergrass scam would be exposed as a fraud. Haase and Bennett's priority was to speed up their release, but they were getting frustrated. For over two years on remand, they had given it their all, played their best shots to get out. The plotting and scheming was so intense that it would give them headaches: the mobile phones, the money, the gun plants, the meetings. They had given everything to Customs and now they wanted payback. Haase wanted to give it one last push, to take some bigger risks. He knew he was so close to getting out that he only needed to close the deal once and for all.

Haase's plan was the oldest trick in the book: the pay-off. He started bribing anyone who had their hand out in the hope that this would speed up the process. The payments would also be useful in fighting a rearguard action against snooping officials asking too many questions about the shady gun plants. Mystery surrounds the movement of millions of pounds in cash from London to Liverpool, of money changing hands between Haase's men and shadowy individuals. Five pay-offs were allegedly sent to officials.

Haase's story is that the first bribe was paid to someone connected to his case. At first, that person refused Haase's offer of money but later took it when it looked like Haase had a good chance of being released.

JOHN HAASE: There was a man involved with our case; he received £100k paid in cash by No-Neck. We had this man's mobile number and I could phone him 24 hours a day. No-Neck had his number as well. No-Neck phoned him and met him and gave him £100k in cash. I'd already sorted this man from day one; the main thing he wanted was information –

money was secondary. Halfway through the case, I offered him money and he said yes. He was a bit shy. I forced this on him but he took the money. He was a bit weak.

I had his personal mobile. Yeah. I could use it whenever.

He received money a year later. The letter to the judge was already getting done before we went to court. Our man on the inside told us that all was going well. We got him paid well before the Paisley Magistrates'. He received £100,000. No-Neck had a payment method. He did it as much as me. There are no tapes of it. But I sorted all this out before No-Neck knew about it. I sorted the man from day one. I asked him from day one did he want any money. He didn't say yes or no. He said, 'Let's get the information first.'

He wanted information first. He couldn't just accept money and go, 'I recommend so and so . . .' He wanted information, even if it was shite like that, the minute of the guns going off [intelligence pinpointing a gun stash and the time it would be at the location]. That's the reason he done it.

He should have twigged from day one that the information was going nowhere. Work it out. You go there, there. Even like, say, London. There was a bad robbery on a pharmaceutical warehouse. How did I know that on the streets of London? I had me feelers out, anything going give me it. If a gun was being used there, dumped there, give it to me, I'll buy it off you. People from Sheffield, Manchester. It was only because I met these people before doing another sentence that I knew what to do. Bennett, he didn't have a fucking clue. He didn't know anyone. He only knows Liverpool and they are useless, that lot.

But the bloke wanted information. Money was secondary. He agreed to accept the dough about halfway through the case. After about 12 months.

The second bribe was £1 million taken by a drug-money courier called John 'Paddy' Scanlon from Chris No-Neck in Liverpool to a Turkish café in Paddington, west London, allegedly under the orders of Haase and Bennett. Scanlon had worked as a professional bagman for No-Neck and Bennett since 1989, before Haase joined the drugs business. His job was purely and simply to ferry drug money between big dealers. Often, the loads were £500,000, for which he was paid about £5,000 a time. He was very conscientious. He wore a shirt and tie and drove an anonymous salesman's car and planned his journeys with precision. He was his own man, autonomous once he had possession of the money. For security reasons, he was allowed to take as long as he liked to drop the money off within a certain timeframe so that he could vary his movements to avoid being followed and intercepted by police or tax-men gangs.

Scanlon received a call from No-Neck, who used The Bank Clerk to move money short distances from the war chest to places in Liverpool. It is believed that The Bank Clerk had delivered the money from the central stash to a food shop on Utting Avenue ready for collection by Scanlon. Scanlon remained quiet about the alleged money-drop for many years but decided to talk after suspecting Haase and Bennett had violated the underworld code by informing on Thomas Bourke, the Turks and others. He first revealed details of the bribe in a phone call to an investigator in which he gave scant details about the alleged bribes.

JOHN 'PADDY' SCANLON: The drop-off was around Edgware Road near Paddington. I drove there. The money was in one of those things, the wheelie suitcases. I knew the man I gave it to because I had a phone call. He would be there, blah, blah, at such and such a time. I was told it was a million pounds.

The person I got it off in Liverpool; I was given the address of the drop then. And off I went. I didn't question what it was for. It doesn't work that way. Fuck all to do with me.

In September 2004, John 'Paddy' Scanlon arranged to tell his story for the first time under strictly controlled conditions at Ken Darcy's house in Stockbridge Village, Liverpool. He feared for his security. In addition, he was worried about criminal charges resulting from a confession. Scanlon, a large man in his late 40s, was seated in the kitchen. He agreed to talk to an investigator in the next room through an open door to preserve a degree of anonymity. He wore a baseball cap and spoke with a thick Scouse accent from the side of his mouth.

––––––––––

JOHN 'PADDY' SCANLON: I used to do the work for them. So I got a phone call to pick dough up from a food shop in Utting Avenue. I had to take it down the smoke to meet someone up from Madame Tussauds, on Edgware Road, on the corner where Paddington busie station is.

The person in the shop, who I knew, handed over the bag and said, 'Here's the bangers.' [Meaning bangers and mash – cockney rhyming slang for cash.] I was told it was a million. I got a phone call the morning of the drop telling me I had to be at the café in London by teatime. The drop-off was at a café in west London.

I picked the bag up at twelve. That gave me four or six hours to get things together. I worked out that it would take me three and a half hours. I used to do it that often, I knew how long it'd take me to get there.

I stuck it in me ma's first because I wasn't ready to go. I'd been on the piss the night before so I was a bit rough. So when they phoned me to tell me the job was a goer, I picked the bangers up, put it in me ma's and said to me ma, because she's a nosy get, 'I'll just put that in your old cupboard.'

And she said, 'What's in it?'

And I said, 'Money, mother.'

She said, 'What do you mean, money?'

I said, 'An awful lot of money. I'll be back in an hour. I'm going to get ready.'

I always used to wear a shirt and tie. So I got off and got

ready. So when's I come back and I was leaving the house, she says to me, 'I thought you were going to show me what was in the case?' So I threw it on the table and opened it up.

I'd seen a million pound before. There was no necessity for me to count it. You must be joking! As a rule, when I took money down, I wouldn't tell them [the bosses or any member of the gang] any of my plans. No one was throwing me in. My work is my work. So long as it gets there, a day late, a fucking week late, as long as it gets there, there's no problem.

At the drop, I had just been told to meet so and so. It was a fella I'd actually met down there before, I think. It was a set time, that one. I met him at a Greek or Turkish café on Edgware Road, next to Paddington Green police station, facing the police station, a bit further up. There's a market there of a Saturday on that road [Church Street Market]. There's all market stalls of a weekend. They block the road on both sides. I know the road well because that is where I'd meet the others, the other people I'd do drops to. I'd meet them about 50 yards away.

The man I handed it to was, I think, a fella I'd met there before. But because it was so long ago, I'm not sure. I just passed it in to him and said, 'Here you are.' I was paid £2,000 for it [by No-Neck]. I think he had a dark complexion. I remember there was two of them. One of them I definitely knew. Just passed it to him in the café. Said, 'Here you are . . .' Then walked out with him and gave it to him.

No one gives a fuck who's carrying what in London. You're just a non-entity. I used to do drops in London where you were given something in exchange. I used to go up and down to London once, twice a month. I knew London well. Me two cousins are posties (postmen). That's how I got to know it well. They took me round and they showed me.

I've always thought since that for what I done for them [Haase and Bennett], I was going to get a pull [be arrested]. That was the money. I didn't know that job was existing. It was only afterwards that the person involved said to me, 'That was the fee. That was the pay-off.' What they [Haase and Bennett] took up [to London]. I was told it was a mil.

I knew who I was making the drop for because I'd done work for them before. But I'm not saying fuck all, lad, about their names. I'd done graft for people, yeah. I was trusted. Fucking hell, I've got kids. It was just work. I was paid a couple of [thousand] quid for it. About two or three quid. For other things, you'd get five quids and seven quids. They [Haase and Bennett] weren't greedy bastards.

I'd done a couple of drops before this one. I was trusted. I don't think fuck all about it [the bribe allegations]. It was just a job. Got nothing to do with me who they [Haase and Bennett] threw in and that they were grasses. They never done me no wrong that way. I've got fuck all against none of them.

I had never done a million-pound drop before. I'd done halves, but I'd never done a full one. It was halves and halves of halves. The big drop was for that one client [Haase]. They were the ones I worked for. To be honest, that was the last one I ever done. Because the shit hit the fan after that, didn't it? I knew exactly what it was about. But it had fuck all to do with me. I thought they were doing a good thing here. I didn't know about the grassing caper. But I thought for what I done for them, I'm going to get a pull here.

When they got out, they weren't indebted to me. But I didn't even see them. Then something else happened. The shit hit the fan [in an unrelated incident] and they left me swinging. [Following the alleged payments, Scanlon was convicted of a crime in Spain for possession of 50 kilos of pot. When he asked his bosses, Haase, Bennett and No-Neck, for money to get him back, they 'let him swing' and refused to help him.] After that, I just fucked them off. It wasn't that they informed on me, but they left me swinging, so we lost contact.

You'd be fucking soft to think No-Neck doesn't know more than he's letting on about the payment. With them two sitting in the big house [prison], who's running the show? He was the conductor. He knew about this thing.

To be honest, I haven't seen him for a long time. He was a good friend of mine. He introduced me to the firm. It was him who trusted me a million per cent. So I wouldn't like to slag the fucker off. No-Neck was The Bank Manager because he orchestrated all the moves. Fucking right he did. I knew about all the gun plants but I've got no comment on whether I did any of the plants for them two fellas. Half the city knew. I'm surprised it wasn't in the *Echo*. But no one knew about the grassing. They've done a boss little move there.

They've walked [been released] and nobody's been thrown in. But then there were rumours that they had informed properly on certain people. John Haase had a fucking good reputation up until then. But he made Eddie [Croker] do the dirty work – put his name to everything. Making him look a cunt.

I started working for No-Neck in '89, '90. I could stop at any time I wanted.

The venue of the handover was most likely the Turkish-run Metropolitan Café, situated right opposite Paddington Green police station. The café has been there for 26 years and is run by a nice guy called Shimel. The owners and manager of the café were not in any way involved with the transaction, nor had any knowledge of any wrongdoing, and the bribes were allegedly paid to government officials connected to the case.

KEN DARCY: I first heard about the money about six years ago [1998]. I've known Scanlon for 20-odd years. This lad has been a staunch friend for 20 years. I've watched his kids grow up and everything.

It wasn't until I came out of jail, spoke to him and it was him that mentioned it to me – that Haase and Bennett paid a million quid to someone who was able to have influence. The reason he hadn't told me before is because he probably thinks I've known about it, having done some graft for Haase and Bennett before. He might have thought, 'He probably knows this already.' But I was fucking gobsmacked.

We were talking in general about the graft and then, you

know, Paddy said, 'I done all kinds for them as well.'

And I said, 'Like what?'

And he said, 'I took money.'

And I said, 'What money?'

And he said, 'I took a million pounds in a bag.'

And I said, 'Fuck off!'

And he said, 'I did.'

They were determined to get out of jail. That's the way I've looked at it. They've paid someone in authority to get out of jail. Big dough, yeah, but they could make that dough back in 12 months.

Paddy was chosen because he had already done graft for them. Drops here, there and everywhere. They knew he could be trusted. The person he picked it up from was a lad called The Bank Clerk. He's just some shitty-arsed kid. That's all he was: a bank clerk – minding money. This kid's straight; that's why he was trusted. Nice kid. Not like us. Straight head, goes to work. He had the money. So that's when I wanted to buy Semtex, firearms. It was that kid who brought the dough around. No-Neck had trained him. He's been well looked after. He was given mountain bikes worth a couple of grand as presents. He was too scared to turn Haase over [steal the money]. He probably thought, 'If I get off with that [steal the money], they'll probably come round and kill me.' And you've got to remember he's had good wages out of it as well.

Paddy drove up to London then, but before he actually went, he left money in his mother's house because he had some business to take care of first. In London, he's passed it over. He's gone his way, the other fella's gone his way. Joe Bloggs has got off to do whatever he does with it. There were several things that helped to get their freedom. It wasn't just the Strangeways gun, it wasn't just the bung, but they were the major factors in the case. Plus the fact that they threw the Turks in.

A million pounds is a lot of money. The people who got it probably thought that nothing was ever going to come of it. They were under the impression that Haase and Bennett were going to come out of prison and lead a normal life. It was stated in their case that their crimes were a one-off. Forty-two armed robberies and it was a one-off? They've made them out to be saints.

Time, scale and process. First it was the firearm plants. They'd already been working a deal with Customs through Nelson, although he didn't know that Haase was doing it deliberately. Then the firearm in a prison puts you in line for the Royal Prerogative. The bung would have been the icing on the cake. It all made sense to me.

The third alleged bribe, of a similar amount of money, was arranged in much the same way. The payment was approximately £850,000. The Liverpool team consisted of three 'organisers' and one minder. One of the organisers was a fence, a trader in stolen goods, who later became a trusted confidant to Haase. The fence, who cannot be named for legal reasons, was chosen because he was essentially a non-criminal, a small businessman who was bright and well organised but who also had an understanding of planning complex underworld activities. In this respect, he was unique. He had grown close to Haase through neighbourhood connections, swearing undying loyalty after Haase had protected him in a dispute with a well-known Liverpool crime family.

According to the fence, the alleged payment was bound for a high-ranking official with foreign connections who claimed that he could influence the case. Furthermore, he believes that some of the payment may have ended up in the hands of a number of lawmen associated with the case, although he is unsure whether the lawmen contacts were simply involved because they may have helped to organise the handover.

For the Liverpool team, the first part of the operation involved a secret meeting with two representatives of the alleged recipients in a pub. The pub, in south-east London, was chosen because it was owned by an expat Scouser, a former professional sportsman, who was used to setting aside quiet parts of his premises for criminals to discuss 'graft'. The Scousers chose the venue because they feared they might be getting set up by the police. So they demanded a safe venue which they knew would be bug-free. It has also been claimed that the Liverpool team chose the venue of the first meeting so that they could secretly video- and tape-record the meeting. Haase was obsessed with covering his back.

The purpose of the meeting was to lay the ground rules of the handover: venue, date, time, action. The two men who came on behalf of the recipient were smartly dressed and well spoken. They asked that the money be handed over at the London Park Hotel, near Elephant and Castle in south-east London. (The staff there were unaware of what was going on.)

After the meeting, the Liverpool team, who did not know where the hotel was, jumped in a cab to do a recce. That was at approximately 1.00 a.m.

THE FENCE: The money was just under a mil, about £850,000. It was just brought down to London in a low-key way by two lads. I went down there separately. When we all rendezed, there was four of us in total. We went to see the fellas from the other side. We met in a pub owned by a mate of ours. That was in the afternoon. They were all right. They were like businessmen. Very straight. We had a drink with them. They were sound. They were relaxed.

We were told that we had to take the money at a later point to the London Park Hotel. I thought it was the Park Lane Hotel, but it wasn't in that part of London. I remember it being near a big shopping centre on a big roundabout, near Elephant and Castle.

Later, we jumped in a private-hire cab to find the hotel so that we knew where it was all going off. I remember the driver was a foreigner and I remember going over a bridge, which didn't make sense. But there were roadworks so we had to jump out rather than him turn round and walk the rest of the way. So we recced it up. It looked quite a nice hotel but it was in a bad place.

Later, at the drop-off, the money was taken to the hotel and handed over to the concierge. That was it. At first, they wanted us to put it in a room, which was sound, but then it got changed to the man in reception. We had someone outside sat off watching everyone that came and went. In fact, we were videoing it for John, just in case.

I know who most of that payment went to. A lot of people have speculated that it was for someone inside the Home Office. But it wasn't; it was someone outside but who knew people in there, who moved in those circles. It was a very high-up fella, someone in the Establishment, an official who knew certain people and might be able to influence them, maybe put a word in without anyone realising. I think that's how it worked. This man was already rich and he had very good foreign connections. He may have given some of the money to someone who could directly help, but once it left us, I don't know – was not my job.

After it went off, an official who John had contacted about all this phoned him to say that he was fine. He also said something about certain people being involved.

Further corroboration of the bribe allegations has come from Suleyman Ergun. He claims that Bennett told him that some of the £1 million the Turks were owed was used to fund the bribes.

SULEYMAN ERGUN: They first told me about the bribe plan when at the meeting in Strangeways prison in which they were trying to get me to plead guilty. I didn't really think they were trying to help us but I gave them the benefit of the doubt. Haase was cunning. He did mention who it was going to – but he was saying less than Ben, not going into detail. But he just said that they had the connection to buy someone off in power.

Then Bennett came to visit me in Norwich later and he told me in detail about the payments. He again told me the name of the powerful man they had targeted with the payment. Bennett would only go into detail when Haase wasn't around. He said money had definitely been exchanged. Eddie [Croker] told me more, because I was banged up with him for a long time. He said that the bung had been done in three drops and that it was over a million. He thought it was more like two million, but he deffo knew it was over one. Haase and Bennett were telling him a lot. Then he'd pass it on to me.

Chris No-Neck has always denied any knowledge of the alleged bribes, claiming that they were invented by Haase to cover his tracks as an actual informer. Although Haase says that he was not a proper grass, and that no criminals were convicted in connection with his bogus gun plants, No-Neck and many other underworld figures believed that Haase also informed on real criminals who later paid the price. For instance, there was Thomas Bourke, the Turks and a controversy over drug dealers arrested in an infamous drug raid called the West Derby Job. Haase knew that his imminent release would raise suspicions that he was a real grass and the bogus gun-plant story would not hold water for very long. So No-Neck's theory is that he invented the bribes to divert the attention of star-struck underworld gossips from the real issues. And he does have a point. For example, there is no direct evidence of the bribes – except for the testimony of the bagmen, members of Haase's gang, underworld figures and Haase himself. Some of the evidence is corroborating but so far none of the videotapes or recordings of the alleged handovers have surfaced. On this basis, sceptics dismiss the allegations as a wild conspiracy theory – one perpetuated by the master of the entangled web of multi-layered deceit: practised liar John Haase.

No-Neck suggested there may have been confusion over cash being sent to London, that it was for money that the government had seized as drug profits. But there were serious contradictions in his story. After initially denying he knew John 'Paddy' Scanlon and The Bank Clerk, he then said he did.

Then he tried to deny that Scanlon's drop was a bribe, explaining that the drop did occur but the payment was for an unrelated matter. He said, 'He did a drop for me, not for them [Haase and Bennett].'

However, Ken Darcy is convinced that No-Neck knows full well about the bribes and that he will not admit it because he fears comeback from sinister corners.

CHRIS NO-NECK: I don't know anything about the bribes, but I think it was just another crazy scheme put around by the other fella to cover his tracks. If it did happen, they never told me that, because I never jumped into bed that way. It was on a need-to-know basis, you understand. You have got to be careful when looking into this, because if they've thrown bodies in, then they've fulfilled their deal and they could use the payments to make people look the other way. That's why I never crossed the line. I'm not going to give them my soul. I never let them control me. John had the influence over everyone. Everyone except me. Ben was scared of him but I wasn't. Knew he was a dangerous cunt. He knew at the same time he couldn't make me do what I never wanted to do. The name he had, that was solid gold. I know that somewhere along the line I am going to get entangled. I've always been like . . . if you don't say nothing, they can't do nothing to you. I know I haven't crossed the line. Why should I not admit it all my life, for friends just to go on record and admit it now? That's the whole point. To avoid jail.

I can't help you with the bung because I know fuck all about it. I know nothing about the bung. What you're hearing and what is reality are two different things. That never happened. People have got this tunnel vision and you've got to remove this tunnel vision. Start to remove that and then clarity will set in. You'll understand the threat is they become grasses.

Now, if he had done a bung: eleven fucking years. Don't you think he would have been pinched over it? Don't you think there would have been an inquiry? The three drops – don't you think that money could have been off the DTOA? Who have they given it to? They have given it to the solicitor and he's gone down to pay it. There was no bung. They got a DTOA, yeah? Before they got released, they had to give money in. I know that because Ben told me that.

He could have paid someone off but he isn't going to tell me. No business of mine; he isn't going to tell me.

As I see it, he's gone down and they've gone, 'You're going to have to pay x amount of . . .' Got to be the brief, the bird, whatever.

Nick me all day long because I haven't done fuck all. If I did a bung, I wouldn't tell them. They aren't going to get fuck all out of me. This situation never went through me. It could have gone through someone else. They aren't going to entrust me with shit like that. It jeopardises their situation.

Go after the bung but it's been given to the Cussies. After '96, they threw bodies in. They are legitimately supergrasses. His bird must have been the only one who sent money anywhere. What kind of a man would do that?

KEN DARCY: No-Neck knows everything. He's prepared to admit to the gun plants even though it's a conspiracy to pervert because that isn't such a big thing. And everyone was a winner – both Haase and the Customs. And at the end of the day it makes him look good, because he hasn't dobbed anyone in. But he won't put his hand up to the bribes because that is fucking heavy. It goes very deep and you don't know who you're messing with. He knows that's a very big charge if the busies ever catch up with him – messing with the powers that be. Why would he want that? He's got a wife, kids, a nice house, a business, wages coming in. He's set up for life. If it comes out, it will be the end of that.

18

BAKERMAN BACKGROUNDER

Simon Marc Bakerman was born on 8 October 1962 at the privately run Lourdes hospital in Sefton Park, Liverpool. This was in Liverpool south's sub-district of Edge Hill – the constituency in which the young Michael Howard would unsuccessfully launch his national political career four years later. In 1966 and 1970, Howard stood as Conservative candidate in the area and lost – a bad omen for the relationship he would have to this day with his young cousin Simon who was born there.

Howard and Simon Bakerman are related and are most probably second cousins. The exact relationship is unclear because some records are not available and some accounts of the link do not go into detail. But the most probable explanation is that they are related through their great-grandparents, the Landys. The Landys' daughter Ada Landy is the mother of Howard's mum, Hilda Kershion. Ada's brother, Mr Landy, is father to Simon's mother, Freda Gloria Bakerman, née Landy. Therefore, Freda and Hilda are first cousins, making their sons Simon Bakerman and Michael Howard second cousins.

Freda runs a ladies' clothes boutique called Landys, just like

Hilda did in Llanelli, in the upmarket district of Woolton – the neighbourhood where Paul Bennett once had his drug-dealing HQ. Simon's father is Warner Bakerman, a 39-year-old chartered accountant at the time of his son's birth, now retired.

Simon enjoyed a middle-class upbringing in the leafy district of Aigbuth in Liverpool. His family moved from Fawley Road in swish Calderstones to a newly built bungalow in a solidly suburban cul-de-sac tucked behind a synagogue. Simon was brought up amongst the thriving but conservative Jewish community which tended to live quietly in this tidy corner of the city. He probably attended the local Jewish secondary school, the well-respected King David school in the Childwall district, coincidentally the school attended by the current Lord Chancellor Lord Goldsmith.

The Bakerman family often visited Michael Howard's family. Bakerman gives a fascinating insight into Howard's background.

SIMON BAKERMAN: They [Michael Howard and his family] haven't always got on. I always remembered when he got married, all the family saying what a terrible thing it was, him marrying a non-Semite. 'Poor Michael. Terrible. Terrible,' they said. In a Jewish environment, they were very displeased he had married a non-Jew. Suddenly Michael's home secretary, though, and it's 'Nice guy, Michael.' The way of Jewish thinking, once he became a politician, was that he was someone again.

Michael is a member of a liberal synagogue. He couldn't be a member of a conservative one. Liberal Jews – because he has married out, hasn't he?

He has been dedicated to the [political] cause. He went to a good school. When my mother took him to the doctor's when he was a child, the doctor used to call him 'Mr Prime Minister'. Just the way he was, very advanced for his years, precocious. Intellectually precocious. But cold and distant. Whereas the other members of his family are very warm hearted.

At family gatherings, we often speak of how Michael used to

shrink his jeans so that he could look like Elvis. He was big into the Rolling Stones, too – not that you would think it to look at him now with his suits and his shirts and ties. Mind you, he was always into politics, even when he was wearing all that gear.

Me and my sister often visited them at their home in Llanelli as children and I remember how well ordered the place was. We used to play in the big garden and often saw Michael roaring about the country lanes in his blue Lotus. He always had a smile and a wave for us as he drew up. His parents were obviously very proud of him. You could tell he was on the up and up. I used to visit regularly.

I was only about six at the time when I first met him. I was playing in the garden when I saw this big flash blue Lotus roaring up the driveway. It was Michael and he looked every inch the country squire even then. I think he was training to be a lawyer at the time, but even then his main interest was politics.

I looked after his mother for a few years. I used to take her food twice a week when I lived in London. When she was in hospital, he would ring her but I never bumped into him visiting her. I remember he was always on the move. Busy, busy, busy.

He started off as minister of Environment. Then he progressed through the Thatcher years. He wasn't popular over the poll tax.

While Howard had a deeply conservative personality, Bakerman had a rebellious nature. Though polite, bright and well spoken, he was drawn to lads from the wrong side of the tracks. Where most of his contemporaries in the friendly, close-knit young Jewish community of the 1980s opted for yuppiedom, he opted for a bit of scallydom. But he didn't fit into either camp completely and regarded himself as an outsider. He was also a bit of an eccentric. He spoke with a deep voice, and though his conversation was interesting, he was often regarded as slightly odd because of his mannerisms.

The underworld, though accepting, viewed his education and middle-class background with curiosity.

A family friend said, 'Simon is a well-educated, well-spoken gentleman, but he was always something of a rebel and was prone to fall into bad company.'

Simon had his first brush with the law when he was 18. He was arrested on several occasions for being drunk and disorderly. Then in 1983 he was charged with deception and received a £50 fine. That was the year that Michael Howard entered parliament as member for Folkestone and Hythe. The thrusting Howard went on to become a junior minister in 1985 – the year after Simon Bakerman was convicted of deception for putting a false signature on a consignment of goods.

SIMON BAKERMAN: When I was seventeen/eighteen, I was gambling madly and the debt accumulated until it was a quarter of a million pounds. My family paid it back. It was my inheritance that was coming to me. I was a playboy, a man about town. That's how I got to know all the gangsters. I was a Champagne Charlie.

Bakerman's family had used some of his inheritance to pay off the bookies. They refused to give him more in case he frittered it away. Simon tried to con money out of them by faking his own kidnapping. He roped in one of the city's biggest gangsters to make bogus kidnap calls to his father. In January 1985, this article appeared in the *Liverpool Echo*.

SON TRIED TO CON WEALTHY PARENTS

A greedy son spun a web of lies to con his wealthy Liverpool parents out of money, a court heard yesterday.

Simon Bakerman (22) claimed he owed £2,700 for a business deal that had gone wrong.

And to back his story up, his parents received

257

threatening phone calls and were told their son would come to harm if they did not pay up.

Bakerman inflicted injuries on himself, slashing his arms and legs with a razor. He also wore a plaster cast on one arm, claiming it had been broken by his disgruntled ex-associates.

His worried parents even wrote him an open cheque to pay off his 'debtors'.

But Bakerman was finally unmasked when, in a phone call to his mother, Freda, he said he was being held in a warehouse and tortured. Mrs Bakerman heard the sounds of a child in the background and accused him of lying.

When he was finally arrested by police, Bakerman, of Fawley Road, Calderstones, made a full confession, saying the whole story was a fiction.

Yesterday at Liverpool Crown Court, Bakerman pleaded guilty to attempting to obtain money by deception from his parents.

Accountant Mr Warner Bakerman said he had met his son while in custody and they were reconciled. He said, 'I think that the episode of the incarceration has left an indelible print on his mind.'

Mr Bakerman said his son had several times tried to start business opportunities, 'which I have had to finance and am still financing'.

Bakerman was sentenced to six months' imprisonment, forty-four days of which have already been served in custody, and the rest suspended.

SIMON BAKERMAN: I was blowing money left, right and centre. I spent half a million quid eventually. Had money. Was working. Money in the bank. Money left to me. At 18, casinos, out, Charlie. Had a few girlfriends at the time.

I'd get up at ten in the morning, sell clothes stock for a few hundred quid, which was a lot of money then. Be in the pub at twelve o'clock with fellas who are all millionaires now. Go gambling then end up in the clubs. Just a circle. Get up and do the same thing again. People knew me.

I only wanted eighteen hundred pound off my family, but because my family said I was spending it too quickly, they said no. They were right, in a way. It wasn't a staged kidnapping. It was money I wasn't allowed to have which was mine and which I wanted a lot earlier. But it backfired on me.

In the family, we had people who were connected to the police. They thought: we'll teach him a lesson. They bloody locked me up for four weeks to teach me a lesson. They told me mum and dad not to withdraw the charges and left me hanging in limbo on a charge. They put me in Risley.

To escape the bad influence of Liverpool, Simon then travelled to Israel. He went to work on a kibbutz to get his head together, encouraged by his family. Almost as soon as he arrived, he joined the Israeli Army and was involved in action on the Golan Heights and Lebanon. He said, 'I was a gunner in a tank and had some very hairy moments. There were times I thought I would die.' He got an Israeli passport in 1987, adopting Israeli citizenship.

After an 18-month stint with the Army, he went to work in Tel Aviv, mainly in finance. Returning to London in 1991, he used his contacts to set himself up in business as a financial wheeler-dealer. He became a millionaire, drove a Bentley and looked after Michael Howard's mum at weekends. But he started snorting cocaine after seeing someone using it in his office. His compulsive personality ensured that his habit got out of control and he let business slip.

SIMON BAKERMAN: I blew a million pounds in two years. I would think nothing of spending £2,000 a week snorting coke and splashing out £5,000 on call girls. I funded it by arranging credit with banks for retailers on a commission basis. I was completely off my face most of the time. If it wasn't drugs, it was booze – mainly champagne. I was keeping four women on the go; my love life was a tangled mess. I was constantly struggling to make sense of my world. Eventually it all got too much for me and I lost everything, and when I arrived back in Liverpool, I didn't even have a penny to my name.

Gripped in a downward spiral of drink and drugs, Bakerman returned home and drifted back into his criminal lifestyle to fund his habit. But he was always on the lookout for the chance to make a quick buck.

THE BUSINESSMAN: When the Soviet Union opened up, Simon went to Moscow to try and sell jewellery over there. He went with some well-known Liverpool fellas, some of whom had connections with the underworld. One of them was a very well-respected, very tough man nicknamed The Pugilist. Very old-school. He ruled Liverpool at the time. But these fellas were mostly just like lads who go the match and graft when they're abroad and whatever. They flew all round the world doing deals. They were real Scouse go-getters, very sharp – fences, touts, market-trader types. That kind of mindset. They were selling British produce to the Russians just after the Berlin Wall came down.

It was very poor over there and the Ruskies just wanted anything that was cheap. There was old women outside the hotel where Simon was staying selling just one potato or an old cardie. That's how skint they were. Simon and the lads knew it was going to be hard graft to make a profit over there. But they stayed the course. They had samples of clothes, all kinds of stuff, cheap jewellery, even ice cream.

Simon was brought in because he was very intelligent. He also had contacts in the clothes trade and he was Jewish, which was good at breaking the ice over there because there was a very big, very lively Jewish community. For instance, there was an Armenian Jew who they did business with over there.

They met fellas in the Russian Mafia who put them in touch with other businessmen. Funnily enough, they found out that ice cream sold very well over there. They had taken samples on spec. You wouldn't think it would, being so cold, but the Russians loved it. Eventually, an ice-cream manufacturer in Liverpool started sending three container-loads of ice cream over there every week. He had to double his workforce to keep up with the orders.

A very close associate of Simon's, who was nicknamed Hyman Roth because he thought he was a bit of a gangster like in *Godfather II*, then asked the ice-cream guy to store two container-loads of jaffa oranges from Spain in his yard. By then, Simon and Hyman Roth had been importing cheap stuff from Spain to sell to Russia. They had returned from Russia to the UK but were now busy exporting stuff back there to make money. They had bought a load of oranges to go to Russia but they said the Russians didn't want them. So Simon's friend Hyman was then going around asking the other fellas who'd been on the Russian trip if they wanted to buy them for sale in the UK. But Hyman Roth wanted too much money. So the other fellas was a bit thingy about it. But he kept trying to get someone to go down to the yard and have a look at these fucking oranges. Then Hyman asked one of the fellas, The Pugilist, whether he wanted to go and have a look at oranges. The fella said to him, 'Why would I want to do that? They're jaffas, aren't they? They all look the fucking same. I'm not interested.'

That's what got him thinking that Hyman Roth was trying to set this fella up [The Pugilist]. I knew that Hyman Roth had been investing in cannabis deals with a friend of mine cos he was skint. Basically there was a load of gear inside this container full of oranges and Hyman wanted some fucking joey to go up and open up the containers to see if the Customs would pounce. He wanted someone to test the water – a very old trick in the drugs game. Hyman was a cunning fella.

As it was, that's what happened. The Customs were on it and

in the end Simon's dad got nicked. Simon's dad was called Warner. He was innocent but he was their accountant. One day, he went down to the yard to look at the produce. Customs thought it was his and he got arrested. But he got let off because he had nothing to do with it. Wrong place, wrong time. At one point, Simon was going to say the gear was his just so that his dad wouldn't be implicated. But Warner was released, so in the end Simon didn't have to put himself on offer.

Simon was always bringing trouble to his dad's doorstep. Just before the cannabis thing, Simon had borrowed £5,000 off The Pugilist. Simon was setting up a video shop in Liverpool but he never paid it back. So every morning, no matter what time The Pugilist got up – whether it was 3 a.m., 4 or 5 – he'd go to the Bakermans' house. He'd ring on the bell, not knock on the door, so he wouldn't wake the neighbours, and say, 'I want my fucking money.' Warner didn't have the money so The Pugilist kept going back to harass him until he came up with the money. After about six weeks of doing this, Warner decided to have a word with a mutual friend who knew The Pugilist as well, with a view to getting him to mediate. This mutual friend lived in Spain, so Warner phoned him and explained the problem. After making enquiries, the mutual friend decided that there was no alternative but to pay The Pugilist, and as a favour to both of them this man in Spain settled the debt. He gave The Pugilist the £5,000 and he got off Warner's case.

The *Sunday Mirror* reported Warner Bakerman's unfortunate brush with the law under the headline:

RELATIVE OF HOWARD GETS OFF DRUG RAP
Today, we can reveal that Bakerman's father, Warner, was arrested in a drugs bust in Liverpool but charges were dropped.

Accountant Warner, 62, was held after the discovery of a consignment of cannabis in a lorry-load of oranges. A local underworld figure said, 'He had heart problems and the next thing was let go – but he soon seemed fine.'

A Customs spokesman confirmed, 'The charges were dropped before it reached the committal stage.'

SIMON BAKERMAN: That was mine. It was me who ordered everything. He [Warner] had nothing to do with it. I was away at the time; he went down for me. He happened to be in the wrong place at the wrong time. And even I was innocent of it all.

Bakerman was soon mixed up in the underworld drugs scene in Liverpool and counted some of the city's biggest dealers as his friends, including heroin baron Tony Murray – once shot by Haase's henchman – and many who had close ties with John Haase. Astonishingly, at the same time Bakerman was working closely with some of these godfathers, they were supplying guns for Haase's phoney plants. Bakerman was a junior partner in crime with a big gangster who helped supply 80 shotguns for the second plant in February 1994. Bakerman also knew members of a notorious gangster family on Haase's Southend patch. Ironically, this family had also supplied guns to Haase.

He blew thousands of pounds a week on drugs. He had a safehouse in Widnes used for underworld deals. At the same time, he was carrying a photograph of Michael Howard around in his wallet. In gangster meetings, he would boast about his famous connection. And to cap it, during this period when he was knee deep in organised crime, he received a visit from the home secretary. Shortly before Christmas in 1994, when Howard was the home secretary and John Haase was busy planting guns and plotting bribes, Howard visited Bakerman's home in Liverpool in his government limo.

SIMON BAKERMAN: One day, Michael turned up at my mum's house in his government limo. He was up from London for the football. He came to watch Liverpool. I was snorting a line of coke in my bedroom. I had been wasted for days.

I looked out of the window and saw this swish government car pulling up. It was a white Rover and there were a couple of police outriders waiting outside. I was so down I didn't care about anything. I realised who it was and I tried to pull myself together.

When I went downstairs, there was Michael sitting down at the dinner table. I was so out of my skull I could hardly focus on him. He took a good look at me as I shambled in. There was a look of total disbelief on his face. I don't know what he must have felt. I just said hello.

He nodded back and said, 'Hello, nice to meet you again, Simon,' but I don't think he knew what to say. I wasn't capable of saying anything. After an awkward silence, I just walked out.

Drug baron Tony Murray probably met Simon Bakerman through a local dance and drama school for children called the McKey School. Bakerman got to know the big-time gangster James Turner through Murray, and he also got to know Paul Bennett. In the tape recording of Haase and Bennett's plea-bargaining session in prison, Bennett referred to his connection, who was himself connected to 'top people'. But Bennett said at that stage that he 'wouldn't mess around in politics and everything else' because he was fearful.

Before they were arrested, Bakerman had visited Bennett's drug-dealing HQ in Woolton and was reputedly dealing medium amounts of cocaine for John Haase's pal, though Haase was not aware of this.

19

BRIBE ALLEGATIONS FOUR AND FIVE – THE ALLEGED BAKERMAN BRIBES

Haase's bodyguard The Enforcer claims that in the winter of '95–'96 a fourth payment of about £920,000 was handed over. He was told that Simon Bakerman was the link. The evidence to suggest that Bakerman (who was later convicted and jailed for a £20-million drug conspiracy) was involved is compelling:

- a confession by Haase;
- the disproving of Bakerman's denials claiming that he was out of the country or confined to a wheelchair at the time;
- Bakerman had known Bennett through the world of drug dealing;
- he knew an alleged bagman called Mr A;
- at the time, Bakerman was working directly for a gangster who was supplying guns to Haase for phoney planting;
- he was also working for a crime family who were planting guns for Haase;
- he had close links with numerous drug dealers and gangsters who were connected to Haase;

265

– the bosses of Bakerman's £20-million drugs gang were connected to John Haase.

There is no suggestion that Michael Howard knew of or received any of the money. The money was taken to a London hotel from a flat in Liverpool owned by Haase. The drop was planned with military precision by a female associate of Haase's known as The Supervisor. She was the woman No-Neck had helped after she'd OD'd on cocaine in front of her children. During the planning stages, she consulted with The Enforcer, who was eventually chosen as the lead bagman in the operation.

The Enforcer recalled how the cash was split into four loads of £250,000. He took one bag and three couriers took the rest. All four bagmen were to pay themselves £20,000 from the cash, leaving a total remainder of £920,000, which formed the alleged fourth bribe. Each courier was told to go to the Forte Crest Regent's Park Hotel (now a Holiday Inn) at different times and take each bag to room 33.

THE ENFORCER: I was one of the couriers who took money to room 33 at the Regent's Park Hotel. I was told by Haase to do it during a prison visit. Prior to this handover, I also helped The Supervisor get £180,000 from a safety-deposit box. That may have formed part of the payment, but I don't know.

The instructions for the handover were given to me by a female associate of his called The Supervisor, because she was visiting him frequently, getting a lot of instructions from him on the gun-planting and the bribes and then putting them into action on the outside.

I picked up the money from The Supervisor in a black holdall with a lock on it and drove it to London. In the days before, both me and The Supervisor had discussed the best way to transport such a big amount of money to London. She wanted to do it all in one go, with just one person taking it all down. But I thought about it a lot. I was really methodical and

I was looking at it from all angles. In the end, I told The Supervisor that it was better to do it in four loads of £250,000 than one. That reduced the risk of getting nicked or being followed. Both I and The Supervisor planned it so that each bagman wasn't supposed to know who the others were. That's so we couldn't identify each other if it come ontop. But I had an idea who the others were. One of them was a long-time associate of Haase's called John, who used to graft with him on the heroin. I later found out that this fella used to travel to France with Haase and Ben to pick up tackle from the Turks. He had known John since he was a kid and he was trusted. One of the others may have been a woman. It was agreed that each of the couriers should take out their fee from each parcel. I think it was £20,000 each. So in total, the net handover would have been £920,000.

I took mine in my car but it was up to each other person to make their own way how they wanted. I think one or two of the others went on the train. I drove it to Regent's Park via Swiss Cottage. The hotel room opposite was being watched by Haase's men and they were also outside the main entrance. There was a tray of leftover food outside the room. It had been arranged beforehand how the handover would work. Each one of the bagmen, including me, would go up to the room at separate times, open the door and go inside. There was no one in the room. Then the bag would be put inside and we would leave. Afterwards, I assumed the people who were picking up the money would come into the room and remove it. This system meant that there was never any contact between us and the other end of the operation, reducing the risk of compromising evidence. It had been arranged with the reception that no one who worked there could disturb the room for a few days, possibly even a week. They were just told that it didn't need cleaning, no room service and that.

Just before each delivery, Haase's men from the room opposite placed a used tray of food and drink outside room 133, like as though someone had room service and then left a tray outside for collection. But it wasn't. This was so a keycard for room 133 could be left under a cup on the tray. I went up to the room and picked up the keycard from the tray. I went in, left the money and then left, watched from the room opposite by Haase's men. After I left, I think that they took the tray away so that just before the next delivery or pick-up the keycard would be left under the tray again. This is so it wasn't left hanging about in the corridor. I was told the people we would be paying the bribe to would come and collect it in the same fashion, when all drops had been done. So I think they took it all in one go.

I was told that Bakerman was the link. That he was the connection between Haase and Bennett and to whoever the money was going to.

Later, I found out that Haase and Bennett may have taped the handovers, possibly using covert recording in the room. But I was more sure that they had a person outside the hotel with a video camera, getting footage of people coming and going. For all I know, they may have had a video trained on the door of room 133. I was fucking furious that I had done this for them and they hadn't told me about this recording stuff, which was compromising. A lot longer later I confronted them about this. They said it was true and that they were only covering their arses in case the other side reneged on the deal. I demanded the tapes. They told me that they had only audio-recorded it. They gave me a bag of audiotapes and I just sat there pulling all the tape out of them and smashing them up.

The Fence, who had paid a separate bribe in London but who claimed to have a working knowledge of this handover, later confirmed that each bagman got £20,000 each. He also suggested that one of the couriers may have been a woman nicknamed The Horsebox, a close friend of Haase's and The Supervisor's. She later carried out a gangland shooting on the orders of Haase, firing at a nightclub doorman in a protection-racketeering dispute. Haase ditched her after she became addicted to drugs.

THE FENCE: The Enforcer later went mad over the fact that Haase had taped the handover. He was threatening all kinds, so we just gave him a bag of tapes to shut him up. I think they were the small ones, microcassettes, but I'm not 100 per cent. We said they were the originals and no other copies had been made. So The Enforcer was happy. He just sat there like a kid pulling them apart. Of course, it was a load of bollocks. The tapes we had given him were copies. In fact, I think some of them just had rubbish on them. We had kept copies. Later, Haase directed all the tapes to Ben. Ben kept a copy and copies were also sent up to someone in Scotland for safekeeping. I heard a rumour that a big drug dealer got caught and was on a big charge and he was threatening to make them public to embarrass the authorities. I don't know whether that's true – all I know is that the Jocks have got a copy. Haase and Ben were very close to them.

But the alleged corruption didn't stop there. Haase claims that he paid a fifth bribe of £400,000 to Simon Bakerman, which he assumed was being passed on to Michael Howard. But even Haase was sceptical about this alleged payment. He says he took the Howard–Bakerman link with 'a pinch of salt'. That could mean one of several things: that Haase did not quite believe that Howard was involved; that Haase did not believe that Bakerman would take the money to Howard or had the influence to approach him; or that Haase saw the whole thing as a pie-in-the-sky long shot with little chance of success. However, Haase claims that he decided it was worth a punt anyway on the basis that anything that increased the chances of getting freedom was worth a shot. Again, he claims to have delegated the details to Chris No-Neck and thought no more about it. Haase claims that Bakerman was paid with two kilos of heroin worth about £40,000 for agreeing to accept the money and help influence Michael Howard.

JOHN HAASE: We were having meetings with Tony Nelson, Bennett and our counsel. Mine was Henriques. I don't know who Bennett's was. We were talking about the letter to the judge which would be recommendations for all the information I had given. It would go from the judge to the Home Office, then to the home secretary, who was Michael Howard at the time, who would ultimately sign it.

Paul Bennett said he knew someone who was related to the home secretary. I took it with a pinch of salt. That person was Simon Bakerman. Bennett had drug dealings with Simon Bakerman before. Bennett came back [to me a few days later, after making more enquiries about Bakerman] and said he reckoned he had relations who knew Michael Howard [reckoned he knew people who were related to Michael Howard]. This [organising the Bakerman link] went on for a couple of months. There were a couple of brothers, one Mr A and one Mr I [the initials of their Christian names], who were very good friends of Bakerman. They deal with him. Drugs. Mr I had always done it. [These brothers were from] Park Road, Liverpool [where Bakerman hung out]. Everyone knows everyone.

I got in touch with them through someone else. I can't name that person. They came back and said Bakerman was kosher. The next thing is Paul Bennett said I reckon we've got a deal on and it was x amount of money. When I asked him how much, he said £400k. At the time, it didn't faze me because, as I said before, our bank account was £1 million to play with and we still had a lot left even after buying the guns.

Chris No-Neck was to handle all this business. As far as I know, in December 1995, Chris No-Neck delivered a holdall to [Haase's home address]. A lady [The Supervisor] there collected the holdall. That same day, the holdall was picked up by Mr A. Inside the holdall was £400k cash and a money-counting machine. I phoned [home] and was told the business had been done. My understanding from Bakerman was that the £400k was to pay off Michael Howard when my judge's letter reached him. [This is only Haase's assumption based on Bakerman's assurance and there is no evidence to suggest that Michael Howard was involved in any wrongdoing or knew of any wrongdoing or that the claim is true.] As far as I know, Mr A told me he delivered this [the £400,000] to Simon Bakerman, to be delivered to Michael Howard [again this is only Haase's claim], to pay him off so that when the judge delivered the recommendation to Michael Howard, he signed the Royal Prerogative [Haase's claim]. Bakerman's reward was a couple of kilos of brown for doing the [alleged] deal with Howard on behalf of me and Bennett. Chris No-Neck had loads of brown – he was like a quartermaster.

No-Neck allegedly dropped the money around at The Supervisor's house at 5 p.m. Two hours later, by 7 p.m., the bag of money had been picked up by Mr A. It was then driven to a location one hour outside Liverpool and allegedly handed over to Bakerman. The Supervisor independently confirmed this version of events and her role in the alleged money transfer in a meeting attended by herself, author Graham Johnson, Peter Kilfoyle MP and one of Haase's main lieutenants.

PART THREE

SCANDAL, CONSEQUENCES AND CONSPIRACY THEORIES

20

RELEASE AND
CONSPIRACY THEORIES

In the early summer of 1996, Michael Howard granted John Haase and Paul Bennett a Royal Pardon each. On 3 July 1996, after all the paperwork had been processed, they were released from prison.

All of their hard work had paid off beautifully. They found themselves back on the street in less than six months after the bribes had allegedly been handed over. Officially, their sentences had been reduced by the Home Office from the original eighteen years to five years. With the standard one-third off for parole, that meant they only had to serve about three years of the five. Since their sentencing on 22 August of the previous year, they had officially served ten and a half months of their new five-year tariff. But taking into account the two years and one month they had spent on remand between their arrests in July '93 and sentencing in August '95, they had spent a total three years in jail – qualifying for immediate freedom.

The walk out was a low-key affair. Haase left Franklyn prison and jumped on a train home. Bennett was met by solicitor Tony Nelson and Customs Officer Paul Cook, signifying that he had now become the favourite, the more coveted Customs contact. This was a slight to Haase's status, and he would have been furious if he'd found out.

As soon as Haase got back, No-Neck gave him the cash that was left from the war chest – between £150,000 and £250,000. Bennett got the same amount. Shortly afterwards, Bennett flew with his girlfriend and children to Mexico to lay low.

JOHN HAASE: In December 1995, I'm in Long Lartin prison. At the end of December, I'm in Hull prison. Then, in January, I'm in Franklyn prison. From December, when I phoned my wife, I don't know anything because I'm in the block [secure wing]. 3 July appears; a lot of screws appear and tell me I'm going. I asked where. They said, 'We can't tell you.' I arrive in a police station in Durham. A couple of people came in to talk to me; I can't remember who they were. One plain-clothes policeman took me to the railway station and I was given my fare home and ended up on Lime Street station in Liverpool.

Haase had got his result. He assumed that all of the bribes he had allegedly paid had got to the right people, that they had pulled whatever strings had needed to be pulled, and that the combined effect was the desired result. But what really happened to the alleged payments, assuming they were made in the first place and were not just a figment of Haase's devious and twisted imagination in an unfathomable bid to confuse, to disguise a dark secret? There are several theories:

1) Michael Howard got the money.

There is no suggestion or evidence that the home secretary was guilty of any wrongdoing or corruption. At the worst, he is guilty of nothing more than, like many involved, not seeing through the scam which released two of the most dangerous criminals in the UK back onto the streets.

2) Bakerman took the money and gave it to some other influential figure(s).

Plausible, but who are they? Within days of Haase's release, the *Sunday Mirror* revealed that Bakerman and Haase had twice been in telephone contact with each other.

3) Bakerman took the money from Haase, falsely promising him that he would hand it over to his second-cousin Howard. This theory would mean he had talked up his relationship with Howard in order to sting Haase into thinking that he could help him. The convicted fraudster, who was schooled in the dark arts of the drug dealers – the double-cross, the self-serving streetwise scam – then pocketed the money, later telling Haase it had gone to Howard.

For a cash-desperate, drug-addicted con-artist like Bakerman, such a high-risk double sting would be second nature, no different from his hare-brained fake kidnapping. Haase would never question the deal because he would be getting the result he wanted. If he didn't get out of prison, there was little he could do about it anyway. Who was he going to tell? If push came to shove, Bakerman could give him the money back or make up an excuse that it hadn't worked for some reason. After all, Haase had known from the beginning that there was a risk of failure.

4) Bakerman and Hyman Roth pocketed the money together. It is known that Bakerman had run up gambling debts of £500,000, which Hyman Roth had helped him to pay off. Pocketing Haase's money may have been a good way of recovering the lost money.

5) Chris No-Neck, bitter that he had not been paid by Haase for organising the gun plants, pocketed the money.

6) Bagmen Mr A and Mr I pocketed the money, threatening Bakerman to go along with the plan and sweetening him with a little dropsy.

7) The insider got part of the money and helped Haase get out of prison. This assumes that bribes were actually paid and were not just figments of Haase's imagination, and that he had not made up the story for his own ends.

8) Haase orchestrated the whole bribe plan as an insurance policy if his bid for freedom backfired and he was kept in jail. This theory – supported by Bakerman himself – states that

Haase was worried in case the gun-planting came to light, or, for some other reason, the home secretary refused to follow Customs' advice and let him out, or, if he was let out, that his Royal Pardon would be revoked in the future. To counter this, vengeful Haase prepared to sling mud at the home secretary by saying that he bribed him through his bent second-cousin. He got his heavies to force Bakerman to go along with a bogus plan to bribe the home secretary using intimidation and blackmail.

9) Some of the payments were decoys. Only one was a proper bribe and the rest were to spread confusion – a common tactic amongst drug dealers.

10) Haase feared that he would be exposed as a real informant. He made up the bribe story to cover his early release. He would be able to say to the underworld that he had bribed the home secretary.

11) Haase made the story up so that he wouldn't have to repay the Turks their £1 million.

12) The secret payments were for completely different reasons than for a bribe. For instance, Haase had to pay £840,000 in drug-related asset recovery. But would such an official payment be made so shadily? Yes, it might, if Haase's men organising the drop on the outside – who were active drug dealers at the time – wanted to protect their identities and their close links with drug money. They may have feared a sting by Customs during such a payment. But couldn't Haase have simply made the payment through his solicitor?

All of the criminals who were allegedly involved have different stories. As for Haase, he is adamant that his man on the inside took the money because, at the end of the day, the proof is in the pudding. He got out of prison. The insider delivered on the promise.

JOHN HAASE: Fucking right. He had to or he'd have been in trouble. He would have got bumped.

But what makes him so sure that the others played by the rules? Why is he so cocksure that No-Neck, the two bagmen or Bakerman didn't sting him for four hundred grand?

JOHN HAASE: They wouldn't have done that. One thing, too loyal. That goes for No-Neck. Another thing, scared. If it [stealing the bribe money] didn't work, they'd have been too scared. Twenty, thirty grand to get them shot. Mr A took it, Bakerman . . . I haven't a clue [about the logistics of it].

But wouldn't Haase know the details? For instance, whether Mr A and Bakerman ever met the intended target of the bribe to give him or her the money?

JOHN HAASE: All I know is that I'm in prison at the end of December. Then, in July, I was taken by a policeman to the railway, given me fare home and I ended up in Lime Street station. A couple of days later, met him, Simon Bakerman, at the Royal Oak, Park Road, Liverpool. It was a couple of days later, with Bennett, after we were released. Mr A and Mr I were there, in the Royal Oak pub on Park Road. Had a little discussion: 'Thank you for that favour,' and all that. Bennett had a chat with him [Bakerman] and then we got off. Just a few seconds.

I didn't really like the guy [Bakerman]. Bennett's talking to Simon; I'm talking to Mr A and Mr I – they were my friends. They were making a fuss of him [Bakerman], saying thanks for that, any favours, just let me know.

But didn't Haase ask Bakerman the details? Did Bakerman tell Haase exactly what he'd done? 'Not in so many words,' says Haase. But what actual proof does he have that the money went from Mr A to Bakerman to the recipient?

JOHN HAASE: Bakerman's word. That's it. Mr A wasn't there. I've got no one else's word but Bakerman's. Bakerman. Well, he doesn't look like he's been riding round in a brand new car, that he's spent four hundred grand, anyway.

For Haase, the bottom line is that he got a Royal Prerogative, a very rare occurrence, used only once by David Blunkett while he was in power.

JOHN HAASE: That's what I'm saying. I can't say he [Bakerman] gave him [Michael Howard] it. It's down to Bakerman. I was talking to Mr A the other week. Mr A now lives out the way with kids. He doesn't want all this brought up again. He said, 'Yeah,' [to talking about it] then he thought, 'Phwooorrr!' [No way.] I can't blame him in a sense there. He's living a good life.

Haase said that he paid Bakerman two kilos of heroin and not just £200, as claimed by some of Bakerman's underworld pals.

JOHN HAASE: Money? Bakerman got nothing at all. Bollocks, two hundred quid! A couple of ki of brown. Deffo. Two hundred quid. That's a load of shit. For doing what he done. For getting in touch with [the man who allegedly took the money]. For doing the deal with him on behalf of me and Bennett. No-Neck gave him the brown. No-Neck. He had loads of brown. With No-Neck it was whatever you want.

But No-Neck denies all involvement.

CHRIS NO-NECK: How could I have orchestrated the

Bakerman bung? I'm not going to get myself into shit over them. I owed them nothing. Haase has made all this up to stop himself being labelled a grass. Do you think John Haase would compromise himself with a fucking smack-head [Bakerman]?

Simon Bakerman denies that he received the money from Haase. But he does admit to 'knowing' Paul Bennett and bagmen Mr A and Mr I. He initially denied being in the UK in the winter of '95–'96, when Haase says Bakerman did the business. But checks on his passport state that he returned from Israel on 14 May 1995, putting him in the ballpark. He then claimed that he was having a nervous breakdown and was in hospital in London. However, his confusion over dates is probably down to his drug-addled brain.

Bakerman claims that the bribe scheme was a plan by Haase to put pressure on him, his family and Michael Howard to ensure his freedom at the time and in the future. He says that his life was used as an insurance policy in a plot to blackmail Michael Howard and that Haase's gunmen have threatened to kill him six times to force him to say that he bribed Michael Howard. He says the pressures have extracted a horrific toll, driving him to a £1,500-a-week cocaine habit and several attempted suicides to escape the underworld and the nightmarish JFK-style conspiracy. Following some of the threats, Bakerman armed himself with a gun for self-protection – but shot himself by accident.

Bakerman thinks he was recruited by Haase in case the gun-planting scam backfired and the Royal Pardons were revoked at the last minute. Haase allegedly told Bakerman that, if Howard saw through the scam, he had to say that he'd bribed his famous cousin in order to get him to back off.

SIMON BAKERMAN: Towards the end of the year [1995 or 1996 – he cannot remember], I was told I was part of a conspiracy and I had to play along with it. I couldn't handle it so I tried to kill myself. I was found in the car half-dead, with a hosepipe from the exhaust. I spent the next few months in the hospital. At the time, Michael Howard was home secretary.

Then I started receiving visits from underworld figures. I was the most important pawn in the game, because I was the link between Michael Howard and John Haase, the one who allegedly paid the money from John Haase to Michael Howard to free Haase. That was invented but I was told to play along with it. And if I don't play along with it, my life is over.

He wants his freedom. But if I was to stand and deny it, it could jeopardise his freedom. But if I am dead, it's just one word against another.

I haven't even seen or spoken to Haase in my life. I've seen Paul Bennett. I haven't spoken to him. He used to frequent the same places.

I can't live like this any more. I can't live looking over my shoulder. I can't sleep at night. I've had a nervous breakdown. I've been in the hospital over this. It's ruining my life. I can't go to work. I'm telling you, I was living abroad in the whole of 1995. I came back for the FA Cup final. I went back to Liverpool towards the end of the year. I was told I was part of a conspiracy and I had to play along with it and couldn't handle it so I tried to kill myself. Spent the next few months in the hospital. Right through to 1996. So there's no way they could have met me or seen me. And that proves I was not part of the conspiracy.

I was once offered a gold Rolex watch – I presume on behalf of John Haase – to make a statement saying I had played a role in the conspiracy. The gold Rolex was there in the box with the offer of money. By this time, I was feeling under threat. I went into hiding. I was even questioned about it inside prison and approached by some heavies saying they had records of me being the key player – that I was a key player and the deal had been done in Southport.

I got paid off to pay Michael Howard the money. I've heard figures from £400,000 to £100,000 to £50,000 – to even a million pound. If I don't play along in the conspiracy, I am looking at a bullet in my head. Can't sleep at night. So many sleeping tablets, so many antidepressants. I'm finished. Emotionally drained. You can't get a proper job because you can't concentrate.

Nothing to do with Bennett, I think.

Their aim is that if I'm ever questioned, if I say, 'Yeah, I did get a payment,' it will help his case. I can't say that. I can't lie. I met Mr I once, years ago. I've never spoken to Michael Howard about it. It was not a major concern to him, obviously. I was advised by my family not to. Just to leave things and let it die. I was advised by solicitors to leave it, let it die. You are dealing with the underworld. And I've tried to leave it but it wouldn't die. The longer it has gone on, the more pressure I am under.

I could walk out today and I could be dead tomorrow. I'm going to be in a coffin. It was down to the judge at the end of the day. Howard just signs the paper. It was a con that came off. Everyone knows that. They pulled the wool over Howard's eyes. It's a great PR stunt to give up arms, isn't it? It's not his job to investigate all these things.

All I said is I didn't know them [Haase and Bennett], but I knew some of their associates. The thing is, the game's so deep, the conspiracy is so big. If I go the wrong way, or something leaks out, I've been told my card's marked, there's a bullet in my head.

I'm going abroad, out the way. I am going to live another life. I'm starting a new life. I've had half a dozen visits. But the faces I've seen have been turning up in places I've been. Maybe that is just to say, 'We are watching you.'

A few months ago, I went high up in the police to make enquiries. And I've even broke down in tears, saying why am I a pawn? Why am I part of the game? But I'm in it and I can't get out of it. I know a lot of underworld figures from different areas.

You've got to admire them for getting out in the first place. It's been a great link in a great plot. And full marks, because it has been a great plot. But at the end of the day, why should I and my family have to suffer? Why should I have to live in fear over something I have nothing to do with? To pay someone to kill me is buttons compared to the price of the freedom he earns. If I'm dead, it's his word against Michael Howard's word. If I deny it, I'd be dead within two days of saying that. But I daren't go to the police for help.

Let's face it, half of the police are corrupt. I've seen it with my own eyes, police getting paid. So who do you turn to? If I pick up a gun, I can't fight 50 people because I'll go to prison. I'm in a corner where I can't get out. If I take my own life, it's showing guilt. I'm just a scapegoat for everyone. All my life, a scapegoat.

In December 1995, he's saying [the deal took place]. I was out the country, so that is all right. Like I told you, in 1995, I came back in May, and in August I was in hospital for four months. In December 1995, I was in Israel. In December 1995 is even better, I was in hospital. Even January 1996, I was in hospital. I was in hospital from July right through to the end of the year. And I was living in London. I wasn't even living here. When I came back from Israel, I went straight to live in London. In Mill Hill.

I know where I was! In December 1995, I was in Clearwater in America for four weeks. Miami. In London, at my sister's. I was in hospital for four months. Napsbury General beside Arsenal's training ground in Colney Hatch Lane.

If it was four hundred grand, why would I be signing on? That's all bollocks. First of all he [Haase] is an informer, then he is planting guns. He chops and changes with the weather to whatever is going to help him that day.

But some of Simon Bakerman's denials are not convincing. At first, he said he was in Israel in the winter of '95 – in fact he was in the UK. Then he claimed to be in a wheelchair at the time of the Royal Oak meeting. But he was confined to a wheelchair after an accident with a gun six months later.

Bakerman claims to have reported everything to the police

as far back as 1997, including regular threats on his life. After becoming embroiled in the conspiracy, fearing for his life, Bakerman got a gun – partly for self-protection and partly on behalf of a big gangster he worked for. The gun was owned by one of the gangsters who had helped supply 80 shotguns to Haase for the second phoney gun plant.

SIMON BAKERMAN: In about February 1996, a few fellas I know were tanked up on cocaine. They had a .9 mm pistol and were planning on going into town with it. I don't know what they were planning but it didn't seem good. Anyway, they were pissing around with it and I saw where it was all leading and decided to intervene. I managed to wrestle it away from the fella who had it. They weren't happy about it but they respected me.

A friend of mine advised me to bury it in case something happened. So I went and buried it in a field. A few days later, I told my friend what I'd done and where I had buried it, and she went, 'My God! That is where a school playing field is. It won't take long before kids find that then.'

I realised that kids might find it and the results could be fatal, so I went back and dug it up. Took it home to the shed and began cleaning it. As I had it, cleaning the barrel with a cloth, it went off in my hand. The bullet passed through my upper leg and passed out through the calf area. I had an operation. When I was discharged, I was arrested by the police. They had found the gun and I was charged with having a gun without a licence. I said I was a gun enthusiast and I got off. I was in a wheelchair until some time in 1997.

So, if I was in the Royal Oak pub at that time meeting Haase and Bennett, they would have had to wheel me in there.

I was in fear for my life. That's when I turned to drugs in a big way. I got into cocaine. Soon I was snorting five grams a day, an ounce and a half a week. That's fifteen hundred pound a week. It ruled my life. It blocked my mind out from all the pressures and threats. It gradually got worse to the stage where

I was getting up in the morning and taking drugs. You go to sleep, then next day comes. In the end, you are spending fortunes of money.

When I didn't have money to take cocaine, I'd get up in the morning and take a sleeping tablet just to waste my life away. I was out of work and started to get the press on my back [as stories of Haase and Bennett leaked out]. Life pressures getting to me. I took drugs to hide away the troubles. They just go out your mind. They wouldn't go away. Gradually got worse to the stage where I was getting up in the morning not knowing what I was doing.

Towards the late '90s, when I was 36, 37, it got worse. To start with, it had been a social thing. Do it once. Might not do it for a month or two. But then I'd do it on my own. People didn't realise. I was a closet person. No one was around me. I would just cover up.

The more you take, the more you need. That ruled my life. That ruled my movements. That came before anything. Make sure I've got something there before I did anything else. Any money I had got blown on that. About a thousand, fifteen hundred pound a week. That's an ounce and a half a week. But buying it in little bits and bobs. Money I had. Didn't have to borrow. But my name was good for borrowing money at the time. I was drawing it all out on credit cards.

Once I started having personal problems, it took over my life completely. It ruled my life. Couldn't deal with the problems. Rumours of the stories going around in the press. My friends stayed away from me. I'd do it in my room, in the toilet. People always asking me why I had a cold. My nose is ruined. Needs a bone put in and everything. It's all gone. If it stays in your nose, it just burns through your bone, doesn't it? If I pressed hard on it [my nose], it would just snap.

21

SCANDAL AND CONTROVERSY

The release was still not publicly known. Most people, including the officers of Merseyside Police, thought that the earliest Haase and Bennett would be considered for parole was 2002, as laid down by the Criminal Justice Act 1991. Failing this, they might qualify for release two-thirds of the way through their sentences in 2005.

No one thought for one moment that under Michael Howard, Britain's biggest drug dealers would be freed earlier. In fact, just three months before Haase and Bennett got out, on 30 March 1996, Howard had reassured the public in his infamous 'prison works' speech to the Conservative Central Council in Harrogate that criminals would serve the *exact* sentences they were handed down. Incredibly, as he launched a White Paper called 'Sentencing', Howard boomed, 'And tough deterrent sentences too for professional drug traffickers. They prey on the young and the innocent. They make money out of other people's misery. And they must be made to pay for it.' He went on, 'When criminals have been caught and convicted, they must be properly punished. And the proper place for the most persistent and dangerous criminals is prison. It's needed to protect the public.

'Let's look at the facts. First, violent crime. The maximum sentence for crimes like rape and attempted murder is life imprisonment. Yet in 1994, 95 per cent of these offenders did not get a life sentence – even for their second conviction.

'If the prisoner is still dangerous, he will not be released. The safety of the public must come first.

'I believe that these sentences need to be much stiffer. Career criminals should not receive the same punishment as many first-time offenders.

'Finally, honesty in sentencing. I propose to abolish automatic early release from prison. Everyone else will serve their sentences in full. No more cases of a criminal being sentenced to ten years in prison and walking out after four or five.'

After saying these words, he released Haase and Bennett. You couldn't make it up! It took two months for the press to get wind of the story. Thomas Bourke's sister Jo Holt had known about the release before it happened and got busy briefing the media. Neil Garrett's brother, who was furious that Neil was being labelled a grass by Haase and Bennett, also got revenge by tipping off a brave journalist on the *Liverpool Echo*. The local reporter in turn sold the story to one of the nationals. When the bombshell dropped, it exploded like a ton of TNT. The scandal sent shockwaves around the nation. The *Sunday Mirror*, the newspaper that broke the story, splashed it across the front page under the headline 'Two-Faced Howard – Heroin dealers jailed for 18 years . . . then HE frees them after 11 months in secret deal'.

On pages four and five, the exclusive revealed: 'The scandalous secret the home secretary didn't want you to know'. The main news story was followed by a strong comment piece on the leader page stating that 'Heroin kills at least 1,000 British youngsters every year' and 'The pair were secretly freed in a strange deal involving the home secretary, the judge and HM Customs – an action that defied all the tough words'.

When the *Sunday Mirror* discovered the truth, a senior Home Office official tried to persuade the paper *not* to publish. Bourke's sister Jo Holt tipped off Sky TV. But ominously, Labour MP Peter Kilfoyle revealed that the home secretary had called him minutes before he was due to go on Sky TV and asked him not to do the interview. Howard told Kilfoyle that lives could be in danger. Not knowing the truth, the fair-minded Kilfoyle deferred to his wishes – a decision he now feels angry about.

Peter Kilfoyle said, 'These two villains were on the streets, bold as brass, up to their old tricks, but I deferred to the home secretary's privileged information and did not go out and get involved in publicising what was happening. We had a situation where a self-styled tough home secretary extraordinarily pardoned these truly vicious serious criminals.'

Furious Haase and Bennett then launched their own PR-limitation exercise by threatening the reporter at the *Liverpool Echo* who was tipping off the nationals. He was put in fear of his life, began drinking heavily and fled Liverpool to live under a different name.

But still the story refused to go away. The exclusive was picked up by *The Observer* and the *Sunday Telegraph* and followed up the next day in The Independent. Unfortunately for the home secretary, the story also made the front page of the middle-England agenda-setting *Daily Mail*. The headline screamed: 'Howard in Drug Gang Deal Shock'. For Howard, it was a total sickener.

Merseyside Police and Members of Parliament vented their anger and surprise. One senior officer told the *Liverpool Echo*, 'I was absolutely flabbergasted when I heard they were out. Deals go on but this is an extreme case.'

Everyone started to put the boot in. Labour deputy leader John Prescott branded the decision 'a disgrace'. He added, 'It's not exactly an example of the Government being tough on crime. The home secretary seems to be more prone to letting prisoners out than keeping them in.'

Even anti-drugs group Turning Point poked fun at the supergrass system. A spokesman said, 'You don't have to win the Lottery to get in the cash these days – just inform for Customs or the police. It is a murky world and I think a very slippery slope for society where drug dealers are rewarded for turning in their own.'

Knowsley North MP George Haworth demanded assurances

that the public were safe from the convicted drug barons. The Labour Home Affairs spokesman said, 'Given the recent history of armed violence on Merseyside, which is often associated with drug barons, I find this decision surprising to say the least. For that reason, I am writing to Michael Howard seeking an explanation.'

Michael Howard defended his decision, describing it as a 'wholly exceptional case' and adding that it would have been 'inconceivable' to ignore the call of Judge David Lynch. In a confusing statement, Howard went on:

> He said that were it not for the special circumstances of the case in terms of the lives of the men and safeguarding future operations, he would have passed a sentence of five years instead of the eighteen years which he has passed. I think we have to look at this in the context of the real world. If I would have taken any other decision, I would have been open to the most serious criticism.

When contacted by reporters, Judge Lynch said, 'I cannot speak to you.'

Two days later, on Wednesday, 11 September 1996, the Haase scandal was still going strong in the national newspapers. *Daily Mirror* reporters Frank Corless and Patrick Mulchrone were the first journalists to track down the recently freed prisoner to his Liverpool 'lair' and ask him for a comment. Haase responded with a threat – 'Get away; I'll hurt you' – followed by a string of four-letter-word abuse. He then landed a kick on terrified Corless as his grinning girlfriend, Debbie Dillon, looked on.

Michael Howard let it be known that information Haase and Bennett had provided 'proved to offer quite enormous and unique assistance to the law-enforcement agencies'. But things got worse for him when a serving police officer wrote to the media revealing the Bakerman link, which thus far had remained a secret. The anonymous source mentioned the bribe and the Strangeways gun. He also said the police had found out about the secret deal on 8 August 1995 – the day before Cook wrote his letter to the judge.

On 25 May 1997, the *Sunday Mirror* added fuel to the fire in revealing how, within days of his release, Haase had twice made contact with shady Simon Bakerman. The paper hinted at awkward questions. Another embarrassing article appeared in the *Sunday Mirror* on 8 June 1997 about Bakerman's dad Warner getting off the cannabis rap.

Meanwhile, Haase and Bennett were worried that the underworld might turn on them for being grasses. They reassured gang-bosses that they had not informed on anything other than phoney gun plants, conveniently forgetting Thomas Bourke. They 'bigged up' the bribe story until everyone was convinced their behaviour had not contravened the underworld code. Haase and Bennett were free to go about their business. Gangsters were briefed to stay on message. One told the *Liverpool Echo*:

> John got people to hide the guns here, there and everywhere in Liverpool while he was behind bars awaiting trial. Police and Customs spent two years doing cartwheels round the city finding them. He's no supergrass – the number of arrests proves that. He tricked the system into letting him off a lengthy stretch in jail. Police and Customs were happy because they got a load of guns to boost their figures.

Customs boss Phil Connelly defended his role of lobbying for Haase even though he suspected he was being conned by saying that he didn't know that so much leniency would be granted.

PHIL CONNELLY: I actually don't care if people get convicted. My job's to catch them. You can't get yourself wound up about convictions. Your job's to catch them, and once they're caught, it is up to the courts.

We'd got the heroin. That's important at the end of the day to me. We probably feel the way a police officer feels about it. We've got the stuff and we've taken the stuff off the street. I couldn't feel remorse or regret about Haase and Bennett because I was aware of what was going on and that they'd produced all this information. Whether it's right, I don't know.

22

ONTOP TO DEATH – HAASE'S SECOND CRIME SPREE

As soon as Haase was released by Michael Howard, he was bang at it again. But now, under the impression that he was a government-sponsored untouchable, the Liverpool Mafia godfather branched out his crime empire to cover five specific money-spinning rackets. Class A drug dealing was still the core business but the other divisions included extortion and protection rackets, mass cigarette smuggling, illegal debt collecting and wholesale gun-running. On the side, when he had time, he also ran profitable lines in money laundering, kidnapping, armed robbery, fencing stolen goods, hijacking and contract violence. Haase's multitude of sins was masked by a legit front in the form of a security company called Big Brother. In '90s Britain, security consultants had become the building blocks of modern organised crime. Bennett also got busy again, setting up his own deals as well as remaining partners with Haase for security reasons.

But despite being master criminals, Haase and Bennett's crime spree was inevitably doomed. In local parlance, they were 'too ontop' to get away with it for too long. For the next three years, between 1996 and 1999, they winged it and milked it for all they could get – but then it all came crashing down again. What occurred in between was a rerun of history – a complex entanglement of organised crime, grassing and deals with the authorities. But this time the betrayal got personal and poisonous. The partners turned on each other as well as everyone else, and supergrass Paul Grimes turned on his old pal Haase.

Meanwhile, Haase and Bennett continued to be informants for Paul Cook, seemingly making a more or less complete transition from phoney grasses to real ones, as revealed by the contact sheets. They passed on information about rival drug dealers including names, dates and details of big deals. But inevitably they were using their status as a shield to deflect heat away from their own crimes. A different branch of Customs and the Merseyside Police soon grew wary and began investigating Bennett for cannabis smuggling, later widening the investigation to cover Haase. Paul Cook was told to back off to avoid a conflict of interest. The official reason was that his relationship might lead to media interest, bearing in mind the huge outcry over their release. But before police pounced in June 1999, Bennett managed to escape to a safehouse in Scotland. One of Bennett's partners then claimed he tried to pull the old gun-planting trick again to wriggle out of the warrant for his arrest. Bennett's right-hand man Barry Oliver said that Ben had persuaded John Haase to sell him some guns so that he could plant them in Scotland for the authorities to find. Haase went along with the plan, but in October 1999 Bennett's courier was caught with the weapons during transit back to Scotland. Haase was later jailed for 13 years for being involved in the gun transaction. Shortly afterwards, the warrant out against Bennett for the cannabis smuggling mysteriously lapsed and he was walking freely around Liverpool. Oliver's theory was that Bennett had sacrificed Haase in order to save himself from the cannabis charge, that he set up the gun deal so that the authorities could catch Haase red-handed.

The road to ruin began in the summer of 1996, as soon as Haase and Bennett were released by Michael Howard.

KEN DARCY: Haase came to see me two or three weeks after being released to say thanks and all that crap for helping with the gun-planting and that. Then he asked me if I wanted to do some graft, to move 100 kilos of pot in the boot of a car for him. I did and the next day it was shipped to Scotland, the whole lot in one go. Got paid well for that. Did this and that – some gear [heroin].

One night, he asks me to come and get some guns. I asked, 'What are you buying guns for, John?'

He said, 'To help Eddie Croker,' who was still in jail, remember.

I thought, 'Fucking hell! What a top fella trying to help Eddie the way we had helped Haase with gun-planting. Many people forget you when you are inside.'

I didn't know at this point that Eddie was a grass, that he had turned QE [Queen's Evidence] against the Turks, otherwise I wouldn't have helped.

But Haase was bullshitting anyway – it wasn't for Eddie Croker at all. He was buying guns for his own firm, or whatever.

Anyway, I went along because at the end of the day I'm a villain. I looked in this car owned by the lads who were selling the guns. They were from the Southend. They've got three handguns, three 9 milly, a .45, a .38 and a pump-action. These lads wanted a bit [a lot of money]. But we offered two and a half [grand] for the lot and they've gone, 'Go on.'

John's given me the cash from a suitcase. He's followed me home and said, 'Bury them. I'll get them moved in a few days.' He phoned me a few days later. 'Can you bring them to the Heritage Market?' he asked. That was his office on the docks.

Cleaned them up, put them in bin bags and took them down there with bags of rubbish on top. The boot fucking stunk.

Took them in the back way of the Heritage Market and threw them in a skip. He was watching me from the stairs. Afterwards, the guns went up to Scotland.

———————

Following Haase and Bennett's release, No-Neck was promoted to a top executive position in the firm but he was denied an equal partnership. To his disgust, No-Neck was to remain effectively an employee, not a shareholder as he had expected. In real terms, this meant forgoing an equity share in Haase and Bennett's growing property empire.

For all his good work for the cause, for the wonderful job he had done of the gun-planting, No-Neck had thought he was made for life. He assumed that Haase and Bennett would make him an equal third partner. After all, not only had he paid his dues and won Haase freedom, but it would right the great injustice he felt he had suffered in 1992 when Haase had squeezed him out of his money-spinning 10-ki-a-time heroin-dealing partnership with Bennett. In addition, the icing on the cake was the £250,000 he had put in Haase and Bennett's 'backbin' the minute they walked out of prison. He'd done it right – that was pure tribute, just like back in the old country. If nothing else, No-Neck figured, that supreme gesture of selflessness, deference and loyalty would buy him a seat at the table.

———————

NO-NECK: Was I fucking wrong or what? Fucking right, I was. I was sucked in like everyone else. I thought I were going to get graft and that, right. I said to him, 'Are we going to be partners like you and Ben are?'

You know what he turned around and said to me? He said, 'No, I want to keep everything like it is.' That meant just Ben and him. Then that twat turned round and said, 'Anyway, you don't deserve it. The bird [The Supervisor] has done more graft than you this year.'

And I said, 'How did you work that one out, John?'

He said, 'She sent a van-load down to Holyhead.' [Referring

to the gun plant.]

And I said, 'Who kept all the hard-cases [the tax men] away from your house and from Ben's house? Who stopped Ben's kid from getting kidnapped [by the tax men after the missing 50 kilos]? Was it the bird who fronted Tommy Gilday?'

This is how much of a fucking rat he is. But I just swallowed it and got on with it. After that, over a three-year period, I did a lot of graft but I was just annoyed that I wasn't an equal partner.

The ink on the Royal Pardon was barely dry when Haase set to work renewing his heroin and cocaine contacts. The Turkish Connection was re-established with a vengeance – but with Kaya and Ergun in prison, he could only manage to buy small loads off low-grade operators. However, in 1997, Haase set to work planning his quantum leap back into the big-time. His strategy was simple: to increase his heroin-dealing volume back to 1992/'93 levels.

Astonishingly, he turned to the Turks he had betrayed to help him. Devious Haase banked on Kaya and Ergun not knowing about his secret deal with Customs and the fact that he had sneakily tried to persuade them to go guilty on behalf of the prosecution, as well as forcing Croker to make a statement against the Turkish mob. It was insult to injury, kicking a man when he was down, a treacherous double betrayal. But only someone like Haase, with more front than New Brighton beach, combined with a lifetime's supply of prison cunning, could pull it off.

Cheekily he went to see Kaya in jail to ask him for an intro to some heavyweight dealers back in Turkey. But Kaya had been forewarned. The sharp-minded Suleyman Ergun had learned of Haase's betrayal and tipped Kaya off. In true Turkish mafia fashion, Kaya said nothing but did not refuse Haase an audience – he kept his enemy close. Kaya welcomed his old partner with open arms and gave him two heroin connections. One was based in north London. The other was his own brother Yalcin, based in Turkey.

Kaya was playing a cute game. He was stringing Haase along. On the one hand, he wished to get Haase exactly where he wanted him, and on the other hand, he was hoping that Haase would be able to repay some of the £1 million debt that the Turks were owed from his future heroin profits. To show their gratitude, Haase and Bennett started to drop off parcels of £10,000 cash to various kebab shops in London connected to The Vulcan, from where they were passed back to Kaya's family.

Haase and No-Neck flew to Turkey to see Kaya's brother Yalcin to set up a heroin deal. They stayed with the Turk's family, who greeted them with open arms. But the proud Yalcin couldn't stomach the pretence any longer. When Haase gave him £40,000 as a down payment on a heroin deal, Yalcin pocketed the money and 'fucked them off'. He didn't let Haase know directly that they thought he was a grass. He fobbed them off with an excuse and sent them packing. On their return to Manchester airport, Haase and No-Neck were stopped by Customs. Haase was let go but No-Neck was found with two false passports on him. He was later convicted, fined and sentenced to community service.

Haase made do with Kaya's contact Salim – but he was relatively small-time and could only supply limited loads. Haase was determined to get back to the days of 100-kilo parcels on demand. In desperation, Haase and his female deputy, The Supervisor, went to see Suleyman Ergun in jail to beg for a contact. The unforgiving but unfailingly polite Ergun declined. Later, Ergun managed to get hold of the legal documents proving Haase's betrayal. He sent them to Kaya's brother Timi in Istanbul with instructions to make sure that Kaya got to see them, with the ominous message to keep Haase close in the meantime. The Vulcan would deal with Haase in his own time.

Meanwhile, Haase was rebuilding other parts of his crime empire at breakneck speed, while the authorities looked on helplessly. Haase's inevitable return to crime made a laughing stock of the home secretary and the Customs officers who had lobbied for his release, wrongly believing that the duo's prison experience would have taught them a lesson.

For Customs and Excise, Haase was too much of a hot potato to take on. He was a ready-made tabloid crime story. His every move seemed to make the papers and humiliate the government. The situation was further complicated by the fact that Haase was technically still a registered informant. Since January 1994, when he had first turned 'supergrass' on remand and begun feeding Customs information on the whereabouts of guns and drugs, Haase was a fully fledged, signed-up official snout.

That meant Haase could use the fact that he was still 'on the books' as a defence at any time to explain away his criminal activity. It wouldn't be the first time a supergrass had turned around and said, 'I was only committing crimes so that I could gather intelligence and turn it over to the authorities.'

The tricky relationship between Haase and Customs and Excise was exacerbated further because Paul Cook continued to meet Haase and Bennett after their release. This was not to warn Haase to desist from gangsterism or to probe him for criminal intelligence, as would be expected of an informant. Cook met Haase and Bennett in order to discuss how they could limit the damage being done to the authorities by adverse publicity, to keep them away from reporters and to return property. Even so, Haase and Bennett were prepared to grass on rival drug dealers. Via their solicitor Tony Nelson, they told Cook about huge shipments of drugs, dates and even names of dealers. But for some reason, Cook did not act on the info and was later criticised in court. These meetings were detailed in a witness statement later given by Cook. Cook revealed:

> My dealings with John Haase and Paul Bennett since that time [of their release] are as follows:
>
> 1. In 1996, I attended the release of Paul Bennett with Mr [Tony] Nelson his solicitor and then returned to

my office.

2. In late 1996, as part of my duty of care after media articles appeared in various newspapers, I attended Manchester airport, where I met Paul Bennett and his family arriving back into the UK from a family holiday in Mexico. I arranged an overt search of their baggage by uniformed Customs officers, after which I took Paul Bennett to a hotel near the airport to meet Mr Nelson and John Haase. The reason for my actions was to allow their legal representatives to discuss matters with them in advance of the press.

3. I subsequently attended the office of Mr Nelson. I believe this was around December 1997, when Mr Nelson, John Haase and Paul Bennett were present. The reason for this was to return property. A general discussion took place regarding how they were contending with any difficulties. At that time, general information relating to other individuals was volunteered by Paul Bennett.

[The National Investigation Service contact sheet timed 1658 hours relating to this meeting reveals that Bennett informed on seven gangsters involved in heroin, cocaine and Ecstasy deals including two heroin dealers from Manchester, an Asian smuggler from Birmingham who uses the ancient system of Hawala banking to wash money, a South African cannabis smuggler and two of Liverpool's top heroin importers.]

4. I have since received a number of calls, that have diminished in time, from Mr Nelson, during which he gave general details of individuals who were concerned in drugs. I have no record of the dates of these calls.

5. At some time in 1998, I received a call from Mr Nelson and then John Haase concerning a threat against an individual. I passed these details to a member of the Merseyside Force Intelligence Bureau.

[During this conversation, recorded on a contact sheet, Nelson revealed details of some Granby Street-based gangsters, another dealer doing 'loads of brown', a 50–80-kilo cocaine importation before Christmas '98 and that one of his clients had been offered a sample. He also promised 'something good' in a couple of weeks.]

6. On 3 August 1998, I received a letter from my Assistant Chief Investigations Officer.

7. On 11 June 1999, I telephoned Mr Nelson to inform him that Paul Bennett was wanted in connection with a cannabis importation. I asked Mr Nelson that, if possible, he contact Paul Bennett and arrange for him to surrender for interview. I received no news after this request.

In 1998, Cook was instructed by his boss to cut all links. A bombshell memo from Customs boss Steve Rowton to Cook, dated 3 August 1998 and referred to in Point 6 of Cook's statement above, read:

> Restricted – Management
> John Haase and Paul Bennett
> We spoke. As you know, there is sustained political interest in the activities of Haase and Bennett. In order to safeguard our position, we must maintain our distance. You are therefore directed to have no further dealings with Haase, Bennett or their representatives. If they should contact you, for whatever reason, you must report the matter immediately to either me or HODO [head of drugs operations].

The memo seemed to sum up the helplessness of the situation. Customs and Excise had their hands tied as Haase ran amok. It seemed as though Haase had them exactly where he wanted them – dancing to his tune.

Haase's security company employed about 100 guards and was a great front company. One branch of the company hired bouncers out to nightspots in Liverpool. The other supplied watchmen for factories and building sites. The business made a profit but more importantly was a ready source of strong-arms for Haase's criminal activities.

In traditional gangster fashion, Haase maintained to his public that he was going straight despite the crippling stigma attached to his past. In an interview with the *Liverpool Echo*, Haase lied, 'I am going straight, running an efficient business and doing it well. I am a poacher turned gamekeeper. Half my life has been spent locked away behind bars. I feel as though I have wasted so many years.'

Haase said that his woman, Debbie Dillon, kept him on the straight and narrow:

> I met Debbie [Dillon] in a pub in the city and it was love at first sight. Suddenly I had a girlfriend who I wanted to be with more than anything in the world. It was a big, big gamble for Debbie deciding whether to stay with me. We spoke and she discussed things with her parents. I promised her that I would go straight and that things had changed. And her parents' view was that if she loved me, she should give it a go. Thank God. I am happier than I have ever been in my life. I get on great with my in-laws and have reconciled with my mam and dad.

In the mould of the Krays, Haase promoted himself as the kind of guy who helped old ladies to cross the road and gave money to charity.

> I sponsor a Sunday football team, Pineapple FC in Dingle, and I enjoy watching them. I keep fit and enjoy skiing. When I got out, I was discussing what to do with my mate John Melvin. We thought about renovating houses. But John suggested that I should go into the security business. After all, I know a lot about security,

having been a criminal for so long.

He added, 'I am endeavouring to provide an expert service to my clients and have not received any complaint from either client or a member of the public,' knowing full well that disgruntled clients often withdrew their complaints after being beaten up or having their houses firebombed.

The climax of Haase's PR coup was a preposterous untruth: 'Life is so different for me now and I just hope that the public will give me the chance to show that I have changed.'

Behind the scenes, Haase continued his orgy of terror and round-the-clock crime. There was so much graft there were not enough hours in the day to fit it all in. But it was well hidden, and Big Brother Security won a string of legit contracts. Astonishingly, Haase's company took over the security at a parish church. The story made national newspaper headlines. An anonymous member of St Mary's Walton-on-the-Hill church in Walton, Liverpool, who was too scared to be named, told the *Sunday Mirror*: 'It's crazy! How can you have a man like this looking after a church? It's like having the Devil to stand at the gates at St Peter.'

Haase's suitablity to run a security company guarding prime sites such as McDonald's at Liverpool FC's Anfield Stadium raised questions in the press and the profession. Some industry bosses called for him to be banned from trading.

Furthermore, police and Customs and Excise were at a loss to figure out how they could bring Haase down. They couldn't get close to him. Evidence to put him away again was almost impossible to find. Putting Haase's 'political protection' aside, there were very definite technical and logistical problems associated with mounting an operation against him.

Haase's organisation could not be penetrated by outsiders. His inner circle were fiercely loyal and as a supergrass Haase knew the threat posed by informants. Haase was an expert in counter-surveillance, with access to anti-bugging devices, secret video cameras, expert trackers, surveillance vans, long-lens cameras and scrambled walkie-talkies. Private detectives could supply him with a wealth of data, including phone bills, medical records, bank details, ex-directory phone numbers and addresses of rival criminals. Corrupt policemen, lawyers and prison officers also tipped him off about operations against him. Bodyguards protected his every move. Even his wedding looked like a presidential cavalcade, with one onlooker saying, 'There seemed to be a lot of bouncers on the door, checking everyone who went into the wedding. Security seemed very strict.'

In short, the outlook for those looking to bring Haase down was bleak. Haase was emerging victorious and there seemed to be nothing or no one who could stop him.

In 1997, however, Customs began to fight back. Officers began to put together an intelligence file on Haase and figure out what he was up to. By the following year, the preparation was complete. In 1998, a full-scale investigation was launched. A unit separate from Paul Cook's, codenamed Operation Octagon, was tasked to carry out the probe. It was initially focused on a nine-handed gang of cannabis smugglers based in Spain, London and Liverpool. Haase's partner Paul Bennett had shown up on the radar as the central figure in the gang 'who everyone bounced off' – in other words, the boss. Haase was only a junior partner in Bennett's cannabis-smuggling ring – he only had £10,000 invested. But as Bennett was still partners with Haase, Octagon's trail soon led them to the dock HQ, where they realised Haase was doing a lot of graft. Under Operation Octagon, Customs were able to get permission to make Haase their number-one target and to start planting bugs at his office. They would take their chances on the political fallout.

But Customs also had an ace up their sleeve – Haase's old pal and pre-heroin business partner had turned supergrass against the drug dealers. Paul Grimes was willing to betray Haase in order to avenge the death of his son from a heroin overdose. He got a job as Haase's right-hand man in Big Brother Security. Grimes would have to face extreme danger every day and the threat of exposure would be constant. If he was caught informing, his punishment would certainly be torture and possibly death.

The first phase of the operation would be the hardest: getting Paul infiltrated into the gang. He had not seen Haase for ten years and Haase may have discovered during that time through his underworld sources that his old pal Grimesy had informed on Warren. It was very high-risk. Against all odds, though, Grimes pulled it off and got a job as a lowly security guard with Big Brother just after Christmas 1998. Then he rose through the ranks to become Haase's deputy – his security manager – about six months later.

The investigation was called Operation Monet – a massive joint venture between Customs and Excise's National Investigation Service based in Manchester, Merseyside Police's Major Crime Unit and the National Crime Intelligence Service (NCIS). Paul's handler was a Customs intelligence officer called John King, assigned to NCIS.

Haase was so switched on that early on in the operation, in July 1998, he got suspicious, no doubt tipped off by one of his bent law-enforcement people. Incredibly, not suspecting Grimes at all, he told him that there was a 'good team watching him and that they had bugged his home phone, office phone and mobile'. He warned Grimes not to talk on the phone. A Customs officer was later grilled in court about an alleged tip-off to Haase's lawyer, but it was never proved. In April 1999, Haase was allegedly tipped off again, this time by an alleged bent copper at the force's Canning Place station, that his office was, or was about to be, bugged.

The tip-off was bang on – a month later, in May 1999, bugs were inserted with the help of Paul Grimes at Haase's Atlantic House HQ. The whole operation came close to being discovered after the building's state-of-the-art alarm was disturbed during their insertion by a covert Customs team. Only a lot of fancy footwork on behalf of Paul Grimes put Haase's men at ease. Monitoring and recording began on 17 May 1999. A few days later, on 25 May 1999, Customs officers trained a secret video camera on the door to Atlantic House.

PAUL GRIMES: When I got the job with Haase, he just mentioned he was doing the ciggies and was doing £1 million-plus deals. He said he was making as much from them as the drugs. Personality-wise, he'd turned into a tyrant. He'd done so much time, he'd gone crazy. Did not give a shit about authority or anyone. He'd hit the self-destruct button.

One day, I walked in the office about half-eight in the morning. Haase was sitting at his desk cleaning two guns. One was an old Army gun, the other was an automatic. I just looked at him and he started laughing. About half an hour later, he asked me to watch while he hid the guns wrapped in a taped plastic bag under the floorboards in an office upstairs. He was wearing gloves. That's when I found out he was gun-running.

He was also doing a lot of contract violence. There was a hard-core of boys whose job was to fill people in, kidnap them, tie-ups, whatever. One day, we went to this fella's house; I think he owed Haase money. One of Haase's henchmen broke his jaw straight-off, no back answers, with one dig. Then they smashed up a solicitor's office who owed someone money. This solicitor was well connected to the busies and the judges. He wasn't a fucking gangster, he was a civilian and a fucking brief to boot. But John didn't care. These were the new rules. 'I'm John Haase – I'm invincible' was his attitude. I watched him torture a guy from Blackpool for losing him a lot of money on a cigarette deal. This guy had been abducted from his cottage in Lytham St Annes and given a hiding.

Haase asked me to make an acid bath from hydrofloric acid in the cellar to torture two very big gangsters called The Iceman and The Security Boss. Haase was going to torture them so that they would lay off Bennett. Bennett owed them money from a drug deal. [Ironically, just a few years before, The Iceman and The Security Boss had helped with the Royal Pardons by supplying gun plants for Haase and Bennett.]

Behind my back, Haase recruited my son Heath as a security guard, but really as an arsonist in the protection rackets. He was in his mid-twenties but he'd done five years for robbery in

1994. I was fucking furious when I found out and told Heath to get out, but he wouldn't listen. I took Heath aside and warned him to stay well clear of Haase, but he just smiled. It was as though he revelled in rebelling against me. Haase was paying him top dough to buy his loyalty.

It was just villainy all the fucking time. Kenny Doorteam ran the door side of the operation. He was a hard-hitter himself but he needed Haase as backing so he could muscle in on the doors all over town. If Kenny couldn't get a door, then Haase used to cause trouble for the people who owned the door until he got it. Haase didn't let up until he got it. That meant stabbings, shootings and firebombs. If clients weren't persuaded, then their businesses simply went up in flames. End of story. Heath was the top arsonist; he became a specialist at it. Heath was getting in too deep. Had a word with him: 'It's fuckin' serious, this fire palaver. Someone will get killed.'

But he was too big for his boots now. Fucked me off, he did. Haase paid Heath £2,000 to burn down the Sporting Club because the fella who owned it owed Bennett money. Heath set another club in town on fire and smashed up another – to force the owners to hand over the door. They did.

Then Kenny wanted to go after the big hotels and clubs. There was this one called the Devonshire Hotel where the door was run by an old pal of Haase's who was old-school. But Haase didn't give a fuck about any friendships. First the club got smashed up and then Haase sent Heath down to petrol bomb it of a night. Heath smashed up the hotel. Then he done all the cars in so that we ended up with the screw on the car park. Every single car in the car park – about 50, including rows of BMs, Mercs, everything – owned by the guests who were staying at the hotel was smashed up. Sledgehammers, baseball bats, the works. The next morning, it looked like a riot scene. Eventually, after a campaign of hassle, we got the full contract for the Devonshire.

After that, Heath had to carry on doing little bits of damage to the hotel and cars so that it didn't look too suss, so that it looked as though we had nothing to do with it in the first place and that we were gradually reducing the damage now. It was textbook protection-racketeering and it worked like a dream. The money rolled in, but Haase wanted more. He was a 24-hour-a-day gangster. He couldn't sleep. He used to phone me up at three and four o'clock in the morning to ask me about jobs.

Then Kenny wanted another club: the Buzz club, where all the footie players and the Spice Boys used to go and that. So Heath did the business there. Haase ordered a drive-by shooting around Christmas 1998 using a beige Peugeot 205 which he bought for the job that day. A security guard got shot in the hand. [Chris No-Neck later revealed that the actual gun person was a female assassin called The Horsebox.]

Then Haase hit on the idea of actually robbing the pubs and clubs he was meant to be protecting. He actually done the heists himself with a shooter and a balaclava. I couldn't believe it. One of the country's top villains, worth millions, doing blags, but he got a buzz out of it. I think it took him back to his youth, like a proper villain again instead of some fucking drug-dealing fucking organised-crime king sat behind a desk.

On another occasion, he robbed a club owned by a fella who was well connected to the Bhoys – the IRA. In May '99, he planned to rob a 'hole in the wall' in Skelmersdale and use a shopping trolley as a getaway with all the money in it.

Then I started to get close to the real action – drugs. I began to see kilos of drugs being ferried in and out of Haase's office. He used to use a half-caste student as a courier. One day, they were sat at his desk and in the middle was four bag-of-sugar-sized parcels of beigish, off-white powder. It was heroin.

One of the Turks Haase used to deal with kept phoning the office. His name was Yilmaz Kaya. But Haase wouldn't take the call. Then his sister kept phoning up. Haase just blanked it. Haase said that he owed their family money and that's why he was fucking them off.

By July '98, Haase had gone security mad – he had an infrared, see-in-the-dark CCTV camera installed on his flat and a fuck-off iron gate behind the main door. He ripped the camera off Ben's house after he wouldn't pay for it. He started wearing a stun gun he'd bought for £65 around the office.

At the end of August '98, I told my handler that Bennett was looking for a map with coordinates on it so he could land a helicopter there [at the coordinate reference, the site of a pre-arranged drugs handover], presumably with a load of gear on it as part of a drug deal he was setting up. Haase thought it was a wild idea. Shortly afterwards, Bennett went to Belgium to check on a container, presumably for a deal.

Haase used to use all kinds of silly codewords for drugs. For instance, one day Haase asked me to pass on a message to someone that he wanted four videos of *Snow White and the Seven Dwarfs*, which I believed to be drugs, probably coke. He was paying 20s for a kilo. By February, the code was 'shirts'. That was then sold by No-Neck. He was selling bush cannabis as well. That day, he also got the main gates fortified with barbed wire – again paranoid about security. A few months later, in December, he had extra steel bars and locks put on all the doors after personally examining every point of entry and exit on the Stanley Dock building. He was getting more and more paranoid, carrying a cosh around the office and asking me to be at his side or nearby all the time. He started using a walkie-talkie to communicate with all his guards in and outside the building. They were under instructions to tell him about every visitor.

In November 1998, the half-caste lad delivered a load of gear in a black rucksack. But Haase went mad and said it was £60,000 worth of shit. Around then, the crew were making a lot of dough – millions. There was always money. Haase was making millions off 've the ciggies. Literally fucking millions. That's what the Customs could never work out. Was making fucking 20 times more off 've the ciggies than heroin and cocaine. No cargo was less than fifty grand's worth. The profit was 1,000 per cent, week in, week out.

One time, Heath was sent to Scotland to pick up £22,000 in cash for a ki of brown and some other bits and bobs. Then, on another day, Haase had off £500,000 worth of designer clobber, which was in a lorry going to a big shop in the city centre. Then one day, Haase bought a .38 mm handgun off've one of the doormen, along with 100 rounds of ammo. Was purely meticulous in his armament deals, he was. Sat there and counted out every fucking bullet on his desk, until he was convinced that he hadn't been ripped off. Then he went downstairs in the cellar of the dock and pinged off a few rounds.

On his contact sheets, Paul gave details about Haase's obsession with elaborate security procedures. One week, he had his main gates fortified with barbed wire and on another, Bennett got an anti-bug device for him to use. But by December 1998, Grimes was reporting to Customs that Haase was becoming increasingly upset with Bennett for letting him down on deals. Before Christmas, Grimes told Customs that No-Neck was expecting a delivery of heroin. During this time, Haase was using the codename 'Christmas trees' to describe heroin.

PAUL GRIMES: In March '99, Haase asked me to take over his security company because he couldn't front it due to his convictions. But I had convictions as well, so I had to think about it.

John was doing a lot of gun-running to a firm in Scotland, but because of all the fucking chaos, I could never get a hangle on it. But Heath kept telling me how it worked – cos he was right in the thick of it. Was simple. Every time the Jocks wanted shooters, they sent a bagman down to Liverpool. Heath got the gear off've Haase and he drove out to meet the crazy Jocks on his motorbike.

Everything was being captured on tape. I kept warning Heath to get out but he was now more loyal to Haase than to me. By May 1999, I was at the end of my tether with him. I told my handlers that I didn't give a fuck whether the info I was giving them got him nicked as well.

Unaware that Paul Grimes was an informant, Chris No-Neck got on with the day-to-day business of violence, robbery and drug dealing.

CHRIS NO-NECK: The Horsebox, the female shooter he used, used to call Haase 'Dracula' because every six to eight weeks he'd need some claret to pacify him. John was a villain. He needed to see blood. On a job, Haase would steam straight in. One job we knocked on the door and the fella answers. Haase goes 'Uuuuggghh!' [a battle cry before attacking him]. One of us has a Magnum.

On another job at a flat in Tuebrook, John and Kenny Doorteam went to lean on someone. It ended up with John putting one in a fella's leg. Kenny turned around and Haase was already down the road. Some of the other jobs he asked me to go on were too risky.

Now, on jobs he put my way, I could have said, 'Yes, I'll do it 100 per cent,' or, 'No.' I've never been in-between. I'd weigh the plot up. Now he wanted us to do the Cream [mount an armed robbery on the superclub Cream]. Now the Cream was in a square. There were several cameras on it. Now he wanted us to wrap the bird up [tie up the manageress], take the printer [the till], empty the printer and fuck off. And there would have been a tidy few quid there. But it would have been ontop because the roads are camera'd up to fuck down there. He said, 'Are you doing it?'

I said, 'No. I'll do a job I know I can get in and out on. The Cream is 75 per cent ontop and I'd rather have the odds on my side.'

Now that Haase was out of prison and back ontop, Haase and No-Neck set about the business of settling old scores against disloyal gangsters who had tried to have him off while in jail. First on the hit-list were the tax men, otherwise known as The

Hyenas, who took advantage of Haase's incarceration by attempting to steal his money. The tax men had attacked Haase's men in their homes.

CHRIS NO-NECK: The tax man Flannagan had been wrapping people up [kidnapping them], burning them, right. He was a dog. They went for Haase and took his money. After Haase was out, Flannagan came to see me and John with his mate. I was leaning on the car. Flannagan goes, 'What's all this?' meaning that he'd heard that I was looking for him [for revenge].

Then it was like a schoolyard, you know, when two kids run off. Scarpered, they did. I ran after them on me own. Caught up with him. Hit him. I thought, 'He's too fucking big to let up.' So I just fucking caned him. Flattened me knuckle on the cunt. Broke my hand. I had Flannagan – pounding him. I never done it for Haase. He burnt my young mate as well, who grafted for me. He burnt him with an iron and took his dough off him. When I dealt with him, his mate was standing there with a fucking iron bar. I was watching the other cunt as I'm banging Flannagan. And he come at me with an iron bar. I goes 'Aaaah!' and he shits himself. I was going to take the bar off him and ram it down his fucking throat. [Then Haase allegedly joined in and cut Flannagan's throat with a knife.] I didn't see the man do it. He waited until Flannagan was unconscious.

Later, the police recorded Haase bragging about beating Flannagan and going back to his beaten body on the floor *six* times to hit him again.

JOHN HAASE (on the police tape): He [Flannagan] ran. We caught him after about four yards. He went down fuck off. [Laughter.] The other fella got up the road and pulled a big crowy out. So I had a go back at him: 'Come on, come on!' It was crunch. Then back to Flannagan. His head on the floor. It was twenty past eight. All the neighbours are out. You want to see No-Neck's hands with fucking knocking him on the head and that. No-Neck had him on the floor. I just bent over and just kept my hand in. [Haase was possibly armed with a Stanley knife.] His face was bleeding. Smashing his hands and feet. Six times I went back.

Afterwards, Haase feared a revenge attack by Flannagan, so he personally took his henchman Heath Grimes to Flannagan's home address and told him, 'If anything happens to me, make sure Flannagan gets it.' But Heath didn't really want to get involved.

On 10 June 1999, Bennett went on the run after the cannabis ring he was operating on the side was smashed by Operation Octagon in London, Liverpool and Spain. Bennett had been busy using the cannabis to make a fast buck to pay off his drug debts – he still owed £150,000 to The Iceman, whom Haase had threatened to acid-bath.

Customs officers who were part of Operation Octagon now wanted to question Bennett in connection with a large importation of cannabis. The other eight men in the gang had been arrested. According to Paul Grimes, Haase had £10,000 invested in the deal and expected 25 kilos of cannabis from Ben. Ben's escape had been nothing short of miraculous – fuelling suspicions that Customs had purposely alerted him because he was an informant. As the officers waited at his front door, Bennett vaulted over the back wall of his house and escaped along a railway line while his girlfriend quickly burned mobile-phone records. His Second World War escape, coupled with the fact that his arrest warrant was subsequently not enforced, as Bennett freely walked around Liverpool even though he was supposed to be on his toes, led Haase to suspect that Bennett was informing on him.

A couple of months later, he returned to Haase's HQ to work

on a cannabis skunk farm in the basement. The CPS later denied that Bennett had given any 'formal assistance' to the authorities, leaving the possibility that he was briefing them ad hoc, that he was providing off-the-record information to Octagon officers. Bennett then moved to a safehouse in Scotland from where he commuted to Liverpool.

For Haase, the bottom line was simple – Bennett's misfortune was the beginning of the end for him. On 22 June 1999, Customs recorded Haase telling a drug dealer called Derek about Bennett. He said, 'He's been using people in Spain without checking them out. They give you gear and then blow you off.' He also suggested that Bennett might be a police informant, hinting that he was involved in the case of a drug dealer who had recently been jailed for ten and a half years. Bennett later tried to wriggle out of the accusation, saying that he had inside info on the case only because he'd been tipped off by his solicitor Tony Nelson that the suspect was under surveillance. But in the same conversation, Haase didn't let Ben's misfortune interrupt business, as would have been wise. He should have closed down shop for a while. Instead, he told Derek that three kilos of heroin were available 'for big dough', while cockily singing the words, 'Here I am, baby.'

However, as a precaution, Haase began distancing himself from Bennett. He was not only suspicious because of Octagon, but also because a large number of recent illegal deals involving Bennett had got smashed by the law. According to Ben's right-hand man Barry Oliver, Haase had every reason to be suspicious. Oliver claimed that Bennett was now trying to frame Haase for gun-running, to trade off with the authorities.

Other businessmen use their briefcases to carry documents. But on 27 July 1999, Haase was carrying two and a half kilos of cannabis, which he was trying to sell for £8,500. Even while he was on the run, Ben was regularly calling Haase to get money and favours. He asked Haase to send some boys to Strangeways to help the cannabis gang, who were on remand.

Meanwhile, Haase's gun-running operation was spiralling out of control. He was supplying so many guns to villains in

Scotland that the Glasgow godfathers were blaming Haase for single-handedly starting wars. Ken Darcy said, 'On the one hand, the Scots loved buying guns off him. But on the other, they were getting worried because everyone was getting shot.'

Sources in the gang claimed that Haase had got many of the guns over the years through Bennett, who was buying them direct from terrorists in Northern Ireland. As part of their gun-running operation, Bennett had recruited the ex-con and former electrician Barry Oliver onto Haase's firm and made him feel indebted by giving him a job, a house, a car, £1,000 worth of clothes and regular spending money. Bennett employed Oliver as a maintenance man for his property empire, babysitter for his kids, personal trainer and chauffeur – Ben was banned from driving. Oliver, then thirty-seven, had been sentenced to eight years in 1994 for manslaughter. Oliver was determined to go straight but he claimed that Bennett began threatening him with death if he didn't take part in gun deals.

Another gun-runner, based on the Wirral, was also supplying Haase. But on 1 June 1999, during a run to drop off a boot-full of weapons destined for Haase, he was nicked at the entrance to the Mersey Tunnel. Other associates of Bennett's included Toxteth tax man The Iceman and Scottish hard-man Ian McAteer, later jailed for killing drug dealer Walter Selkirk in a horrific assassination while Selkirk's children waited in the car. McAteer later blamed Bennett for setting him up.

According to Oliver, one day in July 1999, Bennett hatched a plot to set Haase up by buying a load of guns off him – and shopping Haase at the same time to the authorities in order to get his own Octagon warrant quashed. Bennett allegedly forced Oliver under threats of death to act as intermediary in the sale of guns between Haase and himself. The guns would then be sold by Bennett to the Scottish Connection. Oliver had been trying to back out by turning off his mobile and moving to a new address with his girlfriend Karen. But desperate Bennett had quickly tracked him down and flew into a vicious, threatening rage outside Oliver's house.

At the end of July, Oliver allegedly visited Ben in Glasgow to collect the £1,000 transport money to be given to Haase for the guns. Oliver claims that Haase was expecting another £5,000 for the guns themselves. Paul Grimes did not know about Ben's alleged conspiracy against Haase – he was busy hatching his own.

PAUL GRIMES: In April '99, Haase hid four guns, three pistols and a sawn-off at the dock. Heath was telling me everything. One day, he told me that a load of guns had been sold to a guy in Stoke.

Heath and Haase used to go into the basement to test them. One day, they fired off an Uzi and a Magnum. Heath told me that Haase, even though he was a top gun-runner, wasn't actually a good shot. He had difficulties with the safety catches.

Then in August '99, Heath told me that the next shipment was on the cards. This was the first time he'd told me about a delivery before it went off. Get paid. I gee'd the Customs up good style and told them to be ready. Then Heath went away on holiday. He must have thought it would go off when he got back, but suddenly the Jocks wanted their firearms. They must have had a blag planned or whatever.

It could've easily been done without Heath, but by this time Haase thought so much of him that he put it off until he got back. Could not understand it, la. Only needed someone on a bike. But Haase was insistent – want Heath, la. No back answers.

When Heath got back, John was made up. Then, on 7 September, Haase called me and said, 'Get down the dock for twelve.'

When I got there, he just told me to stay on the gate. Another one of the lads, called Barry Oliver, was guarding the door. Heath arrived on his bike. He told me he was doing a gun drop to the Jocks. He went in Haase's office and when they both come out, Haase put a small bag on top of the bike's petrol tank. That was it. Heath got off.

Fifteen minutes later, Heath comes back after delivering the guns to the Scottish courier. For delivering the guns, which would get him four years in jail, Heath said he was paid just £50. I says to John immediately that I'm getting off, jumps in the van and fucks off. Outside the dock, I phoned Customs and give them the gen.

Paul was not privy to how his information was actually used by Customs and the police. But at about the same time as he was ringing in his intelligence to Customs, the police had stopped the car driven by the Scottish courier. A sports bag containing an Uzi sub-machine gun and a Dirty Harry-style Smith & Wesson Magnum revolver was recovered from the front passenger foot-well. The ammunition included 49 rounds of .38 mm bullets and 170 rounds of .9 mm, including 70 dum-dum-style hollow-point bullets designed to wreak havoc in the body on impact.

In the run-up to the seizure, the police had been on alert to catch the gun dealers red-handed. They had been given a warning by Paul Grimes several weeks beforehand that a gun deal was in the offing and possibly had supplementary intelligence supplied by Paul Bennett. In addition, a Customs surveillance team had video cameras trained on the main entrance to the office to watch the comings and goings. A very useful picture had been built up.

Seconds before Heath had left the dock offices on his motorbike, Haase had been observed with him. A police surveillance team had followed Heath's motorbike to the Atlantic Café in Walter Street, north Liverpool, where he drew up next to a gold Renault Laguna. The Renault had been driven down from Scotland to Liverpool by 46-year-old Walter Kirkwood, a criminal from Dumbarton who worked for one of Scotland's leading underworld figures. Both engines were still running when Heath lifted the black Head sports bag from his shoulder and threw it into the car.

Kirkwood was followed towards the M6 motorway and

intercepted at traffic lights near Kirkby by armed police. As evidence against Haase, the guns were excellent in every respect. But they didn't arrest the Mr Big straight away. The police kept a low profile so that Haase would not be aware that they were closing in on him. When Kirkwood did not return to Scotland, both gangs did not seem to suspect that the police were involved until much later. Haase carried on committing crimes unaware.

A lot of the gun-deal negotiations were on tape purporting to show that Barry was getting the guns on behalf of Bennett under duress. It was rumoured that Bennett was deliberately encouraging the Scottish gangs to kill each other so he could exploit the weakness to sell more drugs – as well as trying to stitch up Haase at the same time. In one conversation, Haase offers four guns for three grand as if he's selling a second-hand car. In-between the negotiations, he casually talks about the Sunday League football team he sponsors.

> Haase: I've got four but I want three grand. The Mac Ten, that's £2,300. The other one is a brand-new Magnum – that was two grand – and there's a sawn-off as well. That's with ammunition, though.
>
> Barry: That's reasonable.
>
> Haase: Sawn-off . . . I might keep it myself. But they are boss, the Mac Tens. A machine gun has a manual [can be fired on manual single shot as well as automatic]. The Mac Ten's not only got a single fire but rapid fire.
>
> Barry: What does he [Bennett] want to do? Start a war?
>
> Haase: They're not for that. I'll keep one of them. I don't really need that many.

Haase was not arrested on the day of the gun deal and didn't realise that the Scottish courier had been nicked. So he kept on committing crimes as if there was nothing wrong. Busily, he set up a deal with his heroin supplier Salim to buy a kilo of heroin from London. He took Ken Darcy with him as a mule to carry the gear.

Haase was arrested at Liverpool Lime Street train station on 25 October after returning from a trip to London. In a massive surveillance operation, officers had followed Haase and Darcy as they set out from Liverpool Lime Street earlier that day and kept close tabs on them using undercover officers disguised as ticket-booth operators, cleaners and even guards on the train.

On arrival at Euston, Haase and Darcy jumped a black cab to a Turkish restaurant in Stoke Newington, north London. In the café, Haase met Salim. Haase had got Salim's number from Kaya, who was still in prison. In a previous phone call, Salim had told Haase that one kilo of gear cost £18,000. During the handover in the café, Salim generously knocked £3,000 off the asking price there and then, telling Haase that it was now only £15,000. He gave the £3,000 back to Haase.

Upon arrest back in Liverpool that afternoon, Haase had the £3,000 in cash, while in the lining of Darcy's coat a plastic BHS bag was recovered containing a kilo of heroin – 984 grams, to be precise. It was the end of Haase. The Scottish notes Haase had were probably from the sale of guns to the Scottish Connection.

KEN DARCY: He said he'd pay for my ticket and I was getting £200 when I returned. I was told to be at the Crown at 7 a.m. and I'd be picked up to go to Lime Street. But I was 45 minutes late because I went to a different Crown pub. He then gives me £200 in Scottish money. I run back to purchase my own first-class ticket.

Over breakfast, he was talking about his business. He had two mobile telephones with him and made several calls. I didn't really hear the conversations, except Haase saying, 'I'll call when I get there.' May have dozed off. Talking about his Sunday League football team. Get in to Euston, we both get off, walk up the platform into the main area, following him because not sure where I was going. Haase puts the bag down and goes to use the phone. Green holdall. When he finishes the call, he walks off, I pick up the bag and follow him. We went to a cab rank downstairs. Waited a couple of minutes because there is a queue. We get into the taxi. Not sure whether he showed the cabbie a piece of paper with the destination or told him. In the taxi for roughly 20 minutes. No real discussion in the taxi. Haase eventually told the cabbie to pull over. There was a guy walking up and down the road. He paid for the taxi. JH said to me, 'Don't let him see me.' I did not really pay much notice and we went into a café. It was quite scruffy. There was about seven people in there. Big guy asked me if I wanted a cup of tea. I said yes. We go to the back of the café – I follow JH. Brought the tea over in a glass with bits of wood so never drank it.

I sat on the end of a table and JH on another about 5 ft away. He sat with the big chap. Another person appeared, about 50, well dressed. Him and JH seem to know each other. They shook hands, had a little laugh and joke and the three sat on a separate table and had a discussion. Seven- to ten-minute discussion. The two men got up and said, 'Won't be long,' to JH and went off.

They went out the front door and into a Mercedes car. Once they left, I said to JH, 'What's happening?'

He said, 'Only be 20 minutes and then we're gone.'

Still sat across from him. Still other people in the café. It was a Turkish café. About half an hour later, I got a bit suspicious because it was late. I was getting a bit restless waiting around. About 45 minutes later, the big guy returns. I could see out of the café onto the road and saw him get out of the Merc with a carrier bag. He walked across the road towards me in the café. He put this bag on the table, on JH's table. JH said to me, 'Kop for that,' as I hold on to it whilst we are standing up getting ready to leave. We go outside, walk 50 yards to a minicab office and go to Euston. I think that whilst in the cab, I asked him what I had and he said, 'Hooky money.' I deemed that to be counterfeit money. I had no reason to believe otherwise. We get back to Euston and straight onto the train and it leaves. A few minutes later, we have tea and sandwiches and after that JH fell asleep most of the way.

So we get in to Liverpool. He has his holdall. Train pulls up, everyone waiting to get off. JH gets off the train, starts walking up the platform. I help old lady with her bags off the train whilst JH goes off to his car. If I had knowledge as to the contents of the bag, then I would not have helped the old lady off the train. I would have left the train straight away to secure the package. JH told me that his car was parked in the Buzz nightclub car park. I assumed he would give me a lift home.

As I then walk onto the platform to go towards the car, I am arrested.

On 26 October 1999, Haase was arrested at his dock office at the Stanley Heritage Market. Firstly, he was charged with conspiring to supply heroin in relation to the kilo from the north London Turks. Then he was charged with a separate firearms offence related to the Smith & Wesson found on 7 September in Walter Kirkwood's car.

Police moved in on the rest of the gang. Drugs mule Ken Darcy was charged with drug offences. Paul Grimes's son and Haase's heavy Heath Grimes was also charged with firearms offences. Barry Oliver, who had allegedly been at Stanley Dock on the day of the gun transaction, was also charged with firearms offences. At the time of the offences, Oliver was on licence after being released early from prison in connection with manslaughter.

During police interrogations, Haase and Darcy did not fold under questioning. As seasoned career criminals, they answered the majority of questions with 'no comment'. On the other hand, scared Heath Grimes, the young father facing a long stretch, weakly tried to talk his way out of it but tied himself up in knots.

Haase's partner Paul Bennett was still technically a wanted man – a further complication in the already difficult case. There was a live warrant out for his arrest in connection with a £1 million cannabis importation tracked by Operation Octagon. Several defendants began to try to get themselves shorter sentences by plea bargaining after finding out the staggering level of secret intelligence against them. But Haase and Heath Grimes were in for a bigger shock when it dawned on them that the man secretly informing on them was Paul Grimes – a lifelong friend to one and father to the other.

Haase first realised that Paul was the grass when, against all odds, police found a secret cache of guns hidden underneath a floorboard in the vast dock warehouse. It would have been impossible for the officers to find the guns during a routine search – they must have been taken to them by one of Haase's close aides. Paul Grimes was the man who'd kept watch while Haase had stowed them away.

Haase then started threatening to set his heavies on Paul Grimes. Grimes told his handlers that if the attack came, he would go after Haase, insisting that he was not scared and would stand up to him. His handlers had to calm him down.

On one occasion, Heath had still not realised that his own dad had 'thrown him in'. Pitifully, he asked his dad to stand surety on his bail. Astonishingly, Paul did so.

On the drugs-related charge, Haase knew the evidence against him was not as strong. After all, the kilo of heroin had not been found on his person – Ken Darcy had been carrying it. Therefore, he decided that he would try to cut a cheeky yet feasible deal on a lesser charge, something like supplying the cash to buy the drugs but not exactly being involved in the illegal purchase – an obscure form of money-laundering.

Haase felt confident on this score because, as he claimed in private to his co-d's, the kilo wasn't technically his anyway. Haase said that it was all the fault of Chris No-Neck, who had set up the deal after repeatedly badgering him for a kilo of brown in the run-up to the trip. He claimed he had first visited the Turks in London on Saturday, 23 October, two days before he was busted, to talk about other business. The kilo of heroin was a side issue, a favour for No-Neck.

Haase said that it had been No-Neck's job to arrange a courier to pick up the parcel, but because of a mix up in travel arrangements he was forced to travel down himself in order not to stand up the Turks. Haase never contemplated revealing the story about No-Neck to the police, but he decided early on that his case strategy would be never to plead guilty to possessing the heroin.

While Haase and Heath were on remand together, Heath believed that Haase would go 'belly up' and 'blow everybody up'. Some of the Scottish criminals connected to Walter Kirkwood threatened to beat Haase but he was saved when Heath stepped in. But then Haase turned on Heath. He suspected that Heath was going to change his plea to guilty. Heath had got a job as a barber in Strangeways cutting prisoners' hair so they could talk. But Haase refused to discuss the case with Heath. Heath was so incensed that he threatened to break Haase's jaw and that of the other co-defendant, Barry Oliver, who was protecting Haase.

Meanwhile, Heath Grimes was facing a raft of extremely serious charges. However, his father, Paul, was not quick to help him. For a while, Paul visited Heath in prison and continued to pump him for information. Heath was open with him because he had not yet realised that his father was the grass. Paul's ex-wife Christine – Heath's mother – was not so gullible. She realised what was going on and accused Paul of the worst kind of treachery.

At that point, Paul had a pang of compassion. He decided to make a desperate bid to save his son. He asked his Customs handlers if they would go easy on Heath if he turned grass as well. Both sides agreed, but Heath backed down at the last minute. He was too scared of Haase.

PAUL GRIMES: At first, Heath decided to turn and he started passing information at a secret meeting at a hotel in Chester. He gave them some pretty useless info about Haase, such as the extortion Haase had put on the Blackpool ciggies fella and how he was abducted, and how Haase had cut the throat of a man in Norris Green over a security contract. But he also told them about leaks at police HQ that were getting back to Haase, a gun-runner who supplied Haase, the drive-by shooting at the Buzz club, Bennett offering to sell the cannabis from Operation Octagon, an armed robbery on a post office and a bank heist. The busies already knew a lot of this because I had told them, but at least it was a start. Later, Heath told me that Haase was involved in an attempted murder and that he had evidence on tape and in writing about this. I told him to tell the police. The police said they would put him and his family on the witness-protection programme and move them away from the north-west. But then, at the last minute, he lost his bottle, fearing a revenge attack by Haase. Haase had got wind of Heath's plan and demanded a meet in the prison to keep him and all the other co-d's in line. After that, I had to turn my back on Heath. On 14 September 2000, I told my handler that I didn't care whether I ever saw Heath again. He was history.

Part of the deal for allowing Heath a break was that I should help the police find the guns hidden in the dock, special fucking SWAT teams or not. It was largest building of its type in Europe. They'd been at it nearly eight days and found fuck all. So I took them to the spot. They found the gear. There was a Colt handgun and a magazine, a Brevett pistol and a mag, a sawn-off Parker-Hale 12-bore shotgun, 200 rounds of ammo and 25 shotgun cartridges. There weren't as many shooters as I'd seen him put in there. Was like a fucking IRA cache at one stage, but he must have been selling bits over the months, getting rid and that.

Everyone knew that Haase wouldn't think twice about killing me, especially after he definitely found out I was a grass. They found out for sure only after I'd tried to persuade Heath to turn.

Astonishingly, many of Haase's guns seemed to originate from police depots. They were guns that had been seized by police in crimes in years gone by but inexplicably found their way back onto the black market – just like the weapons he had used in the gun plants to con Michael Howard. He was obviously still using the same source. Haase had been so meticulous in his deals that he even had the Polaroids from police records to show to potential buyers.

Meanwhile, from his prison cell, Haase was already plotting to kill Grimes – not out of revenge, but to stop him appearing in court. The plan was more complicated than a straightforward assassination. Haase was desperate to find out exactly how much Grimes had told his Customs handlers. At that stage, Haase did not know about the bugging and the masses of intelligence that Customs had on him. What he did know was that if there was such data in existence, much of it would be inadmissible against him, especially without Grimes standing up in court to back it up.

Haase's grand plan was to try to negotiate a deal with the courts. He was a past master at plea bargaining. If he could pull off one moody sentencing deal, then he could pull off another. Haase was totally confident he could do it again. But first he needed to find out exactly how much Grimes had given his masters.

Haase planned to kidnap Grimes, bundle him into a van, torture him to find out what he had told them, kill him and dump him. But the plan was called off at the last minute, according to the Fence, after Haase's team realised Grimes had secret police protection.

Time was running out. If Haase was going to do a deal, he would have to make soundings before the trial started. In a last-ditch attempt to find out who knew what, he tried the same trick with one of the Customs officers who had helped gather the evidence against him. The officer was photographed at his home and outside his office at the Customs HQ in Manchester's Salford Quays, but the plot to kidnap a serving law-enforcement officer was called off after he proved too adept at dodging his pursuers.

As the pre-trial legal manoeuvres gathered pace, Haase told his solicitor, Tony Nelson, to instruct his barrister, the eminent Lord Carlile of Berriew, to start talking to the prosecution. Nelson was the lawyer who had brokered the deal that had freed

Haase from his previous, 18-year sentence. Seemingly, a loose agreement was reached without delay. The nub of the deal hinged on Haase pleading guilty to lesser charges. In return for a cost-cutting guilty plea, the prosecution would throw their weight behind a plan to give Haase a shorter sentence. The jail term would be slashed because of mitigating circumstances. In short, Nelson believed that if everybody did what they said they were going to do, there was a good chance that Haase might get six years or less. This was not exactly 'beating the case', but it would be the best of a very bad situation. Nelson persuaded Haase that it was worth going for. In a letter to Lord Carlile, dated 5 December 2000, Nelson states:

> I have told our client [Haase] that you have very successfully persuaded the prosecution to agree to one substantive charge of selling firearms in relation to Indictment 1 on the following basis:
> a) That there was no harm to the public.
> b) That there was no terrorist link.
> c) That this was an isolated and 'one off' event.

The letter goes on to reveal that 'if one takes into account all the mitigating features that you have agreed with the prosecution towards damage limitation', then Haase could expect a sentence of between six and seven years. Furthermore, Nelson stated that this could be reduced to between four and five years if Haase pleaded guilty to the charge, saving the State the cost of a lengthy trial. Nelson continued:

> I heartily agree with you and did say, if you recall, spontaneously on the telephone that you could not have negotiated a more handsome basis of plea on behalf of your client, short of the prosecution withdrawing from the action.

Intense plea bargaining also surrounded the second charge relating to the heroin deal. Lord Carlile was seemingly successful in having the indictment reduced to a money-laundering charge, reasoning that Haase would admit to putting up the money to purchase the heroin but not to conspiring to actually deal in the drugs. The amount of money said to be laundered, in addition, was reduced from £10,000 to £3,500. In the same letter, Nelson stated to Carlile:

> With regard to the second indictment, again I feel that Leading Counsel [Lord Carlile] once more has excelled, in that the laundering is limited to £3,500 and again the case law would show a sentence of between eighteen months and three years for that level of laundering, and again credit will be given and a one-third reduction after a plea.

To summarise, Haase was being offered four to five years for the guns and approximately eighteen months for the money laundering: a total of about six years. With time off for good behaviour, that could mean four years, and taking into account the time spent on remand, Haase reasoned he could be out in 2003.

He was 51 years old at the time. It meant he would be out by the time he was 54, which was a result by any measure. Haase agreed to the deal and pleaded guilty before the trial got under way. It looked like another extraordinary coup for Haase.

Of course, there were also hiccups. At a critical point in the negotiations, Lord Carlile suddenly resigned from Haase's case after Haase threatened to call Michael Howard as a witness. Outraged Carlile wrote a letter to Haase stating that his demands were contrary to his professional codes and risked dragging the legal profession into disrepute. He had seemingly baulked at the contemptuous, hard-line approach to the legal system displayed by Haase in his threats to involve Howard. After a brief hiatus, though, the problem was smoothed over and Lord Carlile came back on board.

Certain terms and conditions were attached to the plea

bargain. Members of Haase's gang later claimed that a secret clause was inserted into the bargain prohibiting Haase from talking publicly about this deal or the one he had made during his previous, 18-year sentence. The prosecution, Haase's men claimed, were particularly keen to get him to promise never to go public about Michael Howard's role in the affair. With the six-year deal apparently done and dusted, Haase had to sit back and await sentencing while his co-defendants were tried.

First up, in January 2001, was Barry Oliver, the security guard who had allegedly been at the Heritage Market dock offices on the day the guns were handed over. His co-defendants Heath Grimes and Walter Kirkwood, like John Haase, had entered guilty pleas. The court heard how Customs monitored the deal using electronic surveillance. David Steer, QC, prosecuting said:

> The officers obtained authorisation to insert a secret audio transmitter inside the office. They also started to monitor recordings made by a video camera that was trained on the front door of the offices to record all comings and goings. The observations led to Kirkwood being tracked by armed police officers as he drove his gold Laguna along the East Lancashire Road on 7 September 1999. When it stopped at traffic lights at the junction of Moorgate Road, Kirkby, the police swooped and Kirkwood was arrested.

Mr Steer said that Haase, Oliver and Grimes were not arrested at that time and observations continued until 25 October 1999, when Haase was arrested at Lime Street station after stepping off a train from London. Two days later, police searched the market office building at Stanley Dock belonging to Big Brother Security. The search of Haase's office and the surrounding warehouse space lasted eight days.

Liverpool Crown Court heard at another hearing how Customs officers had placed Haase high on their list of targets soon after his surprise release from jail in 1996. Senior

Customs officer Steve Rowton revealed how his unit had acquired an informant within Haase's organisation from early on. Paul Grimes was clearly the informant in question, but for security reasons the statement did not name him. Rowton told the court:

> Between June 1997 and June 2000, I was assistant chief investigator for the National Investigation Service of HM Customs and Excise in the north-west. I was told we had someone very close to Haase. He gave us access to Haase's office premises so that we could carry out the technical work that needed to be done.

On 21 February 2001, John Haase was sentenced. The court was closed to the public; armed cops guarded the door. The official reason given was to protect the officials and the accused. But there had been rumours that Haase's gangster pals were planning to spring him from custody. Incredibly, the rumours were true.

THE DEBT COLLECTOR: There was a very big gangster in Scotland called Harry. He's in jail now. But he's very hard and very well respected and no one fucks with him. I think that was the gangster John was selling all the guns to. He thought a lot of John and he sent a vanload of Jocks down to Liverpool to spring him from the court. He was very loyal. They were sat off round the corner in a van. They were armed to the teeth. They were drinking whisky. They were bad lads. The plan was simple. They were going to shoot all the busies and get John. You wouldn't fucking believe it. But that is how hard-core the Jocks are. They simply do not give a fuck. Anyway, just before they were about to come out shooting, Haase's bird Debbie Dillon got wind of the plot. She went mad because she was convinced Haase had a good chance of getting off. She was running down the fucking street outside court begging the crazed Jocks not to do it, telling them that Haase had a deal, he was gonna get out anyway, that the last thing he needed was a fucking shoot-out. In the end, she found Kenny Doorteam. She was hysterical. She said to him, 'Kenny, please have a word with them. They are going to shoot all the busies for John.' Kenny, who was always the voice of reason, persuaded them to stand down.

Meanwhile, in court, Haase was completely unaware of the commotion. He even looked relaxed. He had an air of confidence about him, born from the certainty that he was getting six years. His contempt for the legal system was plain to see in his smug expression, knowing that everything had been settled in a quiet out-of-court arrangement.

Instead he was jailed for 13 years. Within seconds, the smile had been wiped off his face, quickly replaced by devastation. He was dumbstruck. He had been well and truly turned over. When he recovered his composure, Haase angrily shouted from the dock, 'I didn't plead guilty for this.' But he was quickly sent down. The sentence consisted of seven years for selling the guns and six years for money laundering. Paul Ferris, the Glasgow godfather, reveals the full drama of Haase's shock.

PAUL FERRIS: The courtroom was silent as the official read out the charges. Now it was the last one's turn.

'John Haase,' read the official, 'you are hereby charged with . . .'

'WHO ARE YOU TALKING TO, YE OLD CUNT?' Haase was on his feet, leaning over the rail, spitting venom. 'YOU CAN'T CHARGE ME. THIS FUCKING COURT CAN'T TRY ME.' His face was scarlet, his fists pumping the air.

'Order! Order!' The crashing whacks of the judge's gavel were drowned out by Haase's furious bellows. 'Take that man down . . .'

Two security guards jumped into action. The first was shoved easily aside, the other held on weakly to one arm, praying for reinforcements and soon.

'NO FUCKING COURT CAN TRY ME, YE PRICKS,' roared Haase. 'ONLY THE FUCKING GOVERNMENT CAN TRY ME. GET ME THE FUCKING HOME SECRETARY IN HERE NOW. HE'LL TELL YE – HE'S THE ONLY ONE . . .'

In sentencing him, the judge made reference to the infamous 1996 decision. Judge Holloway said, 'Mr [Michael] Howard is not given to bouts of light-headedness or light-handedness. One is entitled to assume that the Home Office investigated the details before agreeing to accept the Royal Pardon.'

Superintendent Dave Smith of Merseyside Police said, 'We realised Haase was starting up his operations and was beginning to be a threat to society again.'

Mixed fortunes awaited Haase's co-defendants. Heath Grimes, then twenty-six, received four years and Walter Kirkwood, then forty-six, received three years. Barry Oliver snatched the only result – he walked after the jury returned with a not guilty. His defence had successfully argued that he had been involved in the gun deal under duress from Bennett. Oliver put further pressure on the prosecution, asking awkward questions and demanding that Howard be formally questioned. He also threatened to name the gun-running Bennett as an informant in Operation Octagon. Oliver was convinced that Bennett was going to plant the guns in a phoney cache to offer up to the authorities to get off the Operation Octagon cannabis charges. He was saying that it was a rerun of the bogus caches used by Haase and Bennett to con Michael Howard in 1996. It was a nightmare scenario for the authorities and was a lesson on how the supergrass system was a bag of snakes. Haase had tried to force Oliver to go guilty, boasting that he could do a deal – but Oliver stood his ground.

Oliver said, 'It was during these conversations in his office that I began to realise that Haase and Bennett were setting me up. I also wondered why Bennett needed me at all for the task. I suspected and was told that he was seeking a deal and he needed the weaponry to effectively hand over to the authorities. I knew because he had told me that Nelson had brokered the previous deal. He was very close with Eliot. I spoke with Haase about this. Haase said the authorities would not buy it this time and they would need bodies. I then realised I was such a body, a scapegoat.'

Bennett indicated to Oliver that the guns were destined for HM Customs. Oliver revealed that Bennett boasted of his powerful connections inside the police and Customs and Excise, and said that Ben often phoned Paul Cook, whom he referred to as his guardian angel. Oliver claimed that Ben had met several police officers through Nelson's football team. Ben continued to boast of his relationship with Simon Bakerman. On one occasion, at a boxing dinner, Bennett and Haase were present at the same time as bent copper Elmore Davies.

Haase immediately vowed to appeal. His PR campaign kicked in at once. In a letter to the *Echo* from Strangeways prison, Haase cried, 'I am devastated. I feel like my life is over.' But the stunt backfired when the headline 'Whinger' was splashed across first editions. After pressure from Haase's camp, the critical tone of the piece was toned down for later editions.

From behind bars, Haase protested that he had been turned over. He argued that the deal he had agreed to, the six-year sentence, had been a false promise all along. He said that it had deliberately been made to lure him into entering an early guilty plea and stop him from going to trial. Haase said that the conspiracy had been plotted after he threatened to reveal the secrets behind the deal which had freed him from prison in 1996. After he threatened to call former Tory home secretary Michael Howard as a witness, he alleged, the deal was mysteriously put on the table. Haase believed the authorities would have been seriously embarrassed by a trial.

To back up his conspiracy theory, Haase revealed a timetable of events in the run-up to the deal, recorded in the diary of an associate.

Monday, 4 December 2000

Offered deal of ten to twelve years. Refused.

Tuesday, 5 December 2000

Haase tells his counsel Lord Carlile that he intends to call Michael Howard as a witness.

Wednesday, 6 December 2000

Crisis meeting arranged between Haase and Nelson and Ackerley (junior counsel) in Strangeways prison.

Nelson sends letter to Carlile about six-year deal.

Lord Carlile resigns.

Thursday, 7 December 2000

Haase in pre-trial hearing.

Friday, 8 December 2000

Haase offered new six-year deal. Accepts. Carlile takes up case again.

But no one was listening. In the Commons, Liverpool Walton MP Peter Kilfoyle called for an immediate inquiry into how Haase was released from the 18-year sentence in the first place and accused the Home Office of naivety in their assessments of Haase. Kilfoyle said, 'I just ask you to consider whether more damage was done by allowing Haase and Bennett back out onto the streets, or what could usefully be achieved by pretending that you could handle people like these.'

The trial of Kenneth Darcy took place two months later, on 17 April. Darcy, then forty-two, was sentenced to six years in jail after pleading guilty to possession with intent to supply. David Hislop, defending, claimed Darcy believed he was simply there to watch Haase, as he knew the man 'had enemies'.

Epilogue

CAMPAIGNS FOR JUSTICE

It seems from my research for this book that John Haase regarded his 13-year sentence for gun-running and money laundering in 2001 as payback from the authorities for his last jail term being dramatically cut short by his Royal Pardon. To him, he was now the victim of a conspiracy, being punished by the authorities for not playing the game and keeping his head down after he got out in 1996. The way he saw it, dark forces had conspired to put him away, to prevent him from blowing the lid on a spine-chilling, JFK-style corruption scandal.

Unfortunately, for many of his victims, the blame-everyone-else lag logic didn't add up. Many of them still believed that justice had not yet been done, that there was a still-unpaid debt to society to be redeemed, an outstanding balance of crime credit on his account that only he could repay. The victims argued that his latest sentence was punishment for his latest crimes alone. Politicians, journalists, law-enforcement officers and fitted-up criminals all spoke with one voice when they argued that many of the important questions relating to the Royal Pardon still remained unanswered. They believed that John Haase – and all of his co-conspirators – had not yet been brought to account for the crimes they allegedly committed in pursuit of his freedom.

They began campaigning for justice in earnest. First up was Liverpool Walton MP Peter Kilfoyle, who had been asking questions about John Haase in Parliament ever since he had been stopped from asking questions about the Royal Prerogative on Sky News in 1996. In 2001, encouraged by Haase's gun-running conviction, Kilfoyle reinvigorated his investigation into the scandal, probing every aspect, from the role of bent coppers to the protocol of handling Customs and Excise informants to the farce of the alleged phoney gun plants. His crushing assault on all of the agencies involved forced even the most obstructive civil servants to open their files and was felt right at the top of government. It reached a searing crescendo in 2004 when Kilfoyle made a graft-busting speech in a House of Commons adjournment debate naming Michael Howard's cousin Simon Bakerman officially for the first time in connection with the Royal Pardon and the allegations of large sums of money changing hands.

Next into the ring was Thomas Bourke, the garage owner allegedly framed by Haase and Bennett in the Strangeways gun case. Bourke's family, led by his tireless sister Jo Holt, scrutinised every dodgy aspect of the John Haase case, resulting in 2005 in a leave to appeal against Bourke's conviction. His case is expected to be heard in 2007.

Further weight was added to the cause by families campaigning for the release of several drug dealers convicted in connection with an infamous bust known as the West Derby job. The families claim that the hand of Haase had a role in the murky affair and have urged the authorities to come clean. A number of other criminals also came forward alleging that they had been stitched up by Haase, others confessing that they had carried out alleged perversions of the course of justice in Haase's name.

Then came a series of newspaper articles written by me and this book, revealing for the first time credible evidence of gun plants and alleged bribes.

The combination of all four types of campaigns for justice resulted in a Home Office investigation into the Royal Pardons in 2005 led by Chief Inspector of Constabulary Sir Keith Povey. He concluded that there was enough prima facie evidence to warrant a full-blown police investigation. The Metropolitan Police's specialist crime unit were given the job, generously paid for by the Merseyside force. At the time of going to press, the two-year-long probe codenamed Operation Ainstable has resulted in one alleged conspirator being charged. John Haase has been repeatedly interviewed under caution, as have Chris No-Neck and Ken Darcy, who have been bailed while inquiries continue. Police sources state that between six and eleven men and women are likely to be charged as a result of the probe.

Meanwhile, many of the characters revealed in this book are still around and getting on with their lives.

Peter Kilfoyle MP: Still crusading for justice for all of the victims of drug abuse and organised crime in Liverpool.

John Haase: Still residing at HMP Whitemoor near Cambridge. He is due for release in 2007 but if charged under Operation Ainstable he is likely to be arrested as he leaves prison and sent back to await trial.

Paul Bennett: Believed to be in Spain or Portugal, but mysterious sightings in Liverpool have been reported. The Scarlet Pimpernel has been in contact with villains in his old Norris Green neighbourhood.

Chris No-Neck: Running a small trade business in Liverpool. Interviewed under caution in connection with gun plants.

Ken Darcy: Out of prison and living in Liverpool. Interviewed under caution.

Paul Grimes: New life on the witness-protection programme.

Suleyman Ergun: Out of prison. Moved to Turkey to recover from an illness in 2006 but now back in the UK.

Yilmaz Kaya: Released from his heroin sentence in 2006 and moved back to Turkey.

The Vulcan: Serving a long sentence for drug trafficking in Italy. Hoping to be extradited to Turkey to finish it off.

Simon Bakerman: Lives in Liverpool with his parents.

The Enforcer: Lives a legitimate life in Liverpool and has given evidence to Operation Ainstable.

The Debt Collector: Runs a security company in Liverpool.

The Supervisor: Waiting for Haase to get out of prison.

Michael Howard: Stood down as leader of the opposition in 2005 but is still an MP.

The Fence: Lives a normal family life in Liverpool but is worried about being dragged into Haase's investigation.

James Turner: Washed-up old gunslinger sitting out his days in a Liverpool pub.

Colin Borrows: 'Britain's first crack dealer' is still in and out of jail.

The Horsebox: Recovering drug user worried that she might be charged under Operation Ainstable.

Eddie Croker: Lives a quiet life in Liverpool.

Bulent Onay: Whereabouts unknown.

Mehmet Ansen: Whereabouts unknown.

Mark Drew: Whereabouts unknown.

Neil Garrett: Still in contact with Paul Bennett.

The Estate Agent: Disappeared with £1 million of Haase's property.

Phil Connelly: Former Customs chief now works for the UN in Africa as a drugs adviser.

John Scanlon: Keeping his head down in Liverpool.

The author: Threatened by members of Haase's gang on many occasions. Warned by The Supervisor that he was on a 'death wish' if he continued to write about John Haase. Warned by The Fence that his 'face would be stamped all over' if he ever returned to Liverpool. Still here at the time of writing . . .